JOHN GROTE

A CRITICAL ESTIMATE OF HIS WRITINGS

JOHN GROTE

A CRITICAL ESTIMATE OF HIS WRITINGS

by

LAUCHLIN D. MACDONALD

State University of New York
Fredonia, N.Y.

THE HAGUE
MARTINUS NIJHOFF
1966

Affectionately dedicated to my sisters and brothers:
Mary, Chris, Anne, John K., Neil, Katherine
and in memory of N. Allen

TABLE OF CONTENTS

PREFACE

An objective of this book is to discuss some of the contributions made by John Grote to philosophy. This work is an extension of a dissertation written for the doctorate at Boston University. The author wishes to acknowledge the invaluable assistance in many places to Professor Peter A. Bertocci and the late Professor Edgar S. Brightman both of whom read the entire manuscript in its original form. Also, the author acknowledges the encouraging interest and support of his wife, Helen, whose many suggestions have improved the writing and without whose assistance this work would not have been accomplished. The author assumes complete responsibility for whatever errors or deficiencies appear in the book. All known writings of Grote are listed and the more important ones analyzed.

LAUCHLIN D. MACDONALD

CHAPTER I

INTRODUCTION

1. JOHN GROTE'S LIFE

i. Sketch of his life

John Grote will remain best known by reason of the thought formulated in the *Exploratio Philosophica*, or *Rough Notes on Modern Intellectual Science*. To the philosophical world of his own time he was well known as the teacher who ably held the chair of Moral Philosophy in the University of Cambridge from 1855 until the year of his death, 1866, in succession to the Knightbridge Professor, William Whewell whose *Philosophy of Science* is the subject of at least one chapter of the *Exploratio Philosophica*.

Grote's birthplace was Beckenham in Kent, and the date, May 5, 1813. The influence of his devout mother may have been responsible for his leaning toward the clerical profession; he eventually became an ordained minister in the Church of England.

He studied at Cambridge for the first time when he entered Trinity College in 1831. Previous to this, his education was carried on privately with a view to employment in the civil service in India. After spending four years in Cambridge, he graduated in classics in 1835, and became a Fellow of Trinity College in 1837. For eight years longer he continued study in Trinity. Next followed his rather brief career in the ministry before becoming professor in Cambridge. He was ordained as a deacon in 1842, and minister (or 'priest,' in the Church of England) two years later. Between 1844 and 1847, Grote preached for several of his clerical friends and continued his residence in college until 1845. Foreign travel formed certain interludes from study. After 1847 he became curate of Wareside, near Ware. Here he was rector until called to Cambridge in 1855. From the middle of the year 1847, Grote lived near Cambridge and he continued there to the end of his life.

Professor W. R. Sorley [1] classifies John Grote as a rational and religious philosopher, and states that though he was a contemporary of Mill, he was not affected by him. Rather, he criticized Mill's epistemology and ethics, and gave what he considered a necessary supplement to each. Anyone who reads Grote's work entitled, *An Examination of the Utilitarian Philosophy* must conclude that he was an independent thinker, and yet he appears to have been greatly influenced by Immanuel Kant as the *Exploratio Philosophica* reveals.[2]

ii. His brothers

It is interesting to notice that a brother, Arthur Grote (1814–1886), was in the employ of the Bengal civil service after he passed from Haileybury. A like task appeared to be the ambition of John Grote before the death of his father, which circumstance altered previous plans. Another brother was the famed historian, George (the eldest of the family of ten sons and one daughter). George Grote, too, was not uninterested in philosophy; his works on Plato and Aristotle are well known.

Moreover, the Grote family, especially George Grote, was well acquainted with John Stuart Mill to whom George Grote was introduced by Ricardo, and whose writings became the object of John Grote's constructive criticism. Mill introduced George Grote to Jeremy Bentham, and though George was not a member of "The Utilitarian Society" founded by J. S. Mill, he, nevertheless, was in sympathy with it. When the society became altered, in name at least, to form a society in systematic reading and study, George Grote donated the meeting-place.

George Grote was one of the supporters of the new university projected by Henry Brougham, Thomas Campbell, and James Mill. London University, therefore, had its beginning. Bitter controversy was waged before this institution was founded, and a chief impetus for its inauguration may be seen in the following:

Mill, with the approval of Bentham... resolved, in 1813, to start a 'West London Lancasterian Institution' to educate all the children west of Temple Bar on unsectarian principles.[3]

iii. Relationship with Ellis

It should be noted that much of the interest that Grote took in philosophy sprang from the stimulus supplied by Robert Leslie Ellis,

[1] Sorley, HEP, 264, 265.
[2] Cf. Chapter II, of this book.
[3] DNB, 37 (1894), 385.

a friend of his at the University for many years. Grote wrote an appreciation of Ellis [1] in which he claims that Ellis greatly influenced his life. Further information on just how Ellis made a strong impression on Grote is nowhere to be found; apparently no further word was ever written about this influence. Grote, however, does imply that he had very many conversations with Ellis in which Ellis seemed to insist on accuracy in thinking and expression. Moreover, other influences seem to be those which one makes on a close friend. The editors of *The Contemporary Review* [2] make the following statement in connection with the article [3] which Grote wrote:

The friend who wrote this memoir, was laid by his (Ellis's) side in August, 1866, the last of a group of remarkable men, too early lost, and long to be remembered in Cambridge.

Ellis held a fellowship at Cambridge for seven years, and was, up to the time of his death on May 12, 1859, in connection with the university. The last four years of tenure of this fellowship coincided with the first four years of Grote's position as professor of Moral Philosophy at Cambridge. These were only a few of the years of a life-long friendship at Cambridge, where Ellis took up the study of law and carried out detailed research in Roman jurisprudence, while Grote continued his interest in philosophy.

2. WRITINGS

i. Writings enumerated

Besides several volumes, Grote wrote numerous articles. Some of these articles are on specialized topics and will be discussed in the addenda at the close of this dissertation. The most important of Grote's writings is the one which presents the main tenets of his epistemology and metaphysics, the *Exploratio Philosophica*, Part I. Next in importance is Part II, posthumously edited by J. B. Mayor, his literary executor who was married to his adopted niece. Following in importance is *An Examination of the Utilitarian Philosophy* where Grote reveals his idealism. *A Treatise on the Moral Ideals* is next in significance. Here Grote's miscellaneous and loose notes are assembled by Mayor. These reveal his affinity with Aristotle's *summum bonum*,

---

[1] CR, 20 (1872), 56–71.
[2] CR, II (1872).
[3] *Loc. cit.*

and Plato's idealism. The complete list, since it is not extensive, of his known writings, may be given here:

1. "Commemoration Sermon," preached in Trinity College Chapel, December 15, 1849.
2. "Remarks on a Pamphlet by Mr. Shilleto entitled 'Thucydides or Grote,'" 1851.
3. "On the Dating of Roman History," in the *Journal of Classical and Sacred Philology*, vol. I, pp. 52–82.
4. "On the Origin and Meaning of Roman Names," in the *Journal of Classical and Sacred Philology*, vol. II, pp. 257–270, 1855.
5. "Old Essays and New" in *Cambridge Essays*, 1856.
6. "A Few Words on Criticism *a propos* of the Saturday Review." An exposure of an attack made by the *Saturday Review* on Whewell's *Platonic Dialogues*, 1861.
7. "Examination of some portions of Dr. Lushington's judgment in the cases of the Bishop of Salisbury v. Williams, and Fendall v. Wilson," in *Essays and Reviews*, 1862.
8. "A Few Words on the New Educational Code." 1862.
9. *Exploratio Philosophica*, Part I, 1865.
10. "What is Materialism?" in *Macmillan's Magazine*, 1867. Printed as chapters one, two, and three, in Part II, of *Exploratio Philosophica*.
11. *An Examination of the Utilitarian Philosophy*, 1870.
12. "On a Future State," in *The Contemporary Review* (1871), vol. 18.
13. "Thought vs. Learning," in *Good Words*, December, 1871.
14. A small selection of sermons was published by Messrs. Deighton in 1872.
15. "Memoir of (Robert) Leslie Ellis," published in *The Contemporary Review*, vol. XIX, June, 1872.
16. "Papers on Glossology," published in *Journal of Philology*, 1872 and 1874.
17. *A Treatise on the Moral Ideals*, 1876.
18. "Montaigne and Pascal," published in *The Contemporary Review*, July, 1877.
19. "Imaginary Conversation between Mr. Grote and Socrates," published in *The Classical Review*, March, 1889.
20. "Discussion on the Utilitarian Basis of Plato's Republic," in *The Classical Review*, 1889.
21. *Exploratio Philosophica*, Part II, 1900.[1]

ii. Remarks on writings

The article concerning Richard S. Shilleto was an attempt to counteract an attack upon his brother, George Grote, the Greek historian; Shilleto claimed that some of George Grote's statements contradicted views presented by Thucydides. Besides this article and the "Commemoration Sermon" he published only one or two classical articles. After he was elected to succeed William Whewell as Knightbridge Professor of Moral Philosophy, in 1855, he wrote copiously, in the form of notes, the most of which were later incorporated by Mayor in *Exploratio Philosophica* and *A Treatise on the Moral Ideals*.

[1] His chief writings as well as some miscellaneous ones are discussed in this book.

These notes were written more with a view toward clearing his own mind on various subjects than for any other purpose. He did not definitely decide to publish any of his writings till later.

Articles 3 to 8, above, were Grote's only writings until he produced *Exploratio Philosophica*, in 1865, a year before his death. This volume was hurriedly sent to press and became Part I, to which Grote wished to add Part II. However, Part II was not edited till long after his death, in 1900 (and then only in a most unfinished form), by Rev. Joseph Bickersteth Mayor, Grote's literary executor and husband of his adopted niece. Much of Part II of the *Exploratio Philosophica* was written by the year 1865. In 1870, Mayor edited *An Examination of the Utilitarian Philosophy* written by Grote to clear up his own views on Utilitarianism, which is largely a detailed criticism of John Stuart Mill's *Utilitarianism*. In 1876 there appeared *A Treatise on the Moral Ideals* to which Grote had not given a title. This volume is the product of his thought on ethical subjects which he decided to publish after *An Examination of the Utilitarian Philosophy*, and was partially printed in 1863.

Grote seems to have been responsible for coining several new words which have begun to find their way into common use, for example, 'personalism' as a philosophic term,[1] 'relativism,'[2] 'nervicity,'[3] 'hedonics,'[4] and many others. For example, though the Oxford dictionary states that 'relativism' was first used in 1885, Grote used it previous to 1876 in some unpublished papers entitled, "Relativism and Regulativism."[5] He wrote papers "On Glossology," some of which appeared a few years later in 1872 and 1874. Grote's accuracy in questions of philology is the same as that shown throughout all his writings and he probably will be remembered best for the distinction between psychology and philosophy. His able criticism of contemporary characters, such as William Whewell, Sir William Hamilton, John Stuart Mill, and others, was made to a great extent in the light of this clear distinction.

---

[1] Grote, EP, I, 146.
[2] *Op. cit.*, 183.
[3] *Op. cit.*, II, 254.
[4] Grote, EUP, Chap. XI.
[5] Grote, TMI, vii.

iii. Additional information relating to circumstances under which writings were presented

Moral fervor and sensitiveness were outstanding characteristics in Grote, and largely by reason of qualities such as these he attracted to himself the esteem of many people with whom he came into contact, especially in his private life.

In early years, Grote made a special study of history and was urged by his brother, George, in 1849, to make application for the chair of Modern History in Cambridge. However, Grote was unsuccessful in his application, and the office went to Sir James Stephen. John Grote was not married.

3. STATEMENT, AND DIVISION, OF THE PROBLEM

In this book, the problem is to arrive at a critical estimate of the writings or philosophic thought of John Grote. This problem, in the first place, entails a presentation of the distinction which Grote made between 'phenomenalism' and 'philosophy,' and the various shades of meaning of both. The problem becomes mainly an epistemological one and is closely connected with metaphysical considerations. Grote, in treating of this subject, deals with some well-known figures in modern philosophy, who will be treated in this work.

It is designed that a distinction will be made between phenomenal reality and things in themselves. Also, it will be shown that there is a fundamental monism throughout Grote's epistemology where the two factors in any theory of knowledge, namely, 'philosophy' and phenomena, are really only different ways of viewing the same reality. This is a major problem in the book and is basic throughout all the ten chapters. But the first eight chapters are specially epistemological. The last two, dealing with personalism and idealism show a basic epistemological emphasis but are characterized by idealism. The problem in these last chapters is to show Grote's professed position in the history of philosophy and to show how it is related to his 'philosophy' and phenomenalism. What he means by these last two terms will form the subject matter of the following two chapters, and less intensively, the other chapters of the book.

In order to make this present work comprehensive of all the known writings of Grote, articles which appeared in various periodicals are discussed; this part of the work appears at the end of the book, under the heading of *Appendix*.

4. SURVEY OF SOURCES AND OF
PREVIOUS WORK ON THE PROBLEM

i. Sources

a. Plato

Examples of the early use of 'noumenon' appear in the *Republic* and in the *Parmenides*, as a synonym for rational intuition. In early Greek philosophy, 'phenomena' meant the opposite of 'essences' or ὄντα. Hence the early meaning of phenomena was that of a derived type of reality.

b. Kant and other modern philosophers

In Kant, a definite distinction is made between 'phenomenon' and 'noumenon.' It was he who instituted a veritable gold-mine of research in the distinctions and comments he makes upon the use of these ideas and how they are related to reality. Kant greatly influenced Grote, and was himself indirectly affected in his epistemology by such bifurcation as that presented in the Two Worlds theory of Plato.

ii. Previous work on the problem

In carrying out his discussion of phenomena, as he contrasts it with what he calls 'philosophy,' 'mind,' 'spirit,' or 'consciousness,' Grote is carried into a systematic criticism of the positions of many philosophers who do not adhere to the distinctions made by Kant and who confuse what Grote regards as the two sides of the epistemological problem, which may be briefly stated by such terms as form and matter, or subject and object. The epistemological problem is not a simple one and Grote deals with it from many angles. Among those who are guilty of confusion in epistemology and are dealt with at considerable length, are, Ferrier, Hamilton, J. S. Mill, Whewell, Locke, Berkeley, Hume, Spencer, and Dugald Stewart.

Grote makes an original contribution in the clarity with which he attacks the vulnerable position of some of his predecessors and contemporaries. What these positions are, and how Grote deals with them, necessitates an examination of the previous work, on the problem, which is surveyed in the foregoing.

5. TRANSITION TO NEXT CHAPTER

What Grote's original position was, will be presented in the main body of this work, beginning with his view of phenomenalism in the following chapter. In the present chapter four main points were presented and briefly discussed, Grote's life, his writings, statement and division of the problem, and sources and survey of previous work done on the problem.

A brief discussion of Grote's writings seemed to be fitting as part of an introduction to a work designed to deal with these major writings. It is of supreme importance that notice should be taken of the distinction that Grote makes between 'philosophy' and consciousness and the importance of this distinction for his epistemology. Let us, therefore, begin with a presentation of Grote's view of phenomenalism involving a consideration of a distinction amongst terms, such as 'noumenon,' 'phenomenon,' and 'thing in itself.'

CHAPTER II

GROTE'S VIEW OF PHENOMENALISM

1. DISTINCTION OF TERMS: 'NOUMENON,' 'PHENOMENON,' AND 'THING IN ITSELF'

i. Derivation and meaning of 'noumenon,' and 'phenomenon'

a. *'Noumenon'*

As a basis for his constructive criticism of James Frederick Ferrier, Sir William Hamilton, John Stuart Mill, and others, Grote seeks in the beginning of the *Exploratio Philosophica* to show what he means by the term 'phenomenalism.' The use of the word 'noumenon' is, at least, as old as Plato. It is therefore expedient to refer to the use of these words, 'noumenon,' and 'phenomenon', in their earliest connotation. Examples of the early use of 'noumenon' are in the *Republic*,[1] and in the *Parmenides*.[2] The word 'noumenon' is derived from the Greek, νοούμενον, anything known, from νοεῖν, 'to know.' It is the German 'Ding-an-sich.' It is free from all sense, and is the object of rational intuition, or pure thought.

b. *'Phenomenon'*

The word 'phenomenon' comes from το φαινόμενον, meaning something that appears, or is seen; the German word is 'Phenomen' which appears to have the same meaning as the word 'Erscheinung.'

In early Greek, 'phenomena' was the opposite of ὄντα, or 'essences.'

---

[1] τοῦτον τοίνυν, ἦν δ'ἐγώ, φάναι με λέγειν τὸν τοῦ ἀγαθοῦ ἔκγονον, ὃν τἀγαθὸν ἐγέννησεν ἀνάλογον ἑαυτῷ, ὅτιπερ αὐτὸ ἐν τῷ νοητῷ τόπῳ πρός τε νοῦν καὶ τὰ *νοούμενα*, τοῦτο τοῦτον ἐν τῷ ὁρατῷ πρός τε ὄψιν καὶ τὰ ὁρώμενα.

("And this is he whom I call the child of the good, whom the good begat in his own likeness, to be in the visible world, in relation to sight and the things of sight, what the good is in the intellectual world in relation to mind and the things of mind." Jowett trans.). *Republic*, 508.

[2] Εἶτα οὐκ εἶδος ἔσται τοῦτο τὸ *νοούμενον* ἓν εἶναι, ἀεὶ ὂν τὸ αὐτὸ ἐπὶ πᾶσιν.

("And will not the something which is apprehended as one and the same in all, be an idea?" Jowett trans.). *Parmenides*, 132.

Hence it was early considered to possess a derived type of reality. There existed no real chasm between the two though they might readily be contrasted; the reason for the contrast is because the phenomena involve the senses and are changeable, while the essences do not change, are related to reason, and are one and eternal. Such was the distinction in Greek thought, but successive ages brought their modification, so that in modern philosophy the word 'phenomenon' is contrasted with 'thing in itself' or 'noumenon.' (But note the distinction between 'thing in itself' and 'noumenon,' and also affinity of 'thing in itself' to 'phenomenon,' below.) 'Phenomenon' is that which has the appearance (Schein) of reality. Kant regards the thing in itself as that which is basic to all reality.

The true correlate of sensibility, the thing in itself, is not known, and cannot be known, through these representations; and in experience no question is ever asked in regard to it.[1]

Our further contention must also be duly borne in mind, namely, that though we cannot know these objects as things in themselves, we must yet be in position at least to think them as things in themselves; otherwise we should be landed in the absurd conclusion that there can be appearance without anything that appears.[2]

That is, 'phenomenon' depends upon the manner in which 'thing in itself' affects the senses.

The above is, in outline, an indication of the change which the word 'phenomenon' has undergone. But another use of the word should be mentioned, which is really a part or by-product of the gradual unfolding of meaning that time has brought to the word 'phenomenon.' It is used in a positivistic sense, and this is the manner in which John Grote employs the word.

I am about to explain a manner of thought which in various applications, or perhaps misapplications, of it, I have been in the habit of mentally characterizing, and perhaps of speaking of, as 'positivism.' I shall now however not use this term, but the term 'phenomenalism.' I understand the two terms to express in substance the same thing.[3]

The distinction, then, amongst the terms, 'noumenon,' 'phenomenon,' and 'thing in itself,' may be stated as follows: 'Noumenon' is the object for thought, or, "the *object* as it is for *true thought*." [4] 'Phenomenon' is "the object as it appears to the senses." [5] The 'thing in itself'

---

[1] Kant, CPR, 74.
[2] *Op. cit.*, 27.
[3] Grote, EP, I, 1.
[4] Brightman, ITP, 389.
[5] *Loc. cit.*

is "the true correlate of sensibility." It is that which "is not known, and cannot be known." [1]

ii. 'Noumenon,' 'phenomenon,' and 'thing in itself,' as used by Kant

Grote appears to fall into the tradition of Kant, and certain it is that Kant had a profound influence on Grote's philosophy. Grote believes, however, that the distinction between phenomena (as related to us), and, things in themselves as objects in themselves, cannot decisively be made. To meet this difficulty, Kant employed matter and form; but since matter in the smallest detail is subject to quantitative laws, this enployment to distinguish between phenomena and things in themselves is not finally effective.

It is important to observe that Kant employs 'thing in itself' as something which can be thought and yet is not an object of sense. Thought, thus, ascribes limits to the realm of sense and indicates a world of things in themselves. The 'idea' is the word Kant used for the ideal of totality which is characteristic of the world of 'things in themselves.' The world of things in themselves, or the world of 'noumena,' could be reached by practical reason, for it is the object of pure thought. However, through a consciousness of "duty done for duty's sake," theoretically at least, the world of the noumenon (which may be *thought* but cannot be *known*), may become a practical reality. Moreover, teleology in science, Kant holds, attempts to bridge the chasm between 'noumenon' and 'phenomenon' in that it asserts that the latter depends for its foundation upon the former.

This purposive order is quite alien to the things of the world, and only belongs to them contingently; that is to say, the diverse things could not of themselves have co-operated, by so great a combination of diverse means, to the fulfilment of determinate final purposes, had they not been chosen and designed for these purposes by an ordering rational principle in conformity with underlying ideas. [2]

Yet it does not affirm (because it cannot) that 'noumenon' exists, though it treats 'phenomenon' as though the former did exist.

The difficulty then appeared to be as to whether or not there is a road from 'noumenon' to 'phenomenon.' Kant attempted to assert a distinction between the two that would remain firm. There was a difficulty here, and to cope with it did not appear easy.

[1] Kant, CPR, 74.
[2] *Op. cit.*, 521.

Kant had taken the two words, things-in-themselves and noumena as wholly synonymous, and accordingly had called on the one hand, duties things-in-themselves, and, on the other, the unknown cause of our sensations noumenon. Here... Reinhold distinguishes very exactly. Noumenon is never anything else to him than Idea of the reason, a demand. Hence it never signifies anything other than what always remains beyond experience: it is an eternal ought.[1]

iii. Reinhold on 'noumenon,' and 'thing in itself'

Let us look at some critical remarks on Kant's use of the terms, 'noumenon' and 'thing in itself,' in order to bring out the meaning of these terms more clearly. Reinhold [2] was conscious of the confusion between the thing in itself and the noumenon, because if the 'noumenon' was regarded as the ground of 'phenomenon' there was need of an explanation here. Fichte attempted to solve this difficulty as well as did the successors of Kant. Reinhold regarded the thing in itself as the source of the 'matter' for our perceptions as distinguished from the noumenon which stood for the problems and ideals which remain unrealized for the mind and which thought sets for experience. The noumenon is therefore not identical with thing in itself, but rather, the thing in itself has a closer relationship with phenomenon.

2. WHAT PHENOMENALISM MEANS

i. Three ways in which phenomenalism has been regarded

Phenomena may be regarded:

a. As mere appearance – as opposed therefore to objective reality. Into this objective reality human knowledge cannot penetrate. Hence epistemological considerations have only to do with the realm of phenomena. This appears, by far, the most commonly held view of the three, though disciples of Henri Bergson, Shadworth Hodgson, and others might be firm in their claims for either one of the other two views of phenomenalism here presented.

b. From the time of Heraclitus this view has existed. The only reality is flux, or phenomena. Among modern philosophers, Bergson as well as others held to this conception.

c. External existence has no place. All reality may be reduced to

---

[1] Erdmann, HOP, II, 479.

[2] Reinhold, at one time professor of philosophy at Jena, undertook extensive reshaping and transforming of the Kantian philosophy. Cf. Windelband, HOP, 570.

appearance; events or things in space and time are rejected. Shadworth Hodgson ardently supports this view.

ii. Grote's meaning

The point of immediate concern is, what is Grote's view? As already mentioned, Grote uses the term 'phenomenalism' for positivism. Phenomenalism would seek to subordinate the study of philosophy to the special sciences. Or in Grote's own words:

Phenomenalism [is] that notion of the various objects of knowledge which go to make up the universe which belongs to the point of view of physical science.[1]

The reason why Grote uses the word 'phenomenalism' instead of 'positivism' is because in the former there is a 'purely intellectual application' which the term 'positivism' does not possess. The term 'phenomena' is an abstraction because it is a looking, for the time being (that is, from the aspect of 'things'), at the 'objects' of physical science. But 'phenomena' are never wholly unrelated *to us*, otherwise they would not be phenomena at all.

Phenomenalism implies a way of looking at objects. If examination is made as to how man arrives at the knowledge which the facts of phenomenalism give, or if consideration is given to man's conduct with regard to such facts after he has a consciousness of them, then the field is one with which phenomenalism is not directly concerned. Consideration as to how man arrives at knowledge is the task of philosophy and not of phenomenalism, strictly speaking. Phenomenalism, like physical science, deals with the view of the object of knowledge in contrast to philosophy which deals with the logical view of the process of knowledge. What Grote means by 'philosophy' should be described here:

Philosophy, by which I mean the study of thought and feeling not as we see them variously associated with corporeal organization, and producing various results in the universe, but as we understand, think, feel them of ourselves and from within, is something to me of an entirely different nature, and leads to entirely different fields of speculation from the physio-psychology which I have been speaking of. I think that those who have the truest view of the one will also have the truest of the other.[2]

It is very important that these two, phenomenalism and 'philosophy' should be kept separate, otherwise there is likelihood of error like

---

[1] Grote, EP, I, 2.
[2] *Op, cit.,* xi.

that of J. S. Mill and William Whewell who did not keep physical science distinctly separated from 'logic' or consciousness.[1]

iii. Berkeley's meaning

a. General

Grote states that the verb of phenomenalism is, *is*, rather than *feels* – the verb of consciousness. This distinction turns on a possible confusion in two different points of departure, when looking at reality. Grote maintains that the confusion arising from Berkeley's thought is due to lack of realizing that there is this double point of departure. The fact of phenomena, Grote feels, is overlooked. Grote may be seen to deal with Berkeley in more detail in a later part of this dissertation. He notes also that the double point of departure exists when no distinction is made between phenomenal reality, and consciousness (or 'philosophy'), and when it is not expressedly observed that these two aspects of reality may be confused with each other. Grote's criticism of Berkeley is not too well taken, but there are some elements of his criticism that are significant. These will be dealt with in a later chapter.

b. Physiologist denies any distinction between 'philosophy' and phenomena

Of course, the physiologist may deny this distinction when he attempts to demonstrate that such and such will happen when a particular stimulus is supplied. But there is no final assurance that it actually will happen. That it will happen must forever remain in the realm of the unknown. For example, the physiologist cannot experience the sensation of the individual. The feeling of the individual may be quite different than what the physiologist believes that it is.

In connection with Berkeley's position in this chapter the following comment of Grote should be noted:

> The phenomenal assumption is that the world of reality exists quite independently of being known by any knowing beings in it... The Berkeleian idealism is little more than the easy demonstration that this view, from a philosophical standpoint, is untenable: that the notion of existence, as distinguished from perceivedness, is, nakedly and rudely stated, as abhorrent to the philosopher as that of perceivingness and will in any part of the matter the laws of which he is seeking is to the phenomenalist.[2]

Here Grote's analysis of the communication between mind and

---

[1] The position of J. S. Mill and William Whewell will be dealt with in detail in later chapters.

[2] Grote, EP, I, 4.

'external' reality comes sharply to the point. Grote seems to be implying that the notion of existence, in distinction from perceivedness, is abhorrent to any philosopher, and that this is self-evident. He tries to show that the philosopher hasn't got this view of reality at all, but one very close to Berkeley's own. It is interesting to note, that Grote claims, virtually, to be very close to Berkeley since he argues that phenomenalism is not the only view of reality that is possible, and seems to hold also, with Berkeley, that there is *no* reality "without the mind."

Grote is scarcely fair to Berkeley if he has in mind that Berkeley is asserting only a commonplace remark when he contends that Berkeley virtually deprecates physical science. Most idealists, as well as others, would agree with Berkeley, as against physical scientists.

Grote deals with the sentence, "we perceive things," in a manner which reminds one of much of the present-day discussions on theories of value. He speaks of 'sensation' being a misleading term because it suggests an action from without rather than from within (that is, within the mind of a human being) when in actuality it should not give such a one-sided emphasis. The term, 'impression,' he states, is not so misleading because it suggests action from without outwards – more so than from without inwards. Hence the importance, he concludes, of stressing the 'communication' between the senses and objects. By this emphasis Grote has anticipated much discussion upon the subject of value, in maintaining the importance of both subjective and objective approaches. Phenomenal reality rests in the communication, between 'objects' and consciousness. Yet, even though this is so,

phenomenal reality so far as it exists, is what it is quite independently of the manner in which anyone knows it, and even independently of its being known at all by anybody, or of there being any such thing as consciousness, or of mind, to know it, except so far, as I have said, as this 'mind' may produce phenomenal effects.[1]

The existence of consciousness has nothing to do with it except insofar as consciousness may produce the effects of phenomenal reality, for example, as illustrated in discussion of the sentence, "we perceive things."

Knowledge of phenomenal reality is an accident of it, and an inescapable one. Since the reality itself is independent of mind and since the only time we come to *affirm* the existence of objects is *after*

[1] Grote, EP, I, 8.

they are observed as existing, then phenomenal reality cannot be observed in any way by the senses even though it may communicate with consciousness.

What, then, is the difference between this phenomenon and thing in itself? Grote attempts to make the position clear. Apparently Kant had confused the issue somewhat, and certainly he has, according to Reinhold, a Kantian critic, commentator, and contemporary. Kant's blurring of the issue is cleared by Reinhold who regards the thing in itself as the source of matter for our perceptions and therefore distinct from the noumenon, which, for example, has to do with the idea of God or that which never can be known by the senses or that for which the senses can never furnish a background. That is, the noumenon denotes the unrealizable problems and ideals which thought sets for experience. Hence the thing in itself has a closer connection here to phenomenon than to noumenon. But this is not so, according to Kant, for

At the same time if we entitle certain objects, as appearances, sensible entities [1] (phenomena), then since we thus distinguish the mode in which we intuit them from the nature that belongs to them in themselves, it is implied in this distinction that we place the latter, considered in their own nature, although we do not so intuit them, or that we place other possible things, which are not objects of our senses but are thought as objects merely through the understanding, in opposition to the former, and that in so doing we entitle them intelligible entities [2] (noumena).[3]

iv. Grote is specially concerned with 'phenomenon' and 'thing in itself'

Grote does not deal with the 'noumenon' of Kant to any extent, but he was apparently influenced by this concept. For he discusses ideals which, like the 'noumenon' can be *thought* but cannot be *known*. But the concepts 'phenomena' and 'thing in itself' are of prime importance. 'Phenomena' are basic in all his discussions of reality.

3. PHENOMENAL REALITY

i. How it is 'seen'

The difficulty with forming conceptions of phenomena is that these conceptions do not do justice to phenomenal reality. Phenomenal

---

[1] Sinnenwesen.
[2] Verstandeswesen.
[3] Kant, CPR, 266, 267.

reality is judged to be such *after* conceptions have been formed of it, not *before*. In the sentence, "we perceive things," there is communication but consciousness has to intervene before the 'things' are perceived. Or the matter may be put thus: Things as they are (as it were), attempt to communicate themselves (their phenomenal reality), but by reason of the mind of men they are looked at through a glass darkly, and the glass is always there (but a different kind for each individual). That which makes phenomenal reality appear as it is, is the fact that the glass *is* there. "To find phenomenal reality, we must find that which can be known, so far as it is known, in common by all."[1] Generally speaking, therefore, the standpoint of phenomenalism is the same for each one.

We have nothing... phenomenally, to do with the way in which the universe is known to us (because its being known is an accident of it), but we have of course to do with the way in which the different parts of it communicate... with the bodily frame.[2]

And if phenomenalism had nothing to do with the bodily frame it would not be phenomenalism but the realm of things in themselves – which, of course, could not be a sensible realm at all, since it would be out of all relation to life, and could neither be asserted nor even thought.

ii. How it is related to life

It may be stated here that "space and time are phenomenal realities in virtue of this their relation to matter and movement, not otherwise." [3] 'Natural agents' are what are furnished to the realms of space and time. The unity that is in nature, and which 'natural agents' to a certain extent furnish, results in perplexity to phenomenal reality as to what life is. Life suggests unity. Each person may know what life means to himself, but only so. He cannot feel what it is for any other. Phenomenal reality cannot comprehend what life is. This may readily be observed by recalling that phenomenal reality is what it is quite independent of the feeling of any individual.

4. TWO TESTS OF PHENOMENALISM

Moreover, phenomenal reality presents a phenomenal truth test. We are convinced that when we act in a certain manner that certain

[1] Grote, EP, I, 9.
[2] *Op. cit.*, 10.
[3] *Op. cit.*, 11.

results will always readily follow. This is a phenomenal test of truth. Phenomenal reality responds to our actions. There is also another test that phenomenalism presents, namely: We believe that a certain thing exists because we see it; and we believe that it will be found to exist if others, as well as ourselves, see it. This is a belief that what we see could be handled, heard, etc. Bacon believed in the utility of practical knowledge and what was of little or no utility was of little or no consequence as practical knowledge; in fact, it could not be practical knowledge. In so believing, Bacon was simply applying the first test of truth. With reference to the second, it is sufficient to state that the fact that we believe, for example, in the existence of a certain object which we see even before we handle or touch it, is because our sight is ordinarily a safe criterion and what it finds out to be true is verified by other senses in the same individual and also by the same or other senses in different individuals.

In actuality these two phenomenal tests for truth are one. They both include response of phenomenal reality to bodily action, or to a particular sense, or senses. That is, reality, or phenomena, responds to the senses. It communicates with them, but nevertheless does not require the senses for its reality. The phenomenal test of truth cannot be made without communication with the senses or a responding in some manner to bodily form. Otherwise it could not be a *test* of truth.

This phenomenal truth test, of Grote's, does not seem justifiable even on the grounds he has accepted himself, to the effect that there are two different aspects of reality, 'thought' and phenomena. These tests run into the same difficulty as a correspondence theory of truth, that assumes 'objects' as *already* in relation to thought when a correspondence is sought. It would *seem* that these tests presented by Grote are *consciously* presented as unjustifiable, or, Grote is in error in presenting phenomenal truth tests which really are not tests at all. It is, apparently, fairer to assume that the former alternative is the correct one.

5. THE PHENOMENALIST SPIRIT OR MIND

Concerning the phenomenalist spirit or mind, Grote holds that the phenomenalist spirit is not something which man has originally; it is more like a gradual growth which is increasingly observant in that it watches out for new knowledge, and leaves a place for such, and is directly dependent upon phenomenal reality. Moral approval or disapproval in the growth of this spirit should not be countenanced. Grote probably holds that such approval or disapproval is not admissible since the growth of this spirit would seem to be largely biological and epistemological.

Order which the phenomenalist spirit recognizes should not approach in the slightest extent that order which individuals are prone to observe in the universe and give to various events and things in it. Not only should the phenomenalist spirit be on the alert for new knowledge and adjust itself accordingly but also should hold certain events and things exclusively, that is, allowing no other conviction to enter into our belief and yet at other times not formulate any conception about certain things and events which because of their nature should remain in doubt.

However, in all this it is of supreme importance to observe that phenomenal reality is what it is irrespective of being *known*. Nothing should be postulated *of* the universe beyond what is discovered there, otherwise the mind is prone to conceive of unity and order where there actually is none.

6. SUMMARY AND FOREWORD TO NEXT CHAPTER

In the foregoing chapter the attempt was made to show what Grote means by the terms 'philosophy' and 'phenomena,' and to show the relationship amongst the terms 'phenomena,' 'noumena,' and 'thing in itself.' Various traditional usages of these terms were dealt with. Very general remarks were made on the place these terms have chiefly in relation to Plato, Berkeley and Kant. These remarks were intended to be illustrative and indicative rather than exhaustive. It was pointed out that the meanings that Grote gives to 'philosophy' and phenomena are especially important. Neither of these can be wholly abstracted from all connection with the other. Each requires the other. Each is connected in some important way *with us*.

However, neither term can properly be considered even in considerable isolation from the other for the meaning of each is partially to be found in its essential counterpart. Just what the relationship between these terms is requires much comment and exposition. To this task we now turn as we consider 'Grote's interpretation of the relation of phenomenalism to philosophy,' in chapter three.

CHAPTER III

GROTE'S INTERPRETATION OF THE RELATION OF PHENOMENALISM TO PHILOSOPHY

1. EACH IS NECESSARY TO THE OTHER

There are two main parts to Grote's thesis in *Exploratio Philosophica*. The preceding chapter dealt with one and stressed it particularly, though mention was also made of the other. It would be impossible to deal with one to the utter exclusion of the other. These two are entitled phenomenalism and 'philosophy.' Let us recall the distinction which Grote makes between these two terms:

I shall call by the name 'phenomenalism' that notion of the various objects of knowledge which go to make up the universe which belong to the point of view of physical science.[1]

When Grote turns to what he calls 'philosophy and consciousness' [2] he considers the "process of knowing... without any reference to any thing being known." [3]

If we consider simply the process of knowing, or ask ourselves what knowledge is, without any reference to any thing being known, we have again what, in respect of the whole fact, is an abstraction, in the same way in which, on *its* side, phenomenalism is so.[4]

It may be stated that Grote here presents his view of physical things. True to his epistemological monism he regards the reality of physical things as capable of being approached from two sides, that of 'philosophy' and of phenomena. In this view he is a Kantian inasmuch as he recognizes the utmost significance of what Kant refers to as the 'pure concepts of the understanding.' [5] This recognition is manifested in his 'philosophical' approach, an abstraction from reality. Kant, Grote would maintain, should hold that these pure concepts are ab-

[1] Grote, EP, I, 2.
[2] *Op. cit.*, 17–33.
[3] *Op. cit.*, 17.
[4] *Loc. cit.*
[5] Kant, CPR, 104.

stractions from reality which must be regarded also as having a phenomenal side. He differs from Kant in holding that we cannot even
refer to a thing in itself apart from a phenomenon. For such would be
an unwarranted abstraction. In his view Grote is also a Berkeleian
inasmuch as he would maintain that we can never regard any reality
as having *significance* for us without being related to mind in a
meaningful way. That is, it would make no *sense* for Grote to contend
that there are real physical things 'out there.'

2. CONSCIOUSNESS AS ACTIVE AND PASSIVE

i. The phenomenalist view presupposes consciousness passive

Grote states that the phenomenalist view is founded on a supposition, namely that we are passive in the knowing process.[1] This
view supposes that we are present at the communication between
certain natural agents and the parts of our body affected by those
agents. There is a communication between matter on one side (the
object for us), and matter on the other side (the matter of our body).
This communication is *accompanied by* a feeling, or by knowledge
(which is *a sort of* feeling). The communication and the knowledge are
coexistent but they are not identical. The communication is between
phenomenal reality and the bodily organs. Knowledge is a sort of
'inward' end of the communication and its role is essentially to give
meaning to the process.

The *parts* of the communication may be referred to, according to
Grote, correctly, as 'sensation.' But in respect to the whole of the
communication we have 'experience.' The extension of this communication makes possible the extension of knowledge. There is a process
going on, then, according to Grote, which is referred to as 'nature.' This
process is phenomenal because it goes on whether we are conscious
of it or not. Phenomenal reality does not necessarily 'appear' but it
can affect us through communication and adjustments of our bodily
organs to meet the stimuli. In the knowing process Grote holds that
we are *passive* (but also *active*).[2] Bowne maintains that we are active.

A certain sense of effort manifests itself, and we seem so to permeate the body
that our own spiritual force comes in contact with the reality. But the sense of

[1] "The phenomenalist view rests on a supposition, one way of putting which is that
we are thus *passive* in knowledge..." Grote, EP, I, 35.
[2] Cf. '*ii. Consciousness is also active*,' below.

tension and effort in the muscles, in such cases, is but the reaction of the organism against the volition, and has merely the function of teaching us how to measure our activity.[1]

Kant in 'The Deduction of the Pure Concepts of Understanding' says that the pure concepts are like seeds that lie prepared, so that on the occasion of experience they are developed. The mind is active, therefore, for Kant in the knowing process. He states that he has undertaken

the hitherto rarely attempted *dissection of the faculty of the understanding* itself, in order to investigate the possibility of concepts *a priori* by looking for them in the understanding alone, as their birthplace, and by analysing the pure use of this faculty. This is the proper task of a transcendental philosophy; anything beyond this belongs to the logical treatment of concepts in philosophy in general. We shall therefore follow up the pure concepts to their first seeds and dispositions in the human understanding, in which they lie prepared, till at last, on the occasion of experience, they are developed.[2]

a. *Consciousness of a process taking place between the matter of nature and the matter of our bodies*

But the consciousness of the process between the matter of nature and the matter of our body cannot go on without our witnessing, or being present at, or having awareness of, this process. This witnessing is consciousness. This is the particular part of the whole noetic process which Grote frequently refers to as 'consciousness,' 'intelligence,' or 'philosophy.' To pay attention to it alone is to abstract 'philosophy' from that without which there could be no 'philosophy' or 'awareness' at all.

I said, in speaking of the awakening of our consciousness, that the first recognition of our own being is accompanied with the recognition of something besides it, or of an universe into which we are born. It is the same as if I had said, that the first recognition of anything not ourselves, or of the universe, was accompanied by the recognition of our own being. In each case the one is the counter-notion of the other: the notion of the one is formed by distinguishing it from the other. Whichever is the first distinct and affirmative notion is in a manner not the first, for the other is the ground and basis of it.[3]

However, Grote does not hold that both are *equally* immediate. There is 'immediateness,' he maintains, essentially in what he calls the 'self-self' but immediateness disappears in the 'thought-self' when reflection enters.

[1] Bowne, MET, 74.
[2] Kant, CPR, 103.
[3] Grote, EP, I, 47.

b. Kant recognizes phenomenal reality as a necessary supplement to reason

Awakening of our consciousness, or rousing of our awareness, means the awakening of our consciousness of *something*, or the rousing of our awareness of *something*, a witnessing of an essential communication between the matter of nature and the matter of our bodies. One might paraphrase Kant here, by saying phenomenal process without consciousness is *blind*; consciousness without the phenomenal communication is *empty*.

Without sensibility no object would be given to us, without understanding no object would be thought. Thoughts without content are empty, intuitions without concepts are blind.[1]

ii. Consciousness is also active

There is an important sense, Grote would hold, in which the phenomenalist view – which we are regarding as dealing with the intercommunication referred to, in abstraction from that part of the knowing process which is aware of the intercommunication taking place – is *wrongly* phenomenal. For the phenomenalist, consciousness is regarded as *passive*. Grote, on the other hand, calls attention to the fact that the passive side of consciousness is only one part of the field. For consciousness means *activity*, also. It means not only consciousness as in "pleasurable or painful feeling, but also consciousness of willing or acting." [2] The reason why the phenomenal approach is wrong in this respect is because our consciousness of acting or willing is much more difficult for us to conceive than our consciousness as passive. But though it may be regarded conceptually as more difficult, this characteristic of consciousness as active is as real as the passive nature of consciousness.

The roots however of the phenomenalist (that is, the wrongly phenomenalist) view lie deep, going even to the original supposition, that it is feeling (or susceptibility) that makes our being, and not feeling and acting (or willing) as well... We are sometimes inadvertently led to this view by our language, when we say that it is consciousness which shows to us our personality: by this we *should* mean not only consciousness as pleasurable or painful feeling, but consciousness of willing or acting.[3]

This difficulty is due to the great number and variety of things which seem to act upon us, whereas we are very limited in the amount of action which we can carry out on things in contact with us.

[1] Kant, CPR, 93.
[2] Grote, EP, I, 36.
[3] *Loc. cit.*

a. Emphasis on 'philosophy' may lead to epistemological idealism

The 'philosophical,' or consciousness, view, though an abstraction from what Grote regards as phenomenalism, is, nevertheless, an approach that is frequently found in epistemology. Emphasis upon it is, he would seem to agree, epistemological idealism. This emphasis is not mistaken, but it results from an abstraction which is weak only when it overlooks the phenomenalist view. The strength of the abstraction of thought from phenomena is evident in that we are *always* on the side of thought and, conversely, could never be on the side of 'objects' in abstraction from thought or consciousness. Later [1] it will be shown how necessarily idealistic and personalistic this emphasis on consciousness, or the self, becomes in Grote.

b. Sensation, intelligence, and will

(1) These three terms have a close relationship to each other – The idealistic emphasis can be detected even in connection with the term 'sensation' which would not *mean* anything without consciousness. We can speak, Grote would contend, about having sensations only insofar as they have *meaning* somehow *for us*. Grote groups together sensation, intelligence, and will,[2] as representing this 'philosophical' approach. In dealing with these three, he reveals further, the essential relation between phenomenalism and 'philosophy.' This, he does not do briefly and in a few words, but with patience one may discover his argument – an argument that cannot easily be pointed out by referring to any particular passage but which is, nevertheless, present, and once discovered is peculiarly stimulating. Let us, then, turn to his specific discussion of intelligence and will, both of which are inseparable from sensation. The three terms may well be considered together.

(2) Sensation and experience – What sensation is can be indicated in the intercommunication which takes place between particular natural agents and specific parts of our bodies. "The communication, which in respect of the particular portions of it is called 'sensation,' is often in respect to the whole of it called 'experience.' " [3] Grote here reveals the synoptic view.

(3) Contemplation is essentially non-phenomenal; communication is phenomenal – In experience – and sensation, as

---

[1] In chapters IX and X.
[2] Grote, EP, I, 34–52.
[3] *Op. cit.*, 35.

the parts of it – there is a continual process taking place which is called 'nature.' Hand in hand with it goes contemplation. Contemplation is essentially non-phenomenal; the process, or communication between ('outer') phenomenal reality and our bodily organs (as 'inner' phenomenal reality), is phenomenal. One must hold on to this, to lose sight of which is to forfeit the peculiar meaning which Grote assigns to the phenomenal.

There is a process going on which we call 'nature,' and there is a wonderful, extra-phenomenal power of contemplating this process: the whole is knowledge.[1]

(4) Contemplation is both active and passive – Grote takes special care to point out, however, that this contemplation is not simply *passive*. It is *active*. Intelligence and will are active. Moreover, they are essentially non-phenomenal. Yet they deal with the phenomenal, the "process going on which we call 'nature.'" [2] That is, the phenomenal and the 'extra-phenomenal' are inseparable. The 'extra-phenomenal' is the realm of 'philosophy.' To separate it decisively from the phenomenal is an unwarranted abstraction.

(5) Commencement of willing requires particulars – When we wake, we wake into a universe of things. Our waking is not to ourselves, and, specifically, not to our consciousness alone. If it were, then a decisive bifurcation would be justified between thought and the process which thought contemplates. There are commencements of acting and willing which make the universe, that we contemplate, a universe of *particulars* (as well as a *uni*verse). All of this commencement of willing, or intelligent acting, as well as the continuation of it, is involved in the term, 'sensation,' which without some such qualifications, is only loosely used.

(6) Recapitulation on the knowing process – Let us now return briefly to consider the knowing process, generally, in its entirety, and to see the place of sensation, intelligence, and will, in it. Grote contends that there are two extremes in the knowing process, the thought or consciousness end and the 'thing' or phenomenal end. Each considered by itself is an abstraction. There are no things except *for consciousness*, and there is no thought that does not involve that which is *thought of*. Intelligence refers to the extreme of consciousness. Sensation involves both extremes and is certainly neither purely thought nor purely phenomenal reality. The will is *active* and reveals the active nature of consciousness, and that there is that upon which

[1] Grote, EP, I, 36.
[2] *Loc. cit.*

it acts, namely, phenomenal reality. This general and brief summation will be supplemented in what follows.

3. ANALYSIS OF SENSATION

i. Sensing in general

Before considering the relation of these considerations to *time* and *space*, let us look at the term 'sensation' and the analysis which Grote makes of it. Grote holds that

An instance of what appears to me the confusion between philosophy and logic on the one side, and physiology or phenomenalism on the other, appears in the manner in which the whole question of sensation has constantly been treated.[1]

Sensation, for Grote, means sensing in general. But sensing in general must be further qualified.

a. 'Sensation proper' and 'the sensation of our activity.'

Grote refers to 'sensation proper'[2] by which he means *passive* sensing as in our 'sensations' of pleasure and pain. He distinguishes this part of 'sensation' from 'the sensation of our activity,'[3] meaning, by this latter term, sensations of willing, or acting. In either case, namely, passive or active sensing, intelligence or awareness is involved and not merely *sensing*. It is from this sensing in general that intelligence gazes upon phenomenal reality. Without the intellectual elements which are combined in this sensing (i.e. the *intellectual* part of it – for there are intellectual elements involved in the term 'sensing' as it is ordinarily used, Grote states), phenomenal reality would not *mean* anything at all.

b. Philosophy and logic

What Grote means by 'philosophy and logic,[4] is the intellectual end of a process of communication through our various organs of sense, which – were it not for the intellect – would be purely physical. 'Sensation,' as this term is ordinarily used, carries this implication of 'philosophy and logic' with it, Grote believes. Some sensations more than others imply consciousness; others seem to be almost purely physical. But, according to Grote's view of sensation there is never a

---

[1] Grote, EP, I, 19.
[2] *Op. cit.*, 38.
[3] *Loc. cit.*
[4] *Op. cit.*, 19.

complete absence of *knowing* however minute, since phenomenal reality is never wholly unconcerned with 'philosophy' (or 'logic'). The physiologist and phenomenalist treat sensation as physical. They assume intelligence involved in 'sensation' without accounting for it.

ii. Two meanings of sensation

There are two meanings that may be taken from the term 'sensation.' First:

'Sensation,' meaning by the term an affection or modification (however we may style it) of our senses (to use that misleading expression), nerves, and brain, is a phenomenon belonging to the domain of physiology. It is what I have... called 'communication.' [1]

Second:

'Sensation,' meaning by the term a feeling on our part, or a portion or instances of consciousness, which, in whatever manner, grows into knowledge, is a fact so far as we call it one, belonging to a different order of thought, and it is philosophy or logic which must deal with it so far as it can be dealt with.[2]

We will now consider these two meanings in relation to *time* and *space*, in Grote's view.

4. TIME AND SPACE

i. Time, but not space, is necessary for acting and willing

These two meanings implicit in 'sensation' are evident in Grote's comments on *time* and *space*. Grote asserts that we have commencements of acting and willing (or active sensing, or sensation – the physical side of which is sensation with the first meaning above), in *time*. Space is not needed for acting and willing. Motivation is possible even within our minds; we can motivate our feelings alone. By this, Grote seems to mean that we can have reflection without any spatial requirements (excepting, of course, that our bodies must have space which Grote assumes). For in reflection – though he does not actually make this statement – there is the active part of the process of *reflecting* and *that reflected upon*. Both are involved in reflection and both are within the 'philosophical' view (implied in the second meaning of 'sensation,' above).

[1] Grote, EP, I, 19.
[2] *Op. cit.*, 19, 20.

ii. Space adequately reveals to us our active nature

Space reveals to us our active nature more adequately, for postulating space we are aware of acting upon what is not ourselves. Force and matter go together. When we feel that we exercise not only will but force, we become aware of what resists our force, namely, matter. The sensation of matter is, therefore, as intimate and early to us as space.

Space reveals our active nature in this way. When we act on objects in space this action is evident or manifest to others. But, space, according to Grote, does not need to be present in order that we may act in some way or will something. For Grote maintains that only time, not space, is necessary for acting and willing. Now, Grote seems to have in mind merely that an act, as reflective, requires time but cannot be measured. He does not, of course, hold that our bodies do not require space. And our minds, *qua* physical, require space. If he means that thought can take place without any spatial considerations at all – not even for that in which thought takes place – then his view would seem to be untenable. This untenable position, however, does not seem to be implied in Grote's writing.

iii. Sensation as a feeling, and sensation of our activity

Sensation as a feeling should be distinguished from the sensation of our activity, according to Grote. Sensation of our activity is only part of the domain of sensation. Sensation as a feeling he regards as sensation proper, or feeling as *passive*. This distinction is not clearcut, as Grote would likely admit; but it is a sensible distinction. Sensation as feeling is pleasurable or painful. Sensation of time is neutral if it is considered as that which contains our feeling of pleasure and pain. Sensation of space is of the area in which motion operates and may be considered also, as in the case of time, as neutral.

Sensation proper, as a feeling,... is all, in a manner, as I have said, pleasurable or painful. In a manner: for the sensation of time is rather as *containing* our feeling of pleasure and pain, and so far as we have a sensation of time, we must perhaps rather call it neutral. Our sensation of space is as of the continent of our motion, of matter as of the absorbent, or counter-agent of our force: how far these sensations are to be considered neutral, i.e., not of pleasure and pain, seems hard to determine, and not *now* important.[1]

iv. Sensations of pleasure and of pain

Whether there are sensations of pleasure and pain which belong to space and time is doubtful. At least one can say that some sensations,

[1] Grote, EP, I, 38.

other than those of space and time, are sensations of pleasure and pain. In considering sensation as pleasurable and painful, Grote points out that the sensation of taste has attached to it a special pleasure or pain. Here one may see the phenomenal character of sensation, as well as its 'philosophical' nature. For the sensation of taste involves the chemical properties of matter which communicate with our organism. This is the phenomenal aspect of the sensation of taste, namely, the communication. The feeling or subjective part of the sensation is not of activity but of pleasure or pain. Here one is much more passive and susceptible to impressions from what communicates with the matter of our bodies.

v. Time is common to consciousness and phenomena

Time is the one element which is peculiar to both consciousness and phenomenal reality. The reason why Grote seems justified in this view is because consciousness requires time. Also, phenomenal reality being essentially the communication of the matter of nature with our bodies (with such parts as sense organs, nerves, brain, etc.) requires time in order that communication can be carried out. Sensation proper, or passive sensing, according to Grote, requires time for its sensing, passively, to take place, e.g., as in the passive sensing of pleasure and pain. Active sensing, such as willing, etc., also postulates time in which its acting may be carried out. Grote was, no doubt, influenced by Kant in his view of time as pertaining to both consciousness and phenomenal reality.

Time, as the formal condition of the manifold of inner sense, and therefore of the connection of all representations, contains an *a priori* manifold in pure intuition. Now a transcendental determination of time is so far homogeneous with the category, which constitutes its unity, in that it is universal and rests upon an *a priori* rule. But, on the other hand, it is so far homogeneous with appearance, in that time is contained in every empirical representation of the manifold. Thus an application of the category to appearance becomes possible by means of the transcendental determination of time.[1]

Duration is experienced and hence time is in the realm of consciousness or feeling. If time were not felt by us, then it would remain unknown to consciousness. And, if it existed anywhere we would know nothing about it. For utter absence of feeling time (i.e. the passing of time) would mean even the lack of any affection of time on our bodies (through any of the senses). That is, one would neither be conscious of time nor would there be any communication (which required time)

[1] Kant, CPR, 181.

for us, of any kind, on our bodies, and hence there would be no phenomenal reality *for us*. Time, therefore, must be peculiar to both consciousness and phenomenal reality.

vi. Space is only partially common to both consciousness and phenomena

Space, Grote states, is only partially common to both feeling and phenomena. Our bodies, to which our feelings are confined, exist in space. Space is not characteristic of feeling as such. But space is characteristic of bodies. Feeling is located in our bodies which are spatial. This last statement must be qualified. For there is the *meaning* end of feeling and the phenomenal reality end. It is the phenomenal reality side of feeling that is physical, and the physical is spatial. In this sense, therefore, feeling can be said to be located in our bodies which are spatial. Space, then, is not characteristic of feeling *qua* feeling as time is. This justifies Grote's view that time is peculiar to both consciousness and phenomenal reality, whereas space is peculiar only to phenomenal reality, and to feeling inasmuch as it may be considered as that which characterizes our body, or feeling as phenomenal reality.

And 'feeling' itself which necessitates a body in order to exist at all, is a term having implicit two meanings as 'sensation' has, namely, as 'philosophical' and 'phenomenal.' Space, then, is *not* peculiar to awareness only very indirectly, inasmuch as awareness requires a body in order to exist at all, and body is spatial.

vii. Conception of space by analogy

Moreover, we are conscious of the matter of our bodies as spatial and can formulate a conception of the matter of the rest of the universe by analogy. That is, it is by analogy that we have awareness of space; space is, therefore, in this way connected with consciousness. Also, phenomenal reality requires space in order to communicate with the matter of our body. This communication, requiring space, is physical, and phenomenal. We are aware of our bodies as phenomenal. Grote does not specially center attention on how we know our bodies. But if he did so, it would have to be somewhat as follows: There is a sort of network of communication in our bodies (as physical and as 'mental!'). How we know our bodies must always be through our capacity to understand, reason, judge, imagine, etc. We seem to have *some* knowledge at least, even in our feeling of anything, otherwise there would be no registering of any meaning for feeling at all. Feeling is popularly related closely with the physical, but to so restrict it entirely (to the physical) is erroneous. However, it should not be overlooked that the knowing of our bodies has also a phenomenal side where there is the 'object' (or 'objects') of our *physical* selves communicating with that which gives meaning to it.

viii. Résumé

This exposition of Grote's remarks on the relation of space and time to consciousness seems a faithful account of his position and seems in accord with the distinction he makes between philosophy and consciousness on the one hand, and phenomenal reality on the other. His general position, then, regarding space and time is that space is necessary to phenomenal reality, whereas time is necessary both to consciousness and phenomena. Space is not essential to awareness though one may be aware of what is spatial, or may frequently think spatially (i.e., of what exists spatially). One might comment further on Grote's remarks regarding space by stating that many concepts are of entities that are not spatial, e.g., triangularity, roundness, various transcendentals such as truth, goodness, oneness, etc. Grote does not attempt to refute such comments in advance and thus by not contradicting further possible reflections on time and space, he leaves a strong impression of the significance of his views regarding space and time, so far as they go.

But Grote fails to deal with other issues regarding space and time, such as their apparently inseparable relation to each other, and so reveals weakness in not having more adequately circumscribed the subject of space and time. However, he is primarily concerned with the relation of space and time to consciousness. Let us now consider the ascribing of rationality to spatial objects.

ix. Rationality ascribed to spatial objects

Grote observes, regarding spatial objects, that there is a tendency to ascribe rationality to them. Consciousness may be consciousness of selfhood, or it may be an 'extra-phenomenal' *power* of contemplating what is not self. The whole of this consciousness falls within the range of knowledge. This 'extra-phenomenal' *power* whether of contemplating the self or what is not self, is intellect. The awakening intelligence (or will) is aware of what resists our efforts. There is a tendency, therefore, to regard what resists our effort, as living like we do. Thus we ascribe animation to objects in the universe, and ascribe rationality to them. The result is that we 'philosophize' about the phenomenal world, and ascribe unity to it where no unity may be actually present.[1]

5. THE RELATIONSHIP OF PHENOMENALISM TO PHILOSOPHY FURTHER ILLUSTRATED

i. By taste

Again, Grote illustrates the relation of phenomenalism to 'philosophy' by analyzing the sensation of sight. For a clearer analysis let us first look at the sense of taste. Tasting is a sort of handling of the chemical agents by the matter of our body, especially by the tongue. By such 'handling' we get the ideas of the shape of some objects. Sensation proper, then, or sensation as feeling (the *passive* nature of sensation, according to Grote) is concerned with the sensation of space which appeared, as Grote observes, to be neutral – neither pleasurable nor painful.

ii. By sight

a. The eye is virtually a machine

Sensation involving 'handling' becomes much more evident in the case of sight. The eye is virtually a machine for touching or handling, at a distance, the chemical properties of objects in space. Light is the specific physical agent or substance which makes the actual communication possible.

We may now... speak of that which, in the advance of knowledge, is of all the most important organ of sensation, the eye: which is in fact a machine for both handling or touching, and also tasting, that is, appreciating certain chemical qualities of matter removed from us, perhaps widely, in space. The instrument of this communication is the particular physical substance or agent,.... *light*.[2]

Though he does not mention other factors concerned in this communication, e.g., the receptivity of the retina for images, etc., yet Grote is fully aware of the necessity of these factors.

b. Color is subjectively felt

Grote does not claim any special training in optics, and states that

---

[1] This view of Grote regarding unity as an essential characteristic of the 'extra-phenomenal' will be referred to again, below. Cf. pp. 36–37.
[2] Grote, EP, I, 39, 40.

for the purpose of showing the relation between phenomena and consciousness, an intimate knowledge or analysis is not necessary. Suffice it to hold that there are voluntary movements and adjustments of the eye lenses so that space is measured to us. So, in the language already used regarding tasting of certain natural objects, we 'taste' color. That is, the color is, in a certain way, *felt*.

The phenomenal communication being this, the corresponding subjective feeling is, that we, in the language which I have used before, as it were *taste* the colour by means of the nervous surface, in a way in some measure analogous to that in which we taste the taste of anything by the palate.[1]

The color is subjectively felt. The various volitional and physical movements of the lenses of the eye have a sensation of feeling (sensation proper, according to Grote) and a sensation of activity either as acting upon proximate portions of the eye region in the matter of our bodies or upon remote matter as in the objects of nature.

iii. Sensation of space is the same
no matter what senses are used

So the sensation of space, as a whole, is the same whether it has to do with the movement of the eye or of the hand. In the case of light, it is the actual communication of rays upon a nervous surface that is phenomenal, whereas the subjective feeling which corresponds to this is the intellectual, volitional, conscious part of the experience. In handling objects there is also the phenomenal communication which is only part of the process. But there is also the conscious awareness of stimulus from objects or of activity *upon* objects. Either abstracted from the other would be meaningful but its meaning would be necessarily limited.

iv. Concerning the defining of 'phenomenon';
Professor Brightman's definition and Grote's analysis

It is correct to state that "the object as it appears to the senses" is phenomenon.[2] Grote does not seem to take any position that would deny any part of this definition. He seems concerned with pointing out what the implications of such a definition may well be considered to be. The phenomenon, for him, is not 'the object' but the object *as communicating* with our senses or, more particularly, with certain specific parts of our bodies. 'Senses,' unanalyzed, include awareness of some

1 Grote, EP, I, 40.
2 Brightman, ITP, 389.

sort. It is just here that Grote becomes specific and distinguishes, in sensation, between a physical communication which strictly, for him, means the *phenomenal* part of the knowing process, and *consciousness* or awareness through activity (as volition, purpose, etc.) or passivity (as awareness of pleasure or pain). To separate the one from the other is part of a necessary analysis in attempting to understand consciousness and phenomena better. But synthesis is also necessary for a synoptic view of the noetic process.

v. Significance of sight among the senses

The 'sense' (as we use the term in ordinary parlance) of sight is especially complicated because 'sight' is used to mean not only the seeing of objects but also as inward sight or intuition. Imagination is a term derived from seeing, yet applies to touching, handling, smelling, and hearing as well. That is, *sight* has a subjective importance of a wide kind when used to represent other 'senses.' It is a sort of typical sense which enables us to refer to and describe the senses in general, according to Grote.

The sense of sight being thus, with development of the intellect, the most important, takes also a *subjective* importance of a different kind. We use it as the typical sense by means of which we describe, and to which we refer, the operations of sense in general.[1]

Taken as *the* typical sense, the corporeal communication between the matter of objects of nature (which includes, strictly, the matter of our own body) and the matter of our bodies (*not* now considered as an object of nature) is phenomena. This communication simply presents the object to the mind. *Qua* corporeal communication there is no 'philosophy,' or consciousness, or awareness. There is a 'mysterious point'[2] at which the corporeal communication is converted into sensibility. Another way of stating this is that "it is the mind that sees the object, and the real sight is *this*." [3]

vi. Mind 'sees'

Sight, considered in a sense wider than merely physical seeing, where mind is involved, is comprehensive in enabling us to *know*. Sight, in this sense necessarily involves intelligence, consciousness, awareness, or volition. Here the philosophical approach is stressed.

[1] Grote, EP, I, 42.
[2] Grote, *op. cit.*, 44.
[3] *Loc. cit.*

Emphasis on intelligence in 'seeing' enable *us* to '*see around*' objects as well as to *see* them. It seems that Grote would mean by this that we can see, or imagine, because of our *mentality*, the side of a building which is not and cannot be corporeally communicated to us. Here, phenomena are missing but 'philosophy' is present.

vii. Quantity of phenomenal communication

That is, the sensation which we may have is

of a colored *object* having magnitude and figure, and... solid shape and definite distance. This is what we call seeing: this is what we see... the corporeal communication which is the *means* of it is not more elaborate than the logical result of the sensation.[1]

The phenomenal communication may be elaborate (and also the 'sensibility') as indicated in the quotation,[2] or it may be almost entirely missing as in the case of 'seeing' the side of a building opposite to us. The phenomena are inseparably connected with awareness; both are necessary to each other and any separation that may be made results in phenomena abstracted or philosophy abstracted.

6. RELATIONSHIP THROUGH CONTRAST

i. Phenomenalist view reached through an unphenomenal process

It is particularly important to see, Grote states, that the phenomenalist view is an abstraction. One may approach epistemology from the phenomenalist view. But one cannot reach the phenomenalist view except through an unphenomenal process. It would seem that Grote would hold to a non-behavioristic position in psychology. He would seem to say that the behaviorist must reach his position through a non-behavioristic process.

We may hold simply... the phenomenalist view in our developed intelligence, but we never can arrive at it, we never can learn it, except by an unphenomenal process. This amounts to the same as I have formerly said when I called the phenomenalist view an abstraction.[3]

ii. Phenomena as a deposit from our thinking

In contrast to the phenomenal universe, thought is fluid and unformed. Phenomena are a sort of deposit from our thinking. That is,

---

[1] Grote, EP, I, 44, 45.
[2] Immediately above.
[3] Grote, *op. cit.*, 45, 46.

all phenomena require thinking in order to be phenomena *for us*. They cannot affect us so that the affecting can be *for us* (and yet not be for us, as would be the case if phenomena were unrelated to consciousness!). In other words, if we were phenomenalists first, we would never have been phenomenalists at all! Phenomenalism is possible only through the extra-phenomenal.

If we had been phenomenalists and physiologists from the first we should never have been so at all, for we never should have known anything.[1]

iii. Extra-phenomenal elements in sensation make phenomena perceptual

Phenomenalism depends upon our subjective sensation, or upon what is sometimes referred to as 'perception.' It is only because of the mixture in sensation of extra-phenomenal elements, or elements quite independent of phenomena that we can have phenomena at all.

7. MIND PROVIDES UNITY

i. The extra-phenomenal gives unity

What Grote refers to as the 'extra-phenomenal' also makes possible the unity that mind in the universe. Phenomena are essentially greatly lacking in unity.[2] Grote affirms that much of the order and arrangement that people see in the universe is not the order of phenomenal reality alone but the order characteristic of mind also. Much of the demand for unity and coherence which is postulated by the mind is due to a conception essential to the nature of human beings. The influence of Kant could well have affected Grote so that he strongly emphasizes the essential nature of the mind to see unity, or to unify:

This transcendental unity of apperception forms out of all possible appearances, which can stand alongside one another in one experience, a connection of all these representations according to laws. For this unity of consciousness would be impossible if the mind in knowledge of the manifold could not become conscious of the identity of function whereby it synthetically combines it in one knowledge. The original and necessary consciousness of the identity of the self is thus at the same time a consciousness of an equally necessary unity of the synthesis of all appearances according to concepts, that is, according to rules, which not only make them necessarily reproducible but also in so doing determine an object for their intuition, that is, the concept of something wherein they are necessarily interconnected. For the mind could never think its identity in the manifoldness of its representations, and indeed think this identity *a priori*, if

---

[1] Grote, EP, I, 46.
[2] "I said that the notion of unity... is not phenomenal." Grote, *op. cit.*, 49.

it did not have before its eyes the identity of its act, whereby it subordinates all synthesis of apprehension (which is empirical) to a transcendental unity, thereby rendering possible their interconnection according to *a priori* rules.[1]

Man, by investing the universe with unity, concedes to it a mind with conceptions of time, space, etc., derived, not from sight or any other sense,[2] but in some manner so that the *lack of unity, coherence,* and *order* which is characteristic of phenomenal reality, is obscured. However, it must not be supposed that the phenomenal completely lacks unity, for some parts of it are distinctly unified. It seems fair to Grote to say that examples of this unity are the motions inside the atom, the harmonious motion of the planets, the 'law' of gravitation, and the action of chlorophyll in a growing plant.[3]

ii. Phenomenal reality essentially obscured

In other words, as soon as consciousness enters the field, true phenomenal reality is obscured. The reason for this may be seen in the case of space. Space (in daylight) for persons possessed of sight is always lighted space. Phenomenal space that operates on our bodies without any consciousness present is not lighted as all. Consciousness, or mind, makes a specific contribution to our conception of space. Phenomenal reality, *qua* phenomenal, is always obscured. It is obscured because our awareness is very limited, and depends upon the particular viewpoints of various selves. The self is also restricted to awareness through the selective nature of each 'sense' taking in certain aspects to which it is adapted, e.g., the eye assimilates aspects of an object very different from the aspects to which the ear is adapted.

iii. Awareness is not the process of operation of phenomena

And yet one cannot say that these various aspects exhaust the nature of the action taking place between the matter of nature and the matter of our bodies. Indeed, the awareness is *not* the process of operation. This operation belongs to the phenomenal world. At the risk of being understood only literally, one may affirm that Grote seems to be saying that consciousness is the most inward part of

---

[1] Kant, CPR, 136, 137.

[2] "Though particulars of the universe... have not *life* they have that unity, or individuality, or reason why they should be distinguished and separately thought of, which in fact is only suggested to us by our consciousness of our own life and consequent felt self-belonging or independence... is a sort of relic or reminiscence of the life which the infant intellect supposed in *things.*" Grote, EP, I, 48, 49.

[3] "I said that in strictness, unity was phenomenally exceptional rather than un-phenomenal.." Grote, *op. cit.*, 49.

phenomenal reality; consciousness cannot be explained in terms of behavior alone. This is not quite fair to Grote, but it is an attempt to indicate exactly what he means. It is better to say that consciousness is not phenomenal reality at all, and is mental.

This does not mean that the phenomenal is entirely non-mental. But phenomena are non-mental viewed from the aspect of phenomena. Viewed from the consciousness or *'we'* side they are *significant* and have a 'mental' aspect. There is a sort of 'inward' part of the communication of phenomenal reality with our bodies that is mental, namely, awareness. And without this awareness the communication of phenomenal reality would not *mean* anything, not even communication. For even the term 'mental' seems too broad (because there are phenomenal implications in it) to distinguish consciousness (or awareness) from phenomena. The term 'sensation' doesn't make the issue sun-clear either. In saying that "consciousness is not phenomenal reality at all" [1] one must hasten to say that consciousness and phenomena cannot be considered adequately if wholly separated from each other. But one can abstract either from the other to emphasize what is meant by these necessarily inseparable terms.

8. GROTE AVOIDS A BASIC BLUNDER IN BEHAVIORISM

We have said that using the term 'sensation' is not clarifying the issue. Even though we analyze sensation into 'sensing' and 'thing sensed,' this does not sufficiently render Grote's meaning. For even 'sensing' can be looked at behavioristically only. This seems to be one of the great blunders of behaviorism. It *should* grant that there is an awareness without which behaviorism wouldn't *mean* anything at all. It is this *meaning* that Grote refers to as 'philosophy,' and alludes to by such terms as 'intelligence,' 'will,' and even such a term as 'sensing' (and the much vaguer term, 'sensation') when these latter terms are stripped of behavioristic elements. The elements in the whole noetic process that comprise 'philosophy' are 'extra-phenomenal,' the balance are phenomenal. Grote would seem to have as little use for *Ding-an-sich* as Kant did.

---

[1] *Supra.*

9. KANT'S ABSTRACTION OF PHENOMENAL
REALITY FROM REASON

i. Kant stresses reason

It is quite impossible wholly to separate consciousness or the sensing of one's existence from phenomenal reality.[1] Phenomena can be sensed but they cannot be completely known. Knowing, as awareness or intelligence, is a sort of response that we make to the communication of the matter of nature upon our bodies (through the senses). Grote believes that Kant has erred in laying such great stress on a critique of reason to the neglect of that from which reason is inseparable, namely, phenomenal reality. No such abstraction can be carried on with utmost fruitful result, according to Grote. Consideration of consciousness, or *how we came to know*, cannot be separated entirely from *what we* do *know*.[2] Yet this is what Kant has, at least, *sometimes*, apparently done, for he sought "to disengage the action of intelligence from all application and actual use of it, and to see what it is in itself."[3]

ii. Concerning the disengaging of "the action of intelligence from all application and actual use of it"

To say that Kant disengaged "the action of intelligence from all application and actual use of it" and "to see what it is in itself" is not objectionable in one sense. For one can take intelligence by itself even though one may not grant that there could be intelligence of any significance without an empirical world in which it might develop. It must be taken for granted, then, that the intelligence which Kant 'takes' is an intelligence that already is so interwoven with empirical elements and dependent on these that we cannot take it "by itself." And if, by 'intelligence' we mean intelligence already partially born of the empirical world, then, in this sense it *is* objectionable "to disengage the action of intelligence from all application and actual use of it" and seek "to see what it is in itself."

---

[1] By "consciousness or the sensing of one's existence" is meant simply awareness. This awareness is *of* phenomenal reality (including one's own physical being).

[2] Consciousness for Grote is wholly knowing. "Consciousness, excluded from phenomenalism, I now assume as the one thing which we *do* know or are certain of." Grote, EP, I, 18. "The 'we' or 'I' of consciousness is something quite different from the 'we' or 'I,' 'man' of phenomenalism, which, as I said, is a portion of matter organized and variously endowed, with phenomenal sensation... for one of its properties." Grote, EP, I, 19.

[3] Grote, *op. cit.*, 18.

iii. Basic agreement between Kant and Grote

If this latter interpretation of intelligence is considered, then Grote is correct in pointing out that intelligence is never separated *wholly* from what he calls 'phenomenal reality.' It is not so much a case, then, that Grote is correct and Kant wrong, or the reverse. The case is, rather, that there is essential agreement between them. Grote is especially concerned with pointing out that actually one can never separate intelligence from the matter of nature because there is a constant communication of this matter with the matter of our bodies, and this communication is phenomenal reality. And Kant is especially concerned with showing what one can find out by separating intelligence as entirely *as possible* from "application and actual use of it." There seems sufficient evidence from Kant's own treatment that intelligence cannot function in a vacuum, for example, he states that "thoughts without content are empty." [1]

10. ABSTRACTING OF CONSCIOUSNESS FROM PHENOMENA IS UNWARRANTED

Let us now consider the position that Grote would take if he were to criticize some epistemological theories in history.

i. Descartes

So far from believing in Descartes's maxim, *Je pense, donc je suis* (*cogito, ergo sum*),[2] Grote would affirm that the proof of our own existence is no more justified by saying that we are conscious than a statement to the effect that there is proof of the external world, is justified. There is awareness in both cases – of *our* bodies in the case of our own existence, and of *other* bodies in the case of the existence of the external world. Grote *does* affirm that the 'self-self,' is the only entity that is wholly immediate.[3]

By the 'self-self' I mean that which cannot really be thought of, i.e., which cannot be made an object of thought, but which is *with-thought* (mitgedacht), thought along with, or included in, our *immediate* thought and feeling, or which, in other words, is one of the essential elements of such thought or feeling. There is a sort of contradiction here, for by attempting to make the reader understand what it is, I am making it an object of thought.[4]

[1] Kant, CPR, 93.
[2] Descartes, DOM, 26, 27.
[3] Grote, EP, II, 145–228.
[4] Grote, *op. cit.*, 145.

There is a sense in which even our bodies are as much a part of phenomenal reality as any part of the external world is (a part of phenomenal reality). The only portion of ourselves which is not phenomenal is our intelligence, consciousness, or awareness. And this non-phenomenal, or – as Grote sometimes refers to it – extra-phenomenal aspect, is also necessarily present when we are conscious of the external world.

For Descartes to start with his own existence as a thinking being *first*, as Grote implies, rather than with phenomenal reality (*first*) is to be guilty of abstracting consciousness (or, 'philosophy') from that with which it is necessarily inseparable, namely, phenomenal reality. The phenomenal has no *meaning* wholly separated from consciousness. Consciousness is *empty* without phenomena. Simple awareness that is awareness of awareness, considered in the narrowest solipsistic sense, is scarcely worthy of being termed 'awareness.' And if this critical reflection be allowed, there is, therefore, still remaining the question, How do we know even that we *are* (in any respect, mental or physical)? – which is a critical comment on Descartes's first postulate (*Cogito, ergo sum*). This at least is Grote's criticism of Descartes. However, it is not justified, for the 'cogito' of Descartes includes all sense data. Descartes can scarcely be criticized on the ground that he abstracted consciousness from phenomenal reality. For he included phenomena in the *apparent* abstraction through the use of the phrase, '*Cogito, ergo sum.*'

Descartes believed that there was one absolutely independent fundamental substance, in the sense that extended things and thinking things are not comprehensible in themselves but only are so in relation to creation by God. Extended things and thinking things are not comprehensible alone; the former are manifestations of extension and the latter of thought. Thought and extension are relative, and created, substances.

For Spinoza mind and matter are reduced to attributes of one absolute substance, the totality of reality, God. The attributes are the eternal essence of the one substance, and all finite things are modes of these attributes. For Descartes there are actually two relative substances, namely, thought and extension. These two run parallel and do not interact (except in the pineal gland). Generally, interaction between mind and matter was not intelligible to Descartes.[1]

[1] "The world is made up of two ultimately different kinds of reality. Descartes... had an uneasy feeling about this situation, for it rendered interaction between mind and matter unintelligible to him." Brightman, ITP, 222.

Descartes affirmed that an act of the will causes expression of the body and an object of the external world causes an impression within – a thought or sensation. The definite bifurcation which Descartes makes, giving two substances, thought and extension, is unwarranted. For extension, or the external world is not so utterly external as Descartes regarded it. For the so-called (by Descartes) *external* world is always, in some manner, communicating with our bodies whether it be in the adjacent form of motions of the atmosphere as one sits in a room or something as remote as the bursting of a toy balloon by a native on the island of Java.

The point is that the external world is not completely external at all. It is a world whose significance is exhausted in the communication that it makes with our senses, nerves, brain, etc., through the matter of our bodies. Our knowing of the external world is possible because of awareness of this communication.

In fact, there is no external world worthy of being called by any term except the communicating world. Any other existence is the world of things in themselves of which we can neither speak nor think (nor write)! This communication, involving things communicating, and that to which they communicate, includes all that Descartes referred to as extended things.

In short, it is phenomenal reality, which together with the extra-phenomenal character of intelligence, comprises all that is on earth, or sea. The difficulty with Descartes's bifurcation between thought and extension is that it is altogether too decisive. Grote would reflect, it seems safe to state, that the inseparable elements of consciousness and phenomena are a sufficient explanation. In this comment on Descartes's philosophy the assumption is that some such criticism as this would be made by Grote.

ii. Spinoza

Let us now look at some possible comments that Grote would make on Spinoza's philosophy. Spinoza tried to bridge the gap between thought and extension through the introduction of attributes and modes. There are two known attributes of substance, thought and extension. For Descartes there was a problem of two substances interacting in an automatic manner. Spinoza – introducing modes of thought and modes of extension – states that substance could be a mode of thought from the aspect of mind, and a mode of extension

from the aspect of matter. This explanation virtually set up a parallelism where no interaction is possible.

Grote would seem to hold that Spinoza's solution of the mind-body
problem was not much more successful than Descartes's. For we are
still left with the internal and the external worlds. He would appear
to hold that Spinoza's system was better in that it regarded substance
as one. To say that there are two known attributes helps greatly in
giving the particularity that we would expect of a cosmic system
dealing with the variety of life which expresses itself in thinking,
extension, particular objects, etc. But Spinoza's philosophy doesn't
show *how* the modes of extension and modes of thought *actually*
interrelate. It seems that at this particular point Grote presents a
solution. All so-called extended objects, according to him, are phenomena, and all phenomena communicate with us; also, we are aware
of at least some of the communication. Both the communication of
which we are aware, and the communication of which we are not aware,
is phenomena.

11. HISTORICAL RECAPITULATION

Grote believed that Descartes went further than Locke, Cousin and
Hume. Because *cogito, ergo sum* formed the basis for Descartes's
epistemology, then, Descartes argued, there must be a non-ego, or
'circum-ego' to which such thought conforms. Descartes believed that
this non-ego was God along with created substance, according to
Grote.

It should be noted, however, that Descartes's argument may be
more properly, in part, stated thus: God must exist because I have a
clear and distinct consciousness of Him, and the idea of perfection
that I possess of the deity involves the deity's existence. And the
inference can be made from the existence of God to the existence of
corporeal bodies and finite selves. Grote, in fastening on one part of
Descartes's argument, namely, upon the 'cogito' of 'cogito, ergo sum'
– and saying that Descartes tends to abstract consciousness from 'phenomenal reality' – seems to be considerably less than wholly fair to
Descartes's whole position.

God, for Descartes, accounts for the conformity of thought to extended things. Descartes asserted this in the form, namely, God would
not deceive us by having the case otherwise. Cousin blamed Locke,
Grote states, for attempting to make ideas, or thought, conform to

fact. But this method, of representation, which Locke employed, was closer to Descartes's than Cousin's was. Even though Locke denied the existence of innate ideas, his approach was the same as Descartes's, namely, in attempting to find a congruence between thought and things. Cousin declared that thought in conformity with human nature is knowledge. Therefore, Cousin fell into almost the same error as Hume who declared knowledge to be congruent with human custom.

Both Cousin and Hume stated, in effect, according to Grote, that custom furnished the basis for knowledge. But Locke's and Descartes's view was very much different and more fundamental because based for all practical purposes on Descartes's dictum, *cogito, ergo sum* – a pillar which remained unshattered until the time of Kant who criticized thought in the light of pure reason.

Grote asserts that Berkeley regarded the world as we see it to be an inspiration from deity.

Hume is content to leave knowledge as customary thought, without any care to examine the nature of this custom. In the same way Berkeley sees no difficulty, and nothing requiring further probing, in the consideration that two notions, both of which may fairly be called natural, in so far as actual human thought indicates human nature – the vulgar notion, namely, of the independent existence of an unknown substance underlying what we properly perceive – that these two apparently natural notions are prejudices only and not correct; while what is correct is something which the natural, habitual, actual thought of men certainly does not realize at all, viz. that our thought as to what we call the external world is a *quasi-inspiration of the Deity*.[1] I am not disputing Berkeley's being to a great extent right, which I believe him to be: my point only is, that he leaves the question where no philosopher has a right to leave it.[2]

Grote also held that Berkeley's reference to things as divine language does not help us:

Things are *themselves*, or they are nothing: if they are God's words to us, as there is no harm in considering them, they are this in virtue of their being things,[3] and we come most to enter into the meaning of them as God's words by the most thoroughly considering them as things, in the sense in which our mind or nature leads us to view things.[4]

What the vulgar have conceived as things, the wise conceives as a language, i.e. as signs of things. Berkeley's favorite metaphor of language is here singularly unhappy. Though there is no harm in calling the external world a language of God to us, there is no *good* in doing so, if we stop where Berkeley stops, for it is a language entirely unknown to us. We have the letters and words, and are told they are signs: but how are we to find out of what? *We* perversely think the letters and words the things, and then we are told they are not so, but we are not

---

[1] Italics mine.
[2] Grote, EP, II, 37.
[3] Or, as Berkeley would likely say, rather: 'In virtue of their being *ideas*.'
[4] Grote, *op. cit.*, 39.

told what it is of which they are signs, so that we are left without things at all, only with a language telling us nothing.[1]

In saying that there is no harm in considering things as divine language, or, as Grote states, 'God's words,' Grote shows his preference for considering things as 'things.' In other words, Berkeley says things are divine language; Grote says 'things' are such considered from the phenomenal aspect. But they are always, also, things *for us*, and they can never be 'things' out of all relation to us. In speaking this way Grote is humanistic in his epistemology. Berkeley is theistic in a way that Grote sees 'no harm in,' yet "we come most to enter into the meaning of them as God's words by the most thoroughly considering them as things."

Grote sees a similarity between Descartes and Berkeley in their approach to the problem of knowledge from what he calls the philosophical (in contrast to the phenomenal). And from his assumption, 'cogito,' Descartes came to yet another which was much less worthy, namely, "I judge this conclusion to be true only because I clearly see it to be so: therefore clear mental sight is the test of truth." [2] The similarity appears in the phrase "clear mental sight" of Descartes; Berkeley asserted the oneness of appearance and reality. To take clear mental sight as the test of truth is what is responsible for 'mis-psychology.' Hallucination can result; clear mental sight is a good criterion when it *is* clear mental sight, but if it is thought to be so when it is really not, error creeps in. Hence the very evident possibility of 'mis-psychology.' Grote states that this lack of ability to see all the implications in his theory of knowledge was in Berkeley a fault only similar to that of a long line of successors in the Cartesian philosophy, and one in which Descartes himself had become involved.

12. MAIN CONTRIBUTION OF THE CHAPTER, WITH COMMENT

Now, leaving the various illustrations of the relation of phenomenalism to philosophy, which Grote derives from his references chiefly to Kant, Descartes, and Berkeley, let us note the main contribution of this chapter. Both phenomena and 'philosophy' are opposite sides of the same reality. This reality is not properly regarded wholly as phenomenal reality, nor is it sufficient to refer to this reality as adequately

[1] Grote, EP, II, 39, 40.
[2] Grote, *op. cit.*, 41.

accounted for by the term 'philosophy,' 'logic,' or 'consciousness.'

Not 'philosophy' in the sense of 'awareness,' *or* phenomena, but 'philosophy' *and* phenomena, can adequately account for reality. 'Philosophy' or consciousness is that which gives significance or meaning to the reality that is 'seen,' 'felt,' or 'sensed.' Consciousness must always be consciousness *of* something, whether an 'external' object or of the self. Consciousness as *complete* immediateness does not exist. It entails phenomena of some sort, whether these phenomena be external 'objects' or selves. So much for reality considered from the *consciousness*, or *thought*, side. Let us now glance at reality more specifically from the *phenomenal* side.

It should be noted that the phenomenal of Grote is very different from the current view of the phenomenal as "the object as it appears to the senses." [1] The phenomenal, or phenomenal reality, for Grote is simply reality viewed from the side of 'things.' Strictly, however, reality can *not* be viewed entirely from the side of things since such viewing involves consciousness. Phenomena, therefore, are intimately related to consciousness, 'philosophy,' or '*us*.' Phenomena, for Grote, can *not* 'appear' to the senses at all. 'Appearance' is a *thought* word. That is, phenomena are always related somehow *to us*, otherwise they would not be phenomena for us at all. And they couldn't, in that case, 'be,' or exist out of all relation to the consciousness, or thought side of us, which alone justifies the use of the word 'existence,' or 'being,' as applied to reality.

13. TRANSITION TO NEXT CHAPTER

Having already considered Grote's view of phenomenalism in chapter two, and his interpretation of the relation of phenomenalism to 'philosophy' in chapter three, let us now consider specifically 'philosophy' itself, as consciousness and the ego.

---

[1] Brightman, ITP, 389.

CHAPTER IV

PHILOSOPHY AS CONSCIOUSNESS AND THE EGO

1. INTRODUCTION

In considering 'philosophy' itself, as consciousness and the ego, let us turn first of all to a philosopher in history who is a good example of those who confuse 'philosophy' and phenomena to a remarkably small degree, namely, James Frederick Ferrier. We will also deal briefly with consciousness as revealed through the ego of Fichte and Lotze, showing points of strength and possible weakness (according to Grote) in each. First of all, then, we will consider the philosophical and the phenomenalist views as clearly distinguished by Ferrier.

2. FERRIER'S TREATMENT OF PHILOSOPHY AND PHENOMENALISM

i. The philosophical and the phenomenalist views clearly distinguished by Ferrier

The valuable point in Mr. Ferrier, in my view, is, as I have said, his consistency in distinguishing what I have called the philosophical and the phenomenalist view.[1]

Grote is careful to acknowledge Ferrier's invulnerable position on the issue of distinguishing 'philosophy,' from 'phenomena.' He, nevertheless, comments upon Ferrier's manner of presentation in *Institutes of Metaphysics*, and points out both what seems tenable and what is not. To this task Grote now proceeds.

Grote states that to say anything is an object before it is an object to somebody is to deal in meaningless terms. The subject, says Ferrier, should be thought with the object.[2]

---

[1] Grote, EP, I, 71.
[2] Cunningham, IAB, 69.

When Mr. Ferrier says that we think the subject with the object, I rather question the term 'object' in this application: if, till the subject is added to it, there is no knowledge, it is not as yet, or itself, the *object*. And Mr. Ferrier hardly sufficiently explains whether he means to pass from the notion of ourselves as knowing, or from knowledge being "knowledge that we know," which of itself, I think, is not very important, to the notion of ourselves, or part of ourselves, known in the object, which *is* the important one. It is *this* which really leads on, in the chain of thought, to the notion of knowledge being the meeting, through the intervention of phenomenal matter and the conversion of it into intellectual objects, with the thoughts, proceeding in the opposite direction, of mind or a mind like our own, however, wider and vaster.[1]

The view adumbrated in the last sentence of the preceding quotation is the view which, though here attributed with doubtful accuracy to Ferrier, is avowedly accepted by Grote himself.[2]

ii. Subject-object relation

With Ferrier's position as stated above, namely, "that we think the subject with the object," Grote agrees. But Grote adds that in the application here, of 'object,' he rather questions the term.

By the object of knowledge, we are, of course, to understand the *whole* object of knowledge, whatever that may be at any particular time. It is quite possible for the mind to attend more to one part of any given presentation than to another. The mind does indeed usually attend most to that part of every presentation which is commonly called the thing. But the part so attended to is not the whole object; it is not properly *the* object of our knowledge. It is only part of the object, *the* object being that part together with the other part of the presentation (self, namely, or the subject) which is usually less attended to, but which is necessary to complete every datum of cognition. In other words, the object, usually so called, is only part of the object of the mind, although it may be that part which is most attended to. The object, properly so called, is always the object with the addition of the subject, because this alone is the whole object of our apprehension.[3]

The mind, Ferrier states, is "itself-in-union-with-whatever-it-apprehends."[4]

The *me* must in all cases form part of that which we know; and the only object which any intelligence ever has, or ever can have any cognisance of is, itself-in-union-with-whatever-it-apprehends.[5]

Here, 'whatever-it-apprehends' is the 'object' which Grote questions. There is for Ferrier a subject-object relationship. Grote observes, quite correctly, that there is a danger in writing in this way. The perilous shoals appear around the bend when one becomes aware that

[1] Cunningham, IAB, 69, 70, quoting Grote, EP, I, 67, 68.
[2] Cunningham, *op. cit.*, 69, 70.
[3] Ferrier, IOM, 98, 99.
[4] *Loc. cit.*
[5] Ferrier, *op. cit.*, 98.

until there is a subject attached to the 'object,' there can be no knowledge, nor can there actually *be* an 'object.' That is to say, an object
cannot be known until it is known to someone. There is significance,
then, in the reflection, that

Ferrier hardly sufficiently explains whether he means to pass from the notion
of ourselves as knowing, or from knowledge being 'knowledge that we know,'
which of itself, I think, is not very important, to the notion of ourselves or part
of ourselves, known in the object, which is the important one.[1]

What Grote is concerned about here is, again, his distinction between
'philosophy' and phenomenalism. 'The notion of ourselves as knowing' is 'philosophy' which Grote identifies as consciousness. It also
seems to be a correct reflection to make, namely, that the passing from
knowledge as 'knowledge that we know' is not very important. Because
'knowledge that we know' embraces confusion of the 'object' and the
subject. Whereas 'the notion of ourselves as knowing' is 'philosophy.'

Grote related further that taking this consciousness as the starting-
point we pass to something which is the more significant part, namely,
to the "part of ourselves, known in the object, which *is* the important
one."

It is this which leads on, in the chain of thought, to the notion of knowledge
being the meeting, through the intervention of phenomenal matter and the
conversion of it into intellectual objects, with the thoughts, proceeding in the
opposite direction.[2]

Thoughts 'proceeding in the opposite direction' to 'phenomenal
matter' are the factors which make possible the 'part of our selves
known in the object.' 'Phenomenal matter' is not present in consciousness. Its phenomenal nature, *qua* phenomenal, is at the furthest
extreme from consciousness. One might say that 'phenomenal matter'
is almost dissociated from us, but it cannot be wholly dissociated,
otherwise it would not be 'phenomenal matter' for us at all. It is reality
seen as much as possible from the aspect of phenomenal reality (in
contrast with the aspect of 'philosophy' at the other extreme). To use
the terms 'subject' and 'object' without qualification is to leave much
room for ambiguity. Hence Grote is careful to qualify each term
throughout his discussion of the subject-object relationship.

Grote asserts that Ferrier is sometimes confused in respect to
subject-object, especially in his presentation of it, and yet Ferrier
recognizes that 'philosophy' and phenomena should not be wholly

[1] Grote, EP, I, 67.
[2] Grote, *op. cit.*, 67, 68.

abstracted from each other. This recognition is evident where Ferrier
points out two common misapprehensions. These

are chiefly of two kinds; the one that this process of logic or thought is an actual,
historical (imagined) production on our part of things from nothing, a creation:
the other that in such processes, alongside of our thought, we are to suppose
things already existing as we know them. But these misapprehensions are in
reality confusions between what I have called the philosophical and the phenomenalist point of view, of the kind which I have endeavored to prevent.[1]

Grote is aware of the misapprehensions or confusions of the philosophical and phenomenal points of view. Ferrier is also aware of these.
Both see that one cannot speak of an object before it can be an object
to anyone, that is, before the object has a subject which 'knows' or is
conscious of it!

It should be noted that the status of phenomena, whether *in* or *out*
of consciousness, needs clarification. Phenomena and consciousness
are both necessary in order to have reality. This reality can be viewed
either from the consciousness (or thought) side, or phenomena (or
'object') side. The point is that reality is *one*; this is a very important
feature to observe. All reality must be for consciousness, or for *us*, in
some way, otherwise it could not be reality. This reality (or phenomena)
requires consciousness to be regarded as reality or phenomena at all.
In this sense phenomena, *qua consciousness*, is *in* consciousness.

But one must be careful here. For phenomena, *qua phenomena*, are
out of consciousness. And the whole view is that reality has these two
aspects to it. Phenomena cannot be phenomena (or 'objects') at all
without consciousness. Nor does it seem possible that consciousness
can be utterly and wholly separated from phenomena; on this point
Grote expounds at considerable length.[2] In this dissertation a complete
chapter [3] is devoted to this issue, under the topic, "Immediateness
and Reflection."

iii. The ego and the non-ego

Let us now consider the subject and object, and their relation, under
the terms 'ego' and 'non-ego,' in order to see if Ferrier provides a good
illustration of the relationship between what Grote calls 'philosophy' and
'phenomena.' For Ferrier, Grote thinks, succeeds very well in keeping
these two fundamental aspects of 'philosophy' and phenomenal reality
separate; the terms Ferrier uses chiefly are, 'subject' and 'object.'

[1] Grote, EP, I, 55, 56.
[2] Grote, *op. cit.*, 145–228.
[3] Chapter VIII.

Grote believed with Ferrier, that the distinction between these two, the ego and the non-ego is of great importance. The road of objective knowledge is the course of the growth of the non-ego in conjunction with the ego. The non-ego for Grote is that which contrasts with consciousness. It is the other side of reality from the abstracted mental side. It does not exist by itself. It is the universe of what is sometimes referred to as 'physical things.' As it is grows, consciousness, as ego, grows. Each is necessary to the other.

The course of objective knowledge is the growth of the non-ego, which from the first, in conjunction with the ego, we are conscious of, into distinctness. The spring or start in this course is given by (what I suppose we must consider a primary fact of all intelligence) the attribution, in the first instance, to each one of these members of the form of thought under which we view the other: i.e. the attribution of objective knowableness to our felt self, and the attribution of subjective knowingness or mind to the non-ego. The latter of these two facts is the spring of objective knowledge.[1]

The spring of objective knowledge has its origin in the projection of ourselves into the non-ego of confusion which Ferrier calls 'nonsense' or 'the contradictory.' Let us see how this takes place by considering 'sensation.' Sensation regarded as "grown intellectual sensation" [2] may be regarded as the subjective state corresponding to which, there is the object or quasi-object. This object is the 'non-ego of confusion' [3] which Ferrier calls 'the contradictory' or 'nonsense.'

The unity which is given to the 'contradictory,' and which we observe in the non-ego, is a projection or an extension of our subjective selves. Thus there is that "which gives law to the disorderly mass." [4] This knowingness attributed to the non-ego is the starting-point for objectivity in the non-ego conceived in conjunction with this knowingness.

Grote does not appear to make his position much clearer by referring to the ego and the non-ego of Ferrier. But there is a manner of expression in Ferrier that attracts Grote. It seems that Grote agrees with Ferrier that there is a 'non-ego of confusion' and that this is the 'object' before the self is projected into it.

There are two features here that seem important for Grote. The first is that it is not quite a case of 'non-ego of confusion' before the self is projected into whatever this 'confusion' could be for Ferrier. Rather, for Grote, the 'non-ego of confusion' is *nothing at all* out of relation

[1] Grote, EP, I, 56, 57.
[2] Grote, *op. cit.*, 57.
[3] *Loc. cit.*
[4] *Loc. cit.*

with the self. The second feature is that Grote believes that the mind furnishes unity. And what Ferrier says about the original 'non-ego of confusion,' before the self is 'projected' into it, seems to show the essential unifying nature of consciousness.

There is a sense, then, in which this non-ego is unknown to humanity. It is not objectivity, for the objective requires a subject or ego without which we cannot properly speak of the objective at all. This is the 'nonsensical' or 'contradictory' to which Ferrier refers.[1] For Grote, the non-ego as 'nonsensical' or 'contradictory' (to use Ferrier's terms), is simply non-existent. In other words, it is within what Grote would call – if it were to *exist* for him – phenomenal fact. But it doesn't exist for Grote, and to call it the 'nonsensical' into which the self is projected (as Ferrier states), is to give to this 'nonsensical' the existence which Grote does not admit that it should have.

This act of projecting self into the unknown, or into this realm of phenomenal fact (which strictly is *not necessarily not unknown*) is similar to our first uninstructed acts of consciousness. We perceive mind or reason, Grote believes, following Ferrier, in the universe somewhat as the child may imagine animation in inanimate objects around itself. Grote holds that this projection of self into phenomena and consequent observance of unity and coordination in respect to it, is similar to the very first acts performed by the child in gaining a conception of the world about it.

Grote's position here is simply, that phenomenal reality is always related to consciousness, or *with us* in some way, and necessarily so, since it becomes knowledge (*for us*). That is, the world of phenomenal fact *may be* exceedingly disconnected but it is not thus that it is *seen*. This is the point which Ferrier, too, wishes to make. Grote states his essential agreement with Ferrier on this issue.[2]

3. CRITICISM OF GROTE AND FERRIER ON THE BASIS OF LOTZE'S POSITION

i. The Non-Ego is not essential to the Ego

Let us turn now to critical reflections on Grote and Ferrier by considering part of Lotze's view of the Ego and the Non-Ego. Lotze

---

[1] Ferrier, IOM, 503.
[2] In all of this epistemological treatment Grote is concerned, of course, with what R. B. Perry refers to as 'the ego-centric predicament.'

discusses the chief objections which have been put forward concerning belief in the existence of an Ego, apart from the existence of a Non-Ego. His argument is followed here to show the possibility of the existence of the Ego without the existence of a Non-Ego to make it possible. Thus we may consider briefly the Ego and the Non-Ego in relation to the Personality of God.

An Ego (or Self, *Ich*) is not thinkable without the contrast of a Non-Ego or Not-Self; hence personal existence cannot be asserted of God without bringing even Him down to that state of limitation, of being conditioned by something not Himself, which is repugnant to Him. – The objections that speculative knowledge makes to the personality of God fall back upon this thought; in order to estimate their importance, we shall have to test the apparently clear content of the proposition which they take as their point of departure. For unambiguous it is not; it may be intended to assert that what the term Ego denotes can be comprehended in reflective analysis only by reference to the Non-Ego; it may also mean that it is not conceivable that this content of the Ego should be experienced without that contrasted Non-Ego being experienced at the same time; finally, it may point to the existence and active influence of a Non-Ego as the condition without which the being upon which this influence works could not be an Ego.[1]

Now, Grote does *not* admit the possibility of the existence of the Ego without the existence of a Non-Ego to make it possible. In fact, Grote would use other terms for what seems to him to be essential in epistemology, namely, phenomena and 'philosophy.' Grote would hold, if he were to discuss the problem with Lotze, that there is too much involved in the 'Ego' to be useful in epistemology. There are, Grote would say, immediate and reflective (or mediate) elements in it. If the Ego is reflective then there is 'philosophy' and phenomena present, as the two aspects in which the one reality of the Ego may be viewed.

Again, if the Ego were taken as representing the self which involves consciousness, 'thought,' or 'philosophy,' then the complete reality must include the Non-Ego as phenomena. Both 'philosophy' and phenomena are essential to each other, so it would be incorrect on Grote's view to say that the Non-Ego is not necessary in order to make the Ego possible. The Ego cannot stand alone, for Grote, *if he were* to use the terms Ego and Non-Ego. However, he would not use these terms since he would feel that they were inadequate to deal with what is involved in epistemology.

Bowne's view of 'pure being' in isolation, may be noted here; it seems to agree with the essential relativity of knowledge in Grote's epistemology. "Pure being is objectively nothing; and even if it were

---

[1] Lotze, MIC, II, 678.

a possible existence, we could never reach nor use it without bad logic." [1] Grote would seem to agree with Bowne here.

ii. Three interpretations of the objection, to the personality of God, considered

There are three possible interpretations then, of such an objection to the Ego or Personality of God, that Lotze considers. The objection itself is founded on the belief that the personality of God necessitates a Non-Ego "which is repugnant to him." The objector holds that if we assert an Ego then we must also postulate a Non-Ego, and for the following reasons as the three possible interpretations point out:

(1) What the Ego denotes can only be realized by reference to a Non-Ego.

(2) It is not conceivable that the content of the Ego should be experienced without that contrasted Non-Ego being experienced along with it.

(3) The Ego could not be an Ego without the existence and activity of a Non-Ego.

In answer to the first two objections Lotze makes the following significant statement:

We admit that the Ego *is thinkable* only in relation to the Non-Ego, but we add that it *may be experienced* previous to and out of every such relation, and that to this is due the possibility of its subsequently becoming thinkable in that relation. [2]

The third objection must be considered more fully. Lotze does not believe that Fichte's insistence on a Non-Ego is worth considering. Fichte's theory was the "Anstoss" or shock of collision (with the Non-Ego) in which self-consciousness arises.

Selfhood, the essence of all personality, does not depend upon any opposition that either has happened or is happening of the Ego to a Non-Ego, but it consists in an immediate self-existence which constitutes the basis of the possibility of that contrast wherever it appears. Self-consciousness is the elucidation of this self-existence which is brought about by means of knowledge, and even this is by no means necessarily bound up with the distinction of the Ego from a Non-Ego which is substantially opposed to it. [3]

In the nature of the finite mind as such is to be found the reason why the development of its personal consciousness can take place only through the influences of that cosmic whole which the finite being itself is not, that is through stimulation coming from the Non-Ego, not because it needs the contrast with

---

[1] Bowne, MET, 14.
[2] Lotze, MIC, II, 680.
[3] Lotze, *op. cit.*, 687.

something *alien* in order to have self-existence, but because in this respect, as in every other, it does not contain in itself the conditions of its existence. We do not find this limitation in the being of the Infinite; hence for it alone is there possible a self-existence, which needs neither to be initiated nor to be continuously developed by something not itself, but which maintains itself within itself with spontaneous action that is eternal and had no beginning.[1]

Now, it appears that both Fichte and Lotze were concerned with the Ego and the Non-Ego from a more cosmological viewpoint than Grote. Grote is chiefly concerned with epistemological considerations. He discusses the personality of God very little, and where he does speak of God it is more in a traditionally puritanical sense designed for audiences unfamiliar with a more rational theology, as in an article entitled "On a Future State." [2]

But the point is, as far as Grote's philosophy is concerned, whether the self as consciousness is possible without considering what consciousness is *of*. To this question Grote answers with an emphatic 'No.' Lotze would seem to disagree by bringing up the case of 'the personality of God.' Grote would say to Lotze that this illustration does not sufficiently bear upon the epistemological problem. Likewise, he would say the same to Fichte who held that the Non-Ego is necessary to the existence of the Ego, even though Fichte's view and Lotze's were very contrary to each other.

The view that the Ego requires the existence of a Non-Ego is also supported by the fact that the greater the variety and multitude of forces working, the more developed will the self or Ego be. Analogous with this self-existence is the Personality of God.

Perfect Personality is in God only, to all finite minds there is allotted but a pale copy thereof; the finiteness of the finite is not a producing condition of this Personality but a limit and a hindrance of its development.[3]

But care must be taken not to make thought (or idea) equivalent to the Personality of God. What is true of the human Ego is not necessarily true of the divine Ego. The human Ego may possess the necessary potentialities for sensations and feelings, yet require stimulus from without for their activity. With the theistic Ego this is not the case, for this Ego contains within its own nature the causes of every stage of its development. It does not require what is not itself in order to be what it is.

This Infinite Being does not need – as we sometimes, with a strange perversion of the right point of view, think – that its life should be called forth by external

[1] Lotze, MIC, II, 687, 688.
[2] CR (1871), XVIII, 134.
[3] Lotze, *op. cit.*, 688.

deficiency which seems to us to make such stimuli necessary for the finite being, and its active efficacy thinkable. The Infinite Being, not bound by any obligation to agree in any way with something not itself, will, with perfect self-sufficingness, possess in its own nature the causes of every step forward in the development of its life.[1]

The purpose of including Lotze's view of the personality of God, was to consider the relationship of the Ego to the Non-Ego, and to see what difference, if any, such a consideration would make in regard to philosophy as consciousness. For consciousness is basic in the Ego and also fundamental in Grote's epistemology. To overlook all consideration of the Ego and the Non-Ego would scarcely seem appropriate in regard to what Grote is dealing with throughout the *Exploratio Philosophica*, namely, the problem of consciousness as inseparably related to phenomena.

iii. Human mind projected into nature

a. Not necessary for mind to project itself into nature

Grote is not concerned with the affirmation or denial of mind or reason in nature. The mind, he says, is projected into nature. By this he means that, for example, the order we see in nature is an order made possible because of the mind's action. Everything, he implies, is dependent upon being related to mind. If we want to call mind, the 'ego,' Grote would seem to have no objection, unless he would hold that by calling it by the term 'ego' we are much less decisive and descriptive than by using the term consciousness, 'philosophy,' 'logic,' 'thought,' or mind.

Through the projection of mind into nature, there is a constant correcting going on, either through contact with other minds, or through the making of advances in one's own thought by oneself. This correcting leads to the eradicating of the projecting of ourselves into nature. That is, phenomenal reality as communication exists even though we may not be *aware* of it. Phenomenal reality is still reality even though conscious mind is not projected into it.

In short, Grote is trying to show that nature considered as *physical* communication has no relation to the human mind. As purely physical there is nothing mental involved. Pure physical reality is devoid of any relation with mind. Yet there is communication among purely physical things. But the communication as wholly material is utterly *meaningless*, for Grote. It is only when mind is projected into nature that meaning enters. We cannot speak or think of the 'purely physical.'

[1] Lotze, MIC, II, 683.

Hence Grote's frequent references to the crucial necessity of regarding consciousness and the phenomenal as abstractions from a reality that requires them both in order to be *reality*.

b. No projection of mind in the complete view

The complete view (which, of course, is impossible) for the human knowing mind, would occur when a complete eradication of this projection takes place. One may see, then, what Ferrier means by the 'nonsensical' or the 'contradictory.' It is that which by itself, and apart from consciousness makes no sense. It is meaningless, 'nonsense,' the 'contradictory.' It is that condition that would exist if there were no projection at all of the Ego into the Non-Ego. Actually this condition, Grote maintains, is never reached. But if it were reached it would be in the region of phenomena – utterly lacking in consciousness, but still fulfilling its role of *communication* through the senses with the body, and up to (but not far enough to include) consciousness.

The 'nonsensical' or 'contradictory' could never be the complete view *to us*. But it is the complete 'view' for phenomenalism – to which one should add – granting that the phenomenal *could* be entirely divorced (which is not the case) from 'philosophy.'

4. MEANING OF 'KNOW,' AND 'KNOW ABOUT,' IN REFERENCE TO PHENOMENAL REALITY

i. The knowing of phenomenal reality viewed in two ways

What is 'nonsensical' is meaningless; if meaning were added it would no longer to be the realm of 'nonsense.' Meaning, attributed to phenomenal reality, i. e. the knowing of phenomenal reality, may be looked at in two ways. First, we may 'know' objects, and, second, we may 'know about' them. The former is γνῶναι, *noscere, kennen, connaître*, the latter, εἰδέναι, *scire, wissen, savoir*. This knowledge has been referred to as knowledge of acquaintance and knowledge of description, by Grote. The former implies that there is something already known and to know is merely familiarity with this known. It is the bodily communication with an object, e.g., by means of the eye. The latter is more expressedly intellectual and does not appear so directly dependent upon the senses for its existence. It is judgmental, according to Grote. Phenomena refer to what is in contact with bodily existence and yet is what it is apart from any mind. Yet it is possible for mind to communicate with it. But with things in themselves there is no possibility of contact at all by mind and they are not known to any person in any form. If they could be manifested to human intelligence their nature would at once be changed.

Confusion between what we *know* and what we *know about*, should be avoided. Grote believes that Ferrier is not lucid here, as may be observed from the following:

> I am not sure whether Mr. Ferrier, in general so clear, is not in this particular otherwise, when he speaks of our knowledge as the knowing ourselves as knowing or apprehending, or the knowing that we know and apprehend, the object of our knowledge... he seems to lose sight of the necessity of giving an account of the last-mentioned knowledge, or apprehension. Is the word 'know' in the two parts of the sentence used in the same or in different meanings? It appears to me that the notion of a difference between things in themselves, and things as we know them arises in the main from the confusion together of these two views of knowledge.[1]

ii. 'Know,' and 'know about,' in relation to phenomena and things in themselves

It seems safe to state, on Grote's view, that if it were possible to have a notion of things in themselves, then knowledge would be complete so far as it went, however localized it might happen to be. And to have a notion of complete knowledge would be to *know* things. If such a notion were actualized, then to say that we *know about* things could not be admitted. One must speak of either one or the other but not both if one is allowed to discuss knowing in relation to things in themselves at all. For if to know an object would be to know the thing in itself, then this knowing of the object would actually be the subject. Were the thing in itself completely known it could be an object to no subject, but would be a subject to itself. In that case, to speak of 'knowing about' the object would be superfluous.

5. RELATIVITY OF KNOWLEDGE

i. Knowledge is essentially relative

To deal with the relativity of knowledge appears just as much beside the mark as to discuss knowledge of things in themselves. Knowledge, according to Grote, *is* itself relative. Communication between the object and consciousness is essential. To say that knowledge is relative suggests that there *is* already a sort of thing in itself

[1] Grote, EP, I, 60, 61.

that is related to mind. Relativity of knowledge also suggests a re-lation to a *particular* person. A word here might be given concerning the error into which Sir William Hamilton falls. Hamilton's reference to the relativity of knowledge overlooks the necessary distinction that Grote makes between the phenomenal and the philosophical views. To say that knowledge is relative in the sense in which Sir William Hamilton does is to affirm twice, and hence once unnecessarily. Knowledge itself implies relativeness.

And since knowledge is itself relative because there are the two elements of 'philosophy' and phenomena involved, it is superfluous to say again that this knowledge that is relative is relative! This is Grote's criticism of Hamilton's remark that he (Hamilton) is going to consider 'in what sense human knowledge is relative.'

In what sense human knowledge is relative. – From what has been said, you will be able, I hope, to understand what is meant by the proposition, that all our knowledge is only relative. It is relative, (1) Because existence is not cognizable, absolutely and in itself, but only in special modes; (2) Because these modes can be known only if they stand in a certain relation to our faculties; and (3) Because the modes thus relative to our faculties are presented to, and known by, the mind only under modifications determined by these faculties themselves.[1]

ii. Misleading to speak of 'modes of existence'

Sir William Hamilton refers to everything known, as 'modes of existence.' [2] This language tends to obscure the relation between mind and the object known. By 'modes of existence' he really means the various ways in which the thing in itself is presented to the mind through the senses. An equivalent to Hamilton's 'existence' is 'thing in itself.' Grote believes that the 'thing in itself' is a logical figment and nothing more.

The 'thing in itself' if we use that language, or 'existence' if we use Sir William Hamilton's, may be considered either as a simply *logical* entity, a manner of expression necessary for us because we wish to consider knowledge as the knowing *about* something, the forming of judgments, scientia – in which case it is not the *object* of knowledge at all, but simply the logical subject of the judgments and the notion of reality attaches not to *it*, but to the sum of what is and can be known *about* it: or it may be considered as the intended object of the know-ledge, what the mind, acting in the way of intuition, apprehension, kenntniss (not, i.e. judgment *about*) is always aiming at, to whatever degree it succeeds. 'Existence,' says Sir William Hamilton, in the passage already cited, 'is not cognisable absolutely and in itself, but only in special modes.' [3]

1 Bowen, MWH, 95.
2 Bowen, *op. cit.*, 95–97.
3 Grote, EP, I, 65.

This is an attempt to describe what underlies that which we know, "a manner of expression necessary for us because we wish to consider knowledge as the knowing *about* something, the forming of judgment, scientia." [1]

What Hamilton in all likelihood did mean was that the thing in itself ('existence,' according to him) could really never be known, and that it could not exist except as a logical entity. In so considering 'things in themselves' Hamilton seems to mean what Kant does by 'noumena,' namely, 'intelligible entitites.' [2] Reality does not attach to the thing in itself, but only to what can be known. Unfortunately, however, he speaks of 'modes of existence,' all of which may be known, and yet 'existence' (as he uses the term) itself could remain unknown. Where Hamilton uses the term 'existence,' Ferrier uses the term 'matter *per se*.' Ferrier prefers this term to 'thing in itself' or to 'unknowable substratum.' To Grote, 'matter *per se*' seems to refer to something which can be known, even though Ferrier does not mean that it can be known. But matter for Grote is never actually 'matter *per se*.' It always is matter for us. 'Matter *per se*' is matter entirely separate from any human consciousness. Such a term would have no meaning for Grote. '*Per se*' is simply indicative of the view of reality from the side of phenomena.

Ferrier's thought is acceptable in the eyes of Grote but not the language. Grote believes that not only the language is unfortunate but also when Ferrier speaks of "Agnoiology,' or "theory of ignorance" the terms are equally ill-chosen. Ferrier admits that we cannot know the thing in itself so why speak of it as "matter per se"? Also, we cannot be ignorant of it, so why refer to it as 'Agnoiology' or 'theory of ignorance'? In other words to say that we know the thing in itself, or that we do not know it, is useless. All that can be said about our relation to it does not pertain to knowing, but rather to existence, or "our state in regard to it," [3] *if* there is such a state which is neither ignorance of the thing in itself nor knowledge of it.

In reference to... his Agnoiology or theory of ignorance... His manner of thought here, as I understand it, is one which might strike many minds forcibly. We do not know this 'thing in itself,' to be sure, but then, on the other hand, we are not ignorant of it; our state in regard of it is not that of ignorance, which is what all you who talk about it imply, and even say: it is no more ignorance than it is knowledge: if you can find a *third* alternative, *that* is our state in regard to it: if not, *you* have no more right to say, expressly or impliedly, that we are

[1] Grote, EP, I, 65.
[2] Kant, CPR, 267.
[3] Grote, EP, I, 75.

ignorant of it, than *I* have to say we know it. This, as I understand, is in other language what I meant by saying, that the notion of knowledge is not applicable to it: that there is nothing to know: that talking of knowing it is like talking of eating light, or smelling sound: disparate, incongruous.[1]

iii. Misleading view presented by Ferrier in writing about the 'Primary Law of Condition of all Knowledge'

Grote agrees with Ferrier when the latter states that the problems of philosophy are seen very differently to different people and Hamilton's reference to 'modes of existence' as virtual things in themselves, finds a counterpart in Ferrier's view of a strictly personal philosophy.

When Ferrier refers to the difficulty of seeing "the true flesh-and-blood countenance of a single philosophical problem," Grote agrees that "no man, for the last two thousand years, has seen the true flesh-and-blood countenance of a single philosophical problem." [2] But Grote sees error in Ferrier when the latter refers to the possibility of relying, with 'perfect confidence' [3] upon a 'strictly reasoned philosophy.' This position of Ferrier's is similar to Hamilton's and evident in the phrase, 'modes of existence,' used by the latter.

But with his remedy I cannot agree: that is, with the applicability of it. We want, he says, *strictly reasoned* philosophy: and when we have it, we shall be so certain that we have it, it will be so evidently irrefragable, that we shall take our ground with the most perfect confidence as against all possible controversy.[4]

Ferrier stated that,

Besides the ego, or oneself, there is no other identical quality in our cognitions – as anyone may convince himself upon reflection. He will find that he cannot lay his finger upon anything except *himself*, and say – This article of cognition I must know along with whatever I know.[5]

Grote objects that 'himself' is just what 'he' cannot 'lay his finger' upon – upon his body surely, but not on 'himself.' Grote holds that body (*qua* physical) in this connection is a part of phenomenal reality, and at the farthest extreme from consciousness.

iv. 'Ordinary' and 'natural' thinking

Though Grote is so greatly in agreement with Ferrier's main argument, namely that, the self must be apprehended along with the object, the ego requiring the non-ego, yet he cannot agree that this main

---

[1] Grote, EP, I, 74, 75.
[2] Grote, *op. cit.*, 69. Cf. Ferrier, IOM, 10.
[3] *Loc. cit.*
[4] *Loc. cit.*
[5] Ferrier, IOM, 80.

argument, constituting as it does the basis for the philosophy of the *Institutes of Metaphysic*, is in essential agreement with what Ferrier professes is the role of philosophy. Ferrier speaks about "the plausibilities of ordinary thinking," [1] and "that man does not naturally think aright." [2] Against this position Grote directs a potent attack. Grote states in defence of 'ordinary thinking' [3] that there are not so many plausibilities about it as there are in much philosophy. The reason for this statement is that 'ordinary thinking' in the estimation of Grote is only partially phenomenalistic and will therefore represent the ground upon which thought will most likely stand, and the thought of many philosophers is thoroughly phenomenalistic.

Grote points out that Ferrier is right in his assertion that philosophy exists for correction insofar as it prevents an overemphasis on either 'philosophy' or 'phenomenalism.'

So far as philosophy does exist for... correction... its use as to 'ordinary' thinking seems to be to prevent any tendency to what I call 'notionalism,' that is, to prevent people's thinking that the 'qualities,' 'attributes' &c., which they talk about, are the *real things* of the universe. Similarly, its use as to 'natural' thinking would be to prevent phenomenalism trespassing, as I should call it, on morals and religion, and becoming positivism. [4]

Grote further points out, in commenting on Ferrier's position, "that the language of ordinary intelligent communication among men is better than the language of philosophers." [5]

There is a sense in which Ferrier is correct in stating that philosophy serves as a correction to 'ordinary' or 'natural' thinking. For by 'natural' thinking Ferrier probably did not mean anything more than 'ordinary' thinking. That is, he asserts that *naturally*, or *ordinarily*, man does not think correctly. If, by natural or ordinary thinking, he means any non-professional positivistic or naturalistic position, or pre-scientific thought, then philosophy should be a correction for this view. For such positivism (or naturalism) seems very limited in that it does not account for much beyond it, and does not escape the criticism of being phenomenalistic.

Hence, it is evident that Ferrier in holding this view regarding natural or ordinary thinking sees quite clearly the danger of overemphasis on phenomenal reality – a main weakness in phenomenalism as Ferrier and Grote use the term. Yet, on the other hand, Grote

---

[1] Ferrier, IOM, 28.
[2] *Loc. cit.*
[3] *Loc. cit.*
[4] Grote, EP, I, 73.
[5] *Loc. cit.*

properly points out that philosophy is not a corrective for ordinary (or natural) thinking when this latter thinking neither over-emphasizes 'philosophy' nor 'phenomena.' Rather, Grote points out, philosophy can spoil this healthy thinking characterized as 'ordinary' or 'natural.'

In either case – where Ferrier is correct (as pointed out above) and where Grote's criticism of Ferrier is acceptable – one sees that both Ferrier and Grote do not lose sight of the distinction between 'philosophy' and 'phenomenalism.' Both seem to see quite clearly what frequently is overlooked in the history of philosophy through specific emphasis resulting in pan-objectivism, correspondence, sense experience, and many other theories.

6. SUMMARY OF MAIN ISSUES

Let us now recapitulate on the main issues presented in this chapter. Grote states that Ferrier is in essential agreement with the distinction which he himself makes between phenomenalism and 'philosophy.' The ambiguities evident in Ferrier's argument arise from his reference to knowledge in such a way that one cannot be sure whether he is stressing the 'philosophical' or the phenomenal aspects. It also seems not only in Ferrier's statements, but also in much of Grote's writing, there would be considerable more clarity if some use was made of the terms 'knowing' and 'known.'

It is interesting to note that Samuel Alexander attempts to be specific regarding the 'subject' and 'object' in knowledge. He states: "There is no mental object as distinct from a physical object." [1]

As an example which presents the least difficulty take the perception of a tree or a table. This situation consists of the act of mind which is the perceiving; the object which is so much of the thing called tree as is perceived, the aspect of it which is peculiar to that perception, let us say the appearance of the tree under these circumstances of the perception; and the togetherness or compresence which connects these two distinct existences (the act of mind and the object) into the total situation called the experience. But the two terms are differently experienced. The one is experienced, that is, is present in the experience, as the act of experiencing, the other as that which is experienced. To use Mr. Lloyd Morgan's happy notation, the one is an -ing, the other an -ed. The act of mind is the experiencing, the appearance, tree, is that upon which it is directed, that of which it is aware.[2]

Both Ferrier and Grote, as well as Alexander, Morgan, and many others, see clearly the danger in speaking of 'subject' and 'object' as

[1] Alexander, STD, II, 111.
[2] Alexander, op. cit., 11, 12.

though these terms could be used in abstraction from each other. Where Ferrier fails Grote observes that failure is due chiefly to Ferrier's manner of presentation rather than to a fundamental confusion of the philosophical and phenomenal aspects in epistemology.

A further consideration of 'philosophy' as consciousness leads Grote to an analysis of the relation of the ego to the non-ego. His analysis is confined to an investigation of human knowledge. For Grote the ego requires the existence of the non-ego, as consciousness requires phenomenal reality for a basis of communication between consciousness and the 'outside' world, or with the non-ego.

It will be helpful to look a little closer at this relation of the ego to the non-ego. In discussing (above) Lotze's comments on the personality of God, it was observed that the Ego did not require the existence of a Non-Ego to make it possible. Ego here is taken as deity. The deity requires nothing other than himself in order to exist. It was pointed out, that according to Grote and Fichte the ego on the human plane *does* require the existence of the non-ego. But, whereas, for Fichte this is true (as it is for Grote) yet the explanation which Fichte gives is very different from Grote's. In Fichte's theory, the non-ego provides the 'Anstoss' or shock of collision with the ego, and thus consciousness arises.

Strictly, Grote does not actually speak in terms of the ego and the non-ego. But there is a sense in which he could speak of them, if they mean what he regards as consciousness and phenomena respectively. And the relation which consciousness and phenomena have with each other has been discussed extensively in the present work up to this point, and also specifically in chapter three. An example of the difficulty that Grote would have in trying to express himself in terms of the ego and non-ego may be seen in the fact that to talk about the non-ego as phenomena would mean that there would be a sort of inner side to the non-ego which is classed by Grote (when this inner side refers to phenomena) as consciousness. Now it would scarcely make sense to speak of *the inner side* of the non-ego as the ego.

In the case of the ego and the non-ego, there is a dichotomy which seems to separate decisively each from the other. But in the case of what Grote means by 'philosophy' and phenomena there is no decisive bifurcation between the two. And the whole of Grote's phenomenology is built up on the view that reality is one, but can be seen from two very different aspects.

According to Grote the non-ego is not properly regarded as things in themselves, for about these latter we are not qualified to speak or think. Were it possible to do so, then the conscious subject would be the object, and the *known about* would, for us, become the *known*, because things in themselves would be the same as things in themselves *being known*!

Some consideration of the Ego on the theistic plane would have enriched Grote's writing on 'philosophy' as consciousness, especially in the case of the deity. One cannot fail to be impressed by the more restricted vision which remains on the human plane. But Grote cannot be condemned for not being more comprehensive in scope. What applies on the human level would seem to be applicable on the theistic, for Grote. It would seem then, that Grote would not have admitted, if he had gone beyond the human plane in his discussion of the Ego, that the Ego as Personality of God were possible without the contrasting Non-Ego. However, Grote's presentation is restricted to human knowing, and one is left to surmise only, about the possible development of his epistemology if he had Lotze as a fellow colleague.

Grote's reflections, following Ferrier, on the projection of human mind (consciousness, or the ego), into nature (phenomenal reality, or the non-ego), seems very sound. If mind were not projected into nature there would be no consciousness of nature. All that is meant here is that nature to *be for us* requires a mind for it to be *to*. And if mind were not projected into nature, nature would still affect our senses, i.e. the phenomenal would operate on us just as its parts intercommunicate with each other. The intercommunication does not cease though the parts involved lack the characteristic of consciousness.

Sir William Hamilton is the object of considerable comment because of his ambiguous use of terms like knowledge, clearly revealing the fact of the ambiguity of equating of 'existence' with things in themselves. Where Ferrier is clear on this point, Hamilton is opaque. Moreover, Hamilton's writing is deeply vitiated throughout because of his failure to make his epistemology (or metaphysics) clear. Had he distinguished between the possible approaches to epistemology, recognizing the 'philosophical' or the 'phenomenal,' and the possibility of emphasizing either, he would not have confused the subject knowing, and the object known, under such terms as 'knowledge,' and the object known with things in themselves under terms such as modes of existence (where existence is used for things in themselves).

Hamilton's confusion is seen in the fact that he states that we are equally conscious of our reality and of matter. Grote points out that we are immediately conscious of our selves, but that we are not immediately conscious of matter at all. To say that we are conscious of matter is to assume matter as already being in relation to consciousness and *then* to relate this consciousness of matter to our consciousness!

Failure to see important issues in epistemology clearly is characteristic of much writing in the field. Ferrier is basically correct. Hamilton is a good example of considerable failure. There are others who have missed the fundamental distinction between 'philosophy' and phenomena. Grote turns his attention to some of these in subsequent chapters. His immediate concern, however, is with the scale of sensation in relation to knowledge. This subject is taken up in the following chapter.

CHAPTER V

'PHILOSOPHY' AND THE SCALE OF SENSATION

1. INTRODUCTION

In the last chapter the discussion centered on philosophy as consciousness and the ego. The method followed was to deal with Grote's exposition of the positions taken by several philosophers regarding consciousness and the ego, and to show more clearly, by an examination of these positions the various features of his own position. This method provided for consideration of what is sometimes regarded as the subject-object relation, and the relation of the ego and the non-ego, in epistemology.

It was also pointed out that there are two types of knowledge, knowledge of acquaintance, and knowledge of description or knowledge about. The former is immediate and has to do with the consciousness side of knowledge; the latter is concerned with knowledge viewed from the side of 'things.'

The present chapter is concerned with a further exposition of the relation of consciousness with phenomena, showing that there is a scale having two extremes, the one which is as wholly consciousness or 'philosophy' as possible (for example, in self-consciousness) and the other which is as wholly phenomenal reality as possible. We will be particularly concerned in the present chapter with showing the place of 'philosophy' in relation to this scale. Hamilton provides a good illustration of a mixing of the two aspects (the 'philosophical' and the phenomenal) together, for example, in stating that consciousness of our selves and 'consciousness of matter' are equally immediate. But the particular concern in this chapter is with the 'scale of sensation' and its relation to 'philosophy.' So it will be necessary to consider both the extremes of the scale and the gradation between them.

2. IMPORTANCE OF THE SCALE OF SENSATION

i. Meaning of sensation very significant

Grote considers, what he calls, "the scale of sensation or knowledge" very important. It is important because it illustrates his entire epistemology and because, without its being either explicitly or implicitly in his system, his main contribution to epistemology would be negligible.

This chapter is related to the foregoing chapter on "philosophy as consciousness and the ego" as illustrative of the place of 'philosophy' in relation to phenomena. The illustration it provides is logical rather than pictorial. There are two main points served in the relating of this chapter to the previous one: (a) It attempts to solve the problem of how much 'philosophy' is present in various sensations, the amount varying from an infinitesimally small degree to an infinitely large degree. (b) The other purpose served is in the development of the problem of the relationship of 'philosophy' (or consciousness) to phenomena, since this relation is essential and crucial for all epistemology, according to Grote. To discuss this scale of sensation he sets aside a complete chapter.[1] The relation of 'philosophy' to this scale is illustrated by referring to the metaphysics of Sir William Hamilton.

The word, 'sensation,' itself, was used by Grote in a general sense to express feeling, thought, or consciousness.

After all, *sensation* is the general term to express the consciousness, feeling, thought which we have correspondent with... more correctly, *supposed* by us correspondent with, the presence of any portion of existence independent of us.[2]

Kant also used sensation in the sense of feeling, thought, or consciousness. For Kant sensation means the content of sensuous intuition, that is, the way that a conscious subject is modified by an object. He seems to use the term to point out the content that is sensed instead of the sensing process. The process he calls 'intuition,'[3] and the faculty, 'sensibility.'[4]

ii. 'The scale of sensation'

In general one might say that feeling – whether of pleasure-pain, of color, or whatever – is at the bottom, space at the middle and thought

[1] Grote, EP, I, Chap. VI.
[2] Grote, *op. cit.*, 106.
[3] Kant, CPR, 65.
[4] *Loc. cit.*

at the top of the scale of sensation. Further, at the bottom feeling and matter are not the factors, but rather, feeling and the mediation between body and the external world. Present at this end is consciousness though it may be infinitesimally small. But there must be some consciousness present, however small, in order that there may be feeling. How infinitesimal consciousness is, may be judged from the action and reaction, extremely minute, for example, when anything is tasted. That is, consciousness is barely present and so small that it can *almost* be neglected but for the infinitesimal amount that is necessary to complete the scale with feeling at one end. Consciousness can be postulated as present at the feeling end of the scale, otherwise feeling could not be spoken of at all. At the middle of the scale feeling is present but not nearly so great in magnitude as at the lower end. Here feeling is in relation to matter itself because there is a communication between our bodies and the outside world.

What Grote means by feeling should be noted here. Feeling as physical is, of course, phenomenal; feeling as mental (or viewed from the aspect of 'philosophy') is consciousness.

This feeling or consciousness, excluded from phenomenalism, I now assume as the one thing which we *do* know or are certain of. It is evident that this is a higher and a more intimate certainty to us than any phenomenal certainty. Whether anything beyond ourselves exists or not, we are at least certain that we feel, *i.e.* that feeling, pleasure and pain, are realities, and individual to what, in virtue of this feeling or consciousness, we call *ourselves:* and that so far as consciousness is a proof or a fit suggestive of existence, 'cogito' of 'sum,' *we* ourselves exist.[1]

We are conscious of the communication between our bodies and the outside world, and can speak about it. That this is so appears more clearly when the upper part of the scale, which is the reverse of the lower, is observed. Here there is a communication between thought (as judging, reasoning, imagining, etc.) and phenomenal reality into which we project ourselves.

At the upper end of the scale, that of *thought*, the case is exactly the opposite of what it was in the lower. As *there* there was communication between two different forms or modes of mind, and matter, phenomenalism, appears distinct from them, as simply what has brought about the communication. The perception, in its completeness, of an existing object of knowledge, is really a sympathy with its constitution, arising from the fact that we know ourselves more or less as constituted beings, and that we can make or constitute things ourselves for purposes for which we need them. We recognize therefore in the objects, mind kindred to our own.[2]

[1] Grote, EP, I, 18, 19.
[2] Grote, *op. cit.*, 116.

Where 'unity' is attained through perception knowledge is complete. However, since perception is so imperfect as its best knowledge is but fragmentary. Thus consciousness or knowledge is at its greatest magnitude at the top of the scale and gradually diminishes practically to nothing at the lower end.

At the lower or feeling end of the scale of sensation which I gave a short time since the two things which stand opposite to each other are not properly feeling and matter (sensation and body), but are sensation or feeling on the one side, and on the other side a communication between two kinds of matter, that of our body and that which is external to it. It is *possible*, as I have said, that *here* there may be a mechanical measurement and corresponding to it a latent, because infinitesimally minute, consciousness: e.g. that the real character of *taste* might be an action and reaction (the force on the one side being our will) between the separate portions of our organ of tasts and the particles and minute forces of the thing tasted. But this, though we might possibly follow it out on the side of physiology, we could never possibly follow out on the side of feeling, having no microscope for consciousness.[1]

Here, Grote envisages a scale for sensation which has feeling, with attributes of pleasure and pain, of willing, acting, etc., at one extremity. Sensation at this extreme is pure feeling – meaning by 'pure feeling,' feeling as devoid of thought as is possible. At this extremity there is thought with attributes such as magnitude and durability. These attributes *qua* phenomenal are physical, and it is this aspect of the phenomenal that we are concerned with at this end of the scale. But these attributes *qua* phenomenal must have some 'thought' related to them; hence one cannot avoid speaking of thought in this way, that is, as having attributes as magnitude and durability – but it is not thought *qua* thought but rather thought *qua* phenomena.

We may conveniently imagine two kinds of this sensation, in no degree rigidly separable the one from the other, viz. feeling and thought: *feeling*, that kind of it in which selfconsciousness, reflexive attention, pleasure or pain, is strongly present: thought, that in which the attention is directed rather to the non-ego and to the exertion of the will. The former is clearly that in which there is the least approximation to each other, in the qualities of the feeling and those of the matter.[2]

The attribute of time also appears at the thought end of the scale.

Further, at the lower end of the scale, where feeling dominates, space has a place even though its major importance is at the top of the scale where thought predominates. It seems that it would be better to regard space more as at the phenomenal end of the scale than at the thought end. But Grote may be very much influenced by Kant here,

[1] Grote, EP, I, 114, 115.
[2] Grote, *op. cit.*, 106.

as, for example, by such an expression as this: "Space is a necessary *a priori* representation, which underlies all outer intuitions." [1]

On the philosophical assumption the confused mass of chemical or secondary sensation gives the confused and chaotic matter of (in *this* sense), or preparation for, what is afterwards knowledge. To this *time* and *space* (which viewed from *within*, are in fact a higher degree of self-consciousness and so much volitional exertion) give form and order of the first or lower description, in the sense of shape, magnitude, relative position, &c.[2]

Form, whether in Plato or Aristotle would be at the top of Grote's scale of sensation. Form is the λόγος of Aristotle which corresponds to the εἶδος of Plato, or what Grote refers to as the reason, meaning, purpose, etc., which acts as a soul or criterion for arrangement and which constitutes thing, a thing. This reason or meaning which acts as a criterion for arrangement is at the 'thought' or top of the scale. It is not the primary qualities (of Locke) which have this potentiality of creating the form for feeling but rather "form of the higher description, εἶδος, quality, or *qualitiedness*, kind, true reality, is given by a higher self-consciousness, and there begin to be things." [3] The point of the matter is that shape, size, etc., in which the form may be presented are only accessory factors to that which creates the 'things.'

λόγος applies to 'number' also. The exactitude of mathematical calculations does not apply here for this preciseness is only an accident of 'number.' What is important here to notice is the unit which all calculations presume. This unit is the 'individual' which in calculations give arrangement or order to the 'number' and suggests or reveals a 'mind' present in the universe. The 'thought' which lies at the upper end of the scale of sensation is not of space, which appears to be that which reveals the form, but form or εἶδος itself.

iii. The center of the scale

In the center of the scale space – and its relations – is evident. No space appears at the end of the scale where feelings dominate solely, for Grote. At the feeling (*qua* phenomenal) end the mind is passive – the state which Hamilton improperly regards as the unconscious – and receives impressions, such as those which produce pleasure and pain, from the outside world. At the opposite extremity, where thought is supremely dominant, objects of the outside world are acted upon by thought.

[1] Kant, CPR, 68.
[2] Grote, EP, I, 110.
[3] *Loc. cit.*

What can one say, then, about the center of the scale where the dominant characteristic, for Grote, is space? It seems that, here, feeling – which, *qua* phenomenal, is dominant in the feeling end of the scale – is no longer passive but actively mingles with the activity of what is 'outside' itself. Also, thought, which is dominant in the thought end of the scale, is no longer entirely active but becomes somewhat passive as we approach the center of the scale.

It would seem, then, that feelings such as pleasure and pain on the one hand, and thought as involved in willing and acting on the other, do not belong to two different realms but commingle; this is true of the center of the scale. Bifurcation, where thought predominates at one end, and feeling, *qua* phenomenal – or the 'external world' affecting feeling – predominates at the other end, depends upon the emphasis laid upon the extreme ends of the scale. The bifurcation throughout becomes clearer as one compares the extremities emphasized and disregards the portion (including the center of the scale) between (the extremities).

iv. Importance of the scale of sensation
for Hamilton's position

Let us now turn to consider Hamilton's views regarding the extremes of 'thought' and 'object' in order to see the importance of recognizing what Grote presents as a 'scale' of sensation.

It is not the retina which 'feels,' or sees, but the 'ego' or the 'I,' and the specific relationship of matter to this 'I' still remains the problem involved in bifurcation. Hamilton does not solve the issue by referring to '*consciousness* of mind' and '*consciousness* of matter.' Hamilton's argument, then, simply reintroduces in a new form the problem of how mind and matter are related; it does not solve the problem. The problem that Hamilton does not seem adequately to cope with, and where a bifurcation remains, may be observed in the following: "*Knowledge*, in general, *is a relation between a subject knowing and an object known*." [1] For an 'object known' is treated as though it were not in relation to a 'subject knowing' but in such case it could not be an 'object known'!

Grote makes a summary statement covering Hamilton's attempt: "The *idea* of a communication between mind and matter, feeling and space, further than as a relation of contemporaneousness is [2] such, is

---

[1] Bowen, MWH, 139.
[2] Evidently an error. Grote must have meant 'as.'

not reasonable." [1] But Grote makes a concession in Hamilton's favor: Though the statement above reveals the conclusion, concerning the incompatibility of space and feeling (or matter and mind), at which Grote arrives, yet the problem cannot be easily dismissed. And Grote does not attempt to banish it lightly. Where there is an apparent semblance between space and feeling this semblance is due to the manner in which our bodies *seem* to communicate with the 'outside' world.

v. Locke's error resembles Hamilton's

The semblance is not really a semblance at all. Hamilton's solution through 'consciousness of matter' and 'consciousness of mind' is unacceptable, for reasons which we will have occasion to consider later. John Locke was equally unsuccessful in expressing the possibility of 'thinking spatially.' The primary qualities of an object, according to Locke, are in the object as in our perception of the object.

To discover the nature of our ideas the better, and to discourse of them intelligibly, it will be convenient to distinguish them, as they are *ideas or perceptions in our minds*, and as they are *modifications of matter in the bodies that cause such perceptions in us*.[2]

But for Grote here lies a problem to be solved which Locke had overlooked, namely, the compatibility or lack of compatibility of space and the idea of space.

In the scale of sensation at the extreme of feeling, the phenomenal is predominant. Here the emphasis is on communication of the body, through feeling, with phenomenal reality. At the extreme of thought, 'philosophy,' consciousness, idea, etc., are predominant. To say with Locke that the primary qualities of an object are in the object as in our perception of it is a plastering over of the crack by a language composed of 'square ideas,' etc., Grote asserts. Grote is trying to show that it is quite all right to talk (as he does himself) of the relation between *sensation* (on the highest possible level) *as thought* and objects, where a dualism is unavoidable, and, sensation (on the lowest possible level) as feeling (lacking consciousness) and objects, which is the realm of phenomenal reality. The two are at opposite ends of 'the scale of sensation.' The main and necessary qualification in speaking about thought and objects and feeling and objects is to be extremely careful to recognize which end of the scale we are emphasizing.

---

[1] Grote, EP, I, 104.
[2] Locke, ECH, in Burtt, EPB, 264, 265.

3. TWO KINDS OF KNOWLEDGE – 'HIGHER' AND 'LOWER'

i. Meaning of the terms

a. 'Higher philosophy'

'Higher philosophy' is the theory of 'being,' which may be contrasted with the theory of knowing. What this higher philosophy is, Grote tries to show (in the rather imperfect language) in the following:

> My notion of the higher philosophy answers to what might be called, and by many philosophers has been and is called 'Ontology,' or the theory of 'being,' as against the theory of knowing, or the phaenomenology of knowledge, or various other language.[1]

b. 'Lower philosophy'

'Lower philosophy' is the theory of knowing, feeling, or thought, and is existence only insofar as this knowing suggest it.

> It is not existence of any kind, that in the first instance is supposed to be the object of our knowledge, but what is supposed is feeling, thought, knowledge, and *I* as the subject of them, and only existence in so far as this feeling may, in whatever way, inevitably suggest it. This, evidently, is a *deeper* view than phenomenalism, or, in other words, it mounts to an earlier original fact, But, in the first instance, all that we may consider it concerned about is feelings, thoughts, knowledge, of a supposed *I*.[2] While so restrained, however widely it may trace the manner in which we think and the results at which our thought arrives, it is an abstraction, like phenomenalism, in comparison with what we may imagine an entire view of things. This is what I have called the logical (epistemological) or lower philosophical view.[3]

ii. Reid's answer to skeptics is impotent

For both the higher and the lower philosophies the primary fact is not that the universe exists but that we *feel* or *know* that it exists. This is probably the reason why Grote refers to the theory of knowing, or *thought*, as 'lower,' that is, apparently, as the more fundamental, and without which there could be no being *for us*. This is another way of saying that 'philosophy' is all-important in epistemology. The language of philosophy frequently has been to the effect that we are quite convinced about the existence of the world even when the grounds for being convinced are not clear. Reid states the grounds to be 'common sense.'

The method of the Common Sense School was employed to refute

---

[1] Grote, EP, I, 84, 85.
[2] Probably Grote means the 'soul.'
[3] Grote, *op. cit.*, 84.

skeptical doctrines concerning the existence of the world. But refutations on the basis of common sense were accidents of the question as to the grounds of certainty. They were not logical arguments. The Common Sense philosophers, according to Grote, simply affirmed the reality of thought and things without caring too much about specific details of *how* they are related to each other, and without giving reasons beyond intuition. There is no intimation of possible specific emphases sometimes on the 'philosophical' approach, and sometimes on the phenomenal, such as that for which 'the scale of sensation' makes provision. Grote is trying to show in referring to the Common Sense School that one cannot overlook the two different aspects of looking at one reality. And he is trying to show that a lack of distinguishing these aspects from each other is very characteristic of such thinking as Common Sense.

iii. Hamilton regards the 'philosophy' of knowledge as the analysis of consciousness

Hamilton emphasizes the 'philosophical' approach. With his view of the 'philosophy' of knowledge as the analysis of consciousness, Grote agrees. "All our knowledge, as knowledge, is consciousness: Sir William Hamilton has well exhibited the philosophy of knowledge as the analysis of consciousness." [1]

a. Grote points out the defect in Hamilton's use of the term 'consciousness'

'Consciousness,' understood in the wide sense in which Hamilton uses it, may be analyzed in two ways. It may be regarded as self-consciousness or reflection, or as consciousness of what we sometimes speak of as the external world. We know our own selves by self-consciousness or reflection, and we know the not-self from consciousness that we do not comprise the whole universe. One may say that we have consciousness in both cases but the kind of knowledge that we have of ourselves differs from the kind of knowledge that we have of other things.

Here, then, is the point at which Hamilton errs, according to Grote. One should not call the consciousness that we have of the not-self *knowledge* at all, if, following Hamilton, knowledge be what is built up on consciousness. Grote admits in favor of Hamilton that consciousness as reflection is knowledge. But he does not allow Hamilton to regard consciousness of the not-self as the same kind of knowledge as

[1] Grote, EP, I, 96.

that arising out of reflection. In fact, he will not allow consciousness of the not-self to be called by the term 'knowledge' at all. Yet it seems all right to call it 'belief.' For the certainty that we have of the not-self is not the same as the certainty that we have of our own selves. The certainty that we have of the self is immediate, while the certainty that we have of other things is mediate. Grote would seem almost to go so far as to say that it is only the self that we *do* know. And he would hold that to say we know 'things' is to say that we know what already are *things for us* as though we did not know them in this relation at all (by saying that we know them).

Let us look at what Grote is concerned about here, for surely he is concerned about something that is important to him, and he seems correct in taking pains to show what he means, and it seems of much value for his very important epistemological position.

One may therefore paraphrase his meaning in the following. Hamilton and the Scottish School of Common Sense are equally in error in the grounds that they accept for belief or conviction. These grounds are unsound for the same reason in each case. The Common Sense philosophers assert that common sense is the basis for conviction, for example, they could say to us, let us look at objects as we see them. Hamilton would say, we have a *consciousness* of objects. Both views are fundamentally one. They virtually assert a single conclusion. Let us look at objects as they appear to common sense or as we are conscious of them – both assert.

But, Grote asserts that this is exactly what we cannot do in regard to the objects. Hamilton and the school of Common Sense are in error, for we do not know 'objects' in such a simple way. By saying that we know 'objects,' we are assuming that these objects that we know are somehow 'objects' that we don't know when we say we '*know objects.*' All that we know is our immediate selves. The point is we cannot say that an 'object' *is,* without knowing it somehow. And, *then* to say that we *know* it is simply superfluous, or the virtual saying of the same thing twice.

This, then, is the basis for Grote's view that conviction or belief about something has other grounds than actual knowing. For example, the basis of conviction can well be founded on the convictions of others. It has, therefore, no exclusive foundation such as knowing, nor is it exclusively founded upon consciousness of self.

Conviction or belief for Grote may be, strictly speaking, sound or precarious (and therefore possibly sound or unsound). Conviction is sound if based on consciousness of self. It is precarious if it is founded on the doubtful ground which does not know whether it has the character of consciousness of self (or personal knowledge) or the character of convictions of others. If both characters are present the conviction is not precarious but sound. If only the convictions of others are present then there is no justification for saying that one *knows*, or that one is certain, but only (at best) that one has a conviction, or belief.

Hamilton would express himself somewhat as follows. The majority of men do think thus, and that is all that is necessary to convince us that what is thus thought is a fact of consciousness. But the fact that men do think in a certain way is very often convincing as a fact of consciousness, but it may be wholly unjustified, because the majority may be wrong. There is no certainty attached to such a 'proof' of a fact of consciousness, even though it may be a good practical criterion to follow.

We know the form or qualities of this not-self (i.e. the sensible world) as something entirely dissimilar to the form and qualities which in ourselves we are conscious of. This ought not indeed (as I have said) to be called *knowledge*, if knowledge is what is built on consciousness: we may call it belief: by which we need mean no more than that, without the slightest doubt as to matter (the form and qualities of the not-self) existing, the certainty which we have of it is not the same (in kind, i.e. for in degree, for all that I know it may be) as the certainty which we have of our *own* existence.[1]

Grote holds that in all Hamilton's discussion of 'consciousness' he can detect no distinction between the two references to consciousness, namely, self-consciousness and consciousness of other things.

I can see nothing in Sir William Hamilton's doctrine except assertion that it *is* the same, without any attempt at reason for the assertion except what I have already spoken of, the notion (if I may so describe it) of a local coincidence of thinking existence and material existence on the occasion of what we call a sensation in a particular part of the body. We feel that part of our body and what is in contact with it, I understand him to say, – that is, we feel or are conscious of matter – in the same way as we feel or are conscious of mind, our thinking selves. We know thus from the first, in the same way and with a like original knowledge, mind and matter. In different words, we have an immediate knowledge of matter (or the external world), and the establishment of this immediate knowledge Sir William Hamilton looks upon as an important discovery.[2]

Anything like a scale of sensation revealing the relation between 'philosophy' and phenomena is foreign to the whole of Hamilton's

---

[1] Grote, EP, I, 96.
[2] *Loc. cit.*

writing on consciousness. The consciousness which is 'philosophy' and the consciousness of phenomena are not distinguished from each other, by Hamilton. And yet they should be distinguished from each other. We are immediately conscious of the self but to say that we are immediately conscious of the not-self is to overlook the fact that the not-self to be regarded as the not-self must already be in relation to consciousness before we say that we are conscious of it.

b. Grote states a reason for Hamilton's 'consciousness' of the external world

Grote ventures a reason for Hamilton's philosophy concerning consciousness of the external world. The example concerns a pin coming in contact with the finger. Hamilton would say that the knowledge of the pain and of the pin was immediate in both bases. Grote would not agree. The only relation which one bears to the other is that both are contemporaneous, according to Grote. Knowledge of the pin is not knowledge really at all, but simply belief. Knowledge of the pin prick is immediate and is within the realm of consciousness. This illustration is of crucial importance in revealing Grote's view that consciousness of self and consciousness of matter are not properly put together as Hamilton is inclined to do. Hamilton's statement regarding the immediacy of knowledge in both cases is another example of the clash between the being of space, solidity, etc., predominant in the feeling end of the scale, and the being of pleasure, pain, colour, etc., predominant in the thought end.

These factors cannot be brought together on the same plane, and Grote's whole discussion on this subject is to show the fallacy in any attempt to so correlate, what cannot be correlated, on the one and the same level. This particular point is noted by McCosh. Hamilton "attempts far too much by logical differentiation and formalization. No man purposes now to proceed in physical investigation by logical dissection." [1]

c. Hamilton's writing on consciousness vitiated

In view of Grote's criticism of Hamilton's metaphysics in dealing with consciousness, and his mixing indiscriminately the two fundamental aspects in which reality may be viewed, is sufficient to indicate that Hamilton's influence was somewhat exaggerated.

I doubt much whether Hamilton's System of Logic will ever as a whole be adopted by our colleges. We have, however, two admirable text-books founded

[1] McCosh, SP, 417.

on it: – Thomson's 'Outline of the Laws of Thought,' and Bowen's 'Logic.' It will be acknowledged by all, that the discussions he has raised have done more to clear up unsettled points in formal logic than any work published since the days of Kant. These discussions will be looked at by writers on logic in all coming ages.[1]

Sir William Hamilton's own labors in this department, (i.e. Logic) by which he certainly accomplished more for the science than has been done by any man since Aristotle... contains the germs of all his subsequent discoveries.[2]

d. 'Natural Dualism' and 'Hypothetical Dualists'

The name Hamilton gives to his doctrine concerning the immediate knowledge of the external world is Natural Dualism.

Sir William Hamilton calls his doctrine of the immediateness of our knowledge of the external world by the name of Natural Realism or Natural Dualism: the mass of philosophers, who have looked upon this knowledge as, in comparison with our knowledge of our own existence, something which required, so to speak, to give an account of itself, a belief, a mediate knowledge (or however they might express it) – being called by him Cosmothetic Idealists or Hypothetic Dualists.[3]

Grote would call it a monism rather, because Hamilton attempts to place feelings and material qualities together.

The classification here made of philosophers seems of very little value, making, as it does, no account of the purpose and method of the various philosophies, nor any distinction between what a philosopher assumed at the beginning and the results which he considered himself to arrive at. As to the Hypothetic Dualists, it is to be observed that almost all philosophers have been dualists, (nay, have not all?) in admitting a 'besides-self' as well as a self or mind, Berkeley as much so as Sir William Hamilton: our sensations were not in his view causeless or merely self-modifications, only he did not consider the cause of them to be what we are here calling 'the external world.' The name 'Hypothetic' therefore is little applicable to these philosophers, nor, it seems to me, is that of Natural Dualism to Sir William Hamilton's view, which I should rather describe as a sort of Monism (in language of his own), or an attempt to fuse together, as objects of one kind of knowledge, two kinds of things (if they may be called things) so different as feelings and material qualities.[4]

Nor is Hamilton justified in calling philosophers, who see a dualism here, by the name of Hypothetic Dualists because these are far from being 'hypothetic.' They do not affirm the existence of the external world by reason of consciousness of the self. Hamilton, then, according to Grote is actually an epistemological quantitative monist. But those who do *not* hold to dualism on the basis of a consciousness of matter and a consciousness of mind are actually dualists; they admit an irreconcilable bifurcation.

[1] McCosh, SP, 417.
[2] Bowen, TOL, iii, iv.
[3] Grote, EP, I, 97.
[4] *Loc. cit.*

Hamilton's mistake in confusing the two points of view which Grote insists must be kept separate is much in evidence here. Grote would say in criticism of Hamilton that perception is not so immediate (or intuitive) as it appears to Hamilton to be. The only place that it can be considered as intuitive in the smallest extent is in the lower part of the scale. When Hamilton makes the distinction which he does between immediate and mediate knowledge he simply shows that perception in such distinction is mediate – despite the fact that he contends that it is immediate.

e. Matter is only one entity of which we are conscious

In short, according to Grote what takes up a great many pages in Hamilton's philosophy is what has to do with the statement, that what we know is matter (at least it is one of the things we know) and what we know we are conscious of. But matter is only one of the things of which we are conscious and this consciousness is much less intimate than the immediate consciousness of ourselves. And because matter is only one thing of which we are conscious, then consciousness of ourselves is that upon which consciousness of matter is dependent. A study of matter as it affects us is phenomenalism. Grote is especially careful to interpret Hamilton's philosophy correctly – devoting a whole chapter to Hamilton's 'consciousness of matter' – and in so doing fulfills his desire to define his own position.

The net outcome of Hamilton on matter is an untenable position. Hamilton asserts that he knows matter, through an immediate consciousness of it. He affirms that we are equally conscious of our thoughts and of matter. This position is unwarranted in Grote's view. For it is only in consciousness that immediateness can exist. We are not conscious of matter immediately. To say so, after Hamilton, is virtually to affirm that matter first exists or is taken to *be*, and only *after* that are we conscious of it! This is the main issue that Grote belabors in dealing with Hamilton's view of matter as that of which we are immediately aware

f. Hamilton states that he knows matter, even before he examines consciousness of it

In Hamilton's examination of consciousness of matter, matter is regarded as defined and known already, and this altogether independently of consciousness, according to Grote. Hamilton undertakes to examine the 'contents' of consciousness and herein reveals the glaring error in his philosophy. For Hamilton, 'contents' at one time designates will, feeling, etc., and at another light, oxygen with its attributes such as colour, taste, sound, and shape. He concludes that the qualities of matter exist in the same way as thought does; we are immediately conscious of both matter and self (or thought), he holds. Hamilton is not a dualist on the basis of his view that we are equally (immediately) *conscious* of both matter and mind. That is, Hamilton is professing to look at mind and 'matter,' Grote seems to say, from the side of 'philosophy' and *in this sense* he is a monist.

Hamilton has postulated matter spatially to begin with. Then he brings consciousness of this matter into the field. Grote objects to this, and with good reason. Grote states that the only reason why we know that matter exists spatially is because it is related to our consciousness. We cannot bring consciousness in afterwards. Hamilton is not finding matter through consciousness, but knows it already and states what it is. Grote argues that Hamilton is incorrect in doing this. For the more reality is viewed from the phenomenal side the more it is a case of *belief*, and the more it is viewed from the 'philosophical' side the more it is knowledge. Hamilton views it from the side of phenomena and calls it knowledge (rather than belief)!

g. We are immediately cognizant of the non-ego

The above shows how Hamilton came to his philosophic inconsistency. The following is a specific example of his confusion when he attempts to criticize the opposite point of view held by other philosophers. He says that philosophers declare that we are not immediately cognizant of the non-ego. This mistake of Hamilton's is based upon his failure to see the inadequacy of his main thesis. What the philosophers, to whom Hamilton refers, mean, is that we are not cognizant of matter immediately, but only phenomenally. We cannot assume the existence of matter and then say that we are conscious of it to begin with. But Hamilton says that we are conscious of it after we assume it. By this argument it is evident that we are not immediately conscious of the non-ego as he would have us believe. And that we are not immediately conscious of the non-ego is the very argument of the philosophers which he has set about to refute.

4. HAMILTON, MILL, AND REID COMPARED

i. Hamilton and Mill – starting point of each in regard to philosophy and phenomena

The basis of Hamilton's refutations resembles the position of J. S. Mill. Both Hamilton and Mill were equally confused in distinguishing between 'philosophy' and phenomena and were equally monistic.

Sir William Hamilton, starting from consciousness, thinks it a great thing to be able to put the phenomena of matter, by the side of the phenomena of mind, which of course are the first thing he supposes: Mr. Mill, starting from the supposition of the spatial universe, thinks it a great thing to be able to put the facts of mind by the side of the facts of matter, which of course are the first thing *he* supposes. Sir William Hamilton's supposition of our being conscious of matter seems to me to be wrong in exactly the same manner as Mr. Mill's supposition, which I should describe as that we phenomenally know mind – i.e. that we may put *its* facts, and that exhaustively, or as our *only* consideration of them, by the side of physical ones. In respect of Sir William Hamilton – we are conscious of seeing, and just the problem of philosophy is to make out what is our mental relation to the thing we see: what is it but plastering up a crack to say that the word 'consciousness' will cover that also, and that being conscious of seeing is being conscious of the thing we see? [1]

ii. Hamilton and Reid

Reid states that we *know* equally well primary qualities and our perception of them. However, he does not show *how* we know primary (and secondary) qualities of objects. His error is, therefore, as great as that of Hamilton, for the latter believed that the consciousness of mind and the consciousness of matter are equally knowable.

Reid's doctrine of perception, taken in conjunction with his statement of the difference between primary and secondary qualities – that in the case of the former we know equally well both the quality and our perception of it, whereas we know the latter qualities only as powers in bodies occasioning the perceptions, already points in the direction of Hamilton's view. [2]

Reid's view, then, is a sort of occasionalism, without the intervention of deity. Just *how* the powers occasioned the perceptions is left blank. This view is markedly different from the occasionalism of the Occasionalists generally, of whom Malebranche is a typical representative.

The Occasionalists, rejecting Descartes' attempt to explain interaction, held that any direct and natural communication between mind and body was im-

---

[1] Grote, EP, I, 87n.
[2] Forsyth, EP, 114, 115.

possible and invoked supernatural aid to effect it. God, they said, acted as an intermediary. On the *occasion* of the body being stimulated, God aroused in the mind the appropriate sensation and response. And on the *occasion* of that response, God set the body moving in an appropriate reaction.[1]

Malebranche stated:

that God is the cause of our conscious experience as well as of the bodily processes. Matter, being passive, can neither initiate nor transmit physical motion of itself. All movement, whether or not corresponding to mental states, needs the constant intervention of God to set it and to keep it going.[2]

Grote's view regarding the emphasis that is placed now on 'philosophy' and again on phenomena – concerning which the scale of sensation gives an intelligent account – may be substituted for the summary exposition offered by Reid on the basis of common sense alone.

The essence both of body and of mind is unknown to us. We know certain properties of the first, and certain operations of the last, and by these only we can define or describe them. We define body to be that which is extended, solid, moveable, divisible. In like manner, we define mind to be that which thinks.[3]

But the kind of relation which exists between mind and matter is left unexplained.

According to Pringle-Pattison,[4] Hamilton's relativist doctrine is foreshadowed in Reid. "There are not more than one or two passages in Reid which could be cited to show him to be a Relativist; but one of them is so explicit as to be sufficient." [5] This relativistic claim made for Reid is sufficient to show his oversight of phenomenal reality which affects us even when we may not even have capacity for being conscious of it.

iii. Source of Hamilton's error

Grote states that Hamilton makes a somewhat similar error when he does not distinguish clearly between consciousness of self (which is the only place in which the word 'consciousness' can be applied properly) and consciousness of things. In the latter use of the word 'consciousness' Grote cannot concur. To say that we are conscious of things is to say that we are conscious of what already is in a definite relation to mind – without which relation these 'things' would not be 'things' for us.

---

1 Fuller, HOP, II, 68.
2 *Loc. cit.*
3 Hamilton, WTR, 220.
4 Pringle-Pattison, SP, 184.
5 Forsyth, EP, 115n.

Hamilton's procedure might be stated in another way. He regards the phenomena of matter as on the same plane as the phenomena of mind – both alike phenomena. But clearly there is a difference here. One must be careful to note that the phenomena of matter are really phenomena and not something in a definite relation to mind already.

To speak of phenomena is, for Grote, to take a physical approach to reality. *Qua* phenomenal this reality is not consciousness, and as such (namely, as phenomenal reality) it is not in a relation to mind already. Phenomena are not wholly unrelated *to us*, however. But phenomena *qua* phenomena are out of the mind, and phenomena *qua* consciousness is the 'inner' side of phenomenal reality which gives meaning to it (phenomenal reality) and is, therefore, in the mind. This is another way of saying that consciousness of 'things' is not consciousness properly, but rather a looking at reality from the phenomenal side so that we can use the term 'things' with more justification than if we looked at reality from the consciousness side.

To speak of phenomena of matter in the manner in which Sir William Hamilton does is to give matter a prominence in this way of reasoning that it never should have. For the only way that matter is known as matter is because it is seen, touched, etc. Then calling it matter we cannot say that we are conscious of it as we are conscious of self for the very fact that it is matter means that it is so, in relation to mind. Hamilton appears to have been very much attracted by the philosophy of Common Sense – of which Reid is a good example – though it "is not an appeal from philosophy to blind feeling" that he advocates, but rather "it is only an appeal from the theoretical conclusions of particular philosophers to the catholic principles of all philosophy." [1]

John Veitch states that Common Sense philosophy closely resembles analyses of consciousness. "The Philosophy of Common Sense, as held and explained by Hamilton, is none other than the attempt to analyze knowledge or consciousness – our experience, in fact, into its elements." [2] But analyses of consciousness is not necessary in order to give us some of the entities of Common Sense Philosophy where non-conscious entities are assumed.

The chief point of attack, then, made by Grote on Hamilton's philosophy is in reference to the confusion made between 'phenomenalism' and 'philosophy.' Hamilton appears to be guilty of the error of looking upon the 'I' as a part of the phenomenal universe as though it were

[1] Hamilton, WTR, 751.
[2] Veitch, HAM, 103.

capable of dissection. But it is not 'existence' that comes first, according to Grote, but consciousness. What we suppose first is thought,
and secondly, existence. We could not have 'existence' at all except
for consciousness through which all things exist. Here existence must
be interpreted as phenomenal reality, and not as things in themselves
in Hamilton's sense.[1]

iv. Source of Mill's error

The foregoing is an attempt to show wherein the confusion of
Hamilton's thought arises. Mill is guilty of similar confusion. Mill
accepts the phenomena of mind and the phenomena of matter on the
same basis. Here the basic difficulty is that we cannot refer to phenomena of matter without a consciousness of mind.

For Mill 'phenomena of matter' seems legitimate since he approaches
reality from the aspect of phenomena rather than the aspect of
consciousness. To speak of 'phenomena of mind' when dealing with
the phenomenal approach to reality seems as erroneous as to speak of
'consciousness of matter' when dealing with the 'philosophical' approach
to reality. The trouble lies in the fact that in each case there is a professed design to approach reality from either one of two aspects (but
not both), and in actual practice reality *is* approached from the two
aspects at the same time. Thus there is a mixing of 'philosophy' with
phenomena through the use of phrases such as 'phenomena of mind'
(in Mill's case) and 'consciousness of matter' (in Hamilton's). In the
distinction which Grote makes between consciousness and phenomena,
it is illegitimate either to speak of a 'consciousness of matter,' with
Hamilton, or 'phenomena of mind,' with Mill, as shown above.

What appears confused in Mill's method is his manner of dealing
with 'consciousness' and phenomena. He appears to take for granted
(and this is Grote's difficulty in seeing clarity in Mill's argument) that
the phenomena of mind are like phenomena of matter – both alike
phenomena and with equal right, namely, because we are conscious
of both.

5. DESCARTES AND HAMILTON

i. Descartes's epistemological approach, and Hamilton's

It is interesting to reflect that Descartes would not have regarded
consciousness of matter and consciousness of mind as worthy of equal

[1] Cf. pp. 74, 75, above.

acceptance. In *cogito, ergo sum* he recognizes the necessary priority that consciousness (of mind) must receive.

But immediately upon this I observed that, whilst I thus wished to think that all was false, it was absolutely necessary that I, who thus thought, should be somewhat; and as I observed that this truth, *I think, hence I am*, was so certain and of such evidence, that no ground of doubt, however extravagant, could be alleged by the Sceptics capable of shaking it, I concluded that I might, without scruple, accept it as the first principle of the philosophy of which I was in search.[1]

Grote concludes that this is "the logical (epistemological) or lower philosophical view." [2] It may be said that Descartes would regard the phenomena of Grote as in consciousness in the sense that such phenomena have *meaning* only insofar as they are *in* consciousness. But for Grote, phenomena are in consciousness only *qua* consciousness and not *qua* phenomena. On this basic issue Descartes would seem to agree with Grote. However, Grote seems to think that in Descartes's 'cogito' there is a great tendency to emphasize the 'philosophical' approach.

While so restrained, however widely it may trace the manner in which we think and the results at which our thought arrives, it is an abstraction, like phenomenalism, in comparison with what we may imagine an entire view of things.[3]

But if Descartes meant that 'cogito' embraced all processes of consciousness, including sensing, then phenomena are in consciousness, for Descartes. It appears that Descartes *did* mean this by the use of the term 'cogito.' The point, however, that Grote wishes to make here is that consciousness, strictly speaking, should not include any more of 'sensing' than is required for *meaning*, and that the remainder of 'sensing' belongs to phenomena – to the phenomenal aspect of reality. Grote appears to be narrowing down the meaning of Descartes's 'cogito' so that it covers, for him (Grote), the *thought* side of reality when Descartes actually meant that 'cogito' should also include sensing. Grote might remark to Descartes, your 'cogito' is too *mental* to cover the field that you allow it to cover. Descartes could retort – evidently you misunderstand the wide area that 'cogito' covers in my epistemology. Hence, Descartes might continue, I am justified in using it the way I do.

Descartes's *cogito, ergo sum* was an abstraction as was Hamilton's view of the ego in contrast with the non-ego. Hamilton is much less restrained than Descartes. For he talks of 'the phaenomena of mind'

---

[1] Descartes, DOM, 26.
[2] Grote, EP, I, 84.
[3] *Loc. cit.*

side by side with 'the phaenomena of matter.' [1] In order to justify this procedure he states "that we have a consciousness of matter similar to the consciousness which we have of mind or self." [2] Grote would say that this is not even true of matter, as phenomena, not to mention of matter as *Ding an sich*. Grote declares in refutation of such a view that

mind is above matter, because even if there could be established a parallel consciousness of phaenomena of mind with the phaenomena of matter, it is mind which has that consciousness. There would still be a phaenomena of mind at the head of all, namely, this double consciousness itself.[3]

ii. Hamilton's imperfect application of consciousness

Again, it is not possible to consider both the ego and the non-ego as possessing the same relation to consciousness, because consciousness of the ego has to do with feeling, desire, etc., whereas consciousness (to use the word as Hamilton does) of the non-ego has to do with solidity, magnitude, space, etc.

If we have one sort of knowledge in which the forms of the knowledge or the qualities of the things known are space, solidity, etc. (whatever language we use) and another kind of knowledge in which such forms or qualities are pleasure, pain, etc. – knowledge then is not a common ground upon which the things which are known can meet – not a way in which they can be brought together: there are two worlds: and though we may *think* of space and solidity, and though we may *see* the space or the solid body in which we understand the pleasure and the pain to be, we cannot bring the characters of the one world into relation with those of the other, or (in different words) establish any relation except a very imperfect one of contemporaneousness, between them.[4]

Moreover, this confusion may be noted further when Hamilton refers to consciousness of seeing which brings up the question, "What is our mental relation to the thing we see?" [5] Being conscious of seeing is very different from being conscious of the thing we see. The former refers to consciousness of a state within the mind primarily; the latter to consciousness (in Hamilton's use of this word) of matter.

---

[1] Grote, EP, I, 85.
[2] *Loc. cit.*
[3] *Loc. cit.*
[4] *Op. cit.*, 91.
[5] *Op. cit.*, 87n.

6. PROPER USE OF CERTAIN TERMS IN RELATION TO
THE SCALE OF SENSATION

i. 'Presence' and 'presentation'

Let us now look at certain terms the specific meaning of which helps to reveal their misuse by Hamilton, and their proper use by Grote, such as 'presence' and 'presentation,' and 'inward' and 'internal.' With regard to the first two of these – phenomenally they mean nothing more than being contemporary with feeling. At the top of the scale mind is dominant and contemporaneousness is infinitesimally small. Again, 'presence' or 'presentation' may be local, referring to our bodies where feeling, as mind, is in some way related to the corporeal. In the statement 'a tree affects the mind' or 'a tree is presented to the mind,' there is the philosophical application which differs from the tree 'being present at the *eye*' or 'affecting the *eye*'; this latter application is phenomenal. That is, the philosophical application has to do with the top of the scale where thought reigns supreme, and the phenomenal with the bottom where, not thought, but feeling, is dominant.

ii. 'Presentation' and 'representation'

'Presentation' and 'representation' are frequently used without an adequate knowledge of their meaning, e.g., as in 'presentative consciousness.' By 'presentative consciousness' is meant a feeling of ourselves as phenomenally existential and a feeling of an object, in the outside world, in communication with our bodies. By 'representative consciousness' is meant something quite different. In this we feel ourselves to be a part of phenomenal existence as in 'presentative consciousness' and then a consciousness of the existence of something in our thought that appears as if it could be in communication with our bodies as phenomenal existence. Moreover, representative consciousness has to do with two objects, one outside of the mind and the other within. It is only by virtue of the image within the mind that the external object can be known. One of these objects, the one in the mind, is what is *thought*, the one outside, is *thought of*.

iii. 'Mediate' and 'immediate' [1]

It should be oserved that the words 'mediate' and 'immediate' are much wider in scope than the words 'presentative' and 'representative.'

[1] A more detailed discussion of immediateness is found in Chapter VIII of this book, under the title "Immediateness and Reflection."

'Immediate' indicates that there is no break between our knowledge of the outside world and our own consciousness, or rather it refers only to our own consciousness and not to the outside world. 'Representative' indicates a break. In 'representative consciousness' the mind is regarded as presenting an object from the external world to the mind; this object is different from the object within the mind. Knowledge may refer to the object within the mind while 'belief' (or some other word) refers to the object of the outside world. When we speak about knowledge being immediate we deal with that which treats of ourselves; the term 'immediate' cannot be used in reference to the outside world. Moreover, the mediateness of bi-objective knowledge such as in representativeness is only one form of mediateness, this mediateness is possibly, generally, one that comes through the organ of the body, namely, the eye.

Grote differs with Hamilton over the word 'mediateness.' "Sir William Hamilton seems to me to make all knowledge, even as knowledge, mediate." [1] Insofar as knowledge cannot be other than of phenomena, and an object of the phenomenal world may be represented by its bi-objectival counterpart, Grote would agree with Hamilton. At the lower end of the scale (where feeling predominates) this mediate knowledge becomes immediate for the body comes into contact with external objects and the external objects, then, where thought or will is at a minimum, are the knowledge. In this sense the knowledge is immediate and this pertains to outward objects, and not to inner objects (that which is *thought of* the object) as would apply when dealing with the upper part of the scale where thought predominates.

7. CRITICAL REFLECTION ON THE FOREGOING CHAPTER

Grote uses the scale of sensation as a mental device to show the relation of 'philosophy' and phenomenal reality to each other. When 'philosophy' as consciousness, mind, thought, is emphasized we are at the top of the scale where knowledge is mediate. Here phenomenal reality enters progressively less and less, as one approaches this thought end of the scale. Self-consciousness has a large place here. Time and space considered as forms of the understanding enter into this end of the scale.

The first main issue in this chapter concerns space and time. There is a similarity between Grote and Kant regarding the character of

[1] Grote, EP, I, 121.

both. "There are two pure forms of sensible intuition, serving as principles of *a priori* knowledge, namely, space and time." [1]

For Grote time seems to be 'viewed from *within*.' [2] Time then has a large place at the top, or thought, end of the scale. It seems that Grote should have allowed time to have a prominent place at the bottom of the scale also. For if phenomenal reality is more prominent at the lower end, and carries out communication with the body, time is necessary for this communication to take place, even though we might not be aware of the communication. Grote admits that time is essential at the thought end of the scale, because thought requires time. But with as much justification it seems that one could say that time is essential at the phenomenal end of the scale, because, for example, communication of phenomenal reality with the body requires time. Space cannot *mean* anything at the bottom of the scale but is necessary there for the communication of phenomenal reality with, for example, our bodies. Space has *meaning* at the top of the scale. It is a form for thought. But there is a strong objection [3] to holding that space is more predominant at the top than it is at the middle of the scale. Grote seems to infer that it is more prominent at the center of the scale.

To say that space is more significantly attributed to the thought-end of the scale is to face the following difficulty. If space were located at the top of the scale it would seem natural to speak of 'thinking spatially' which would make no more sense than to say that 'thinking redly' is possible, or that square ideas may be assumed.

To say 'we think spatially,' which is the kind of language we ought to use on the supposition of space being a form of thought, seems to me language in some respects of (exactly) the same kind as the supposition of a square idea. The way we think spatially, so far as we do so, is to will a certain amount of exertion, which exertion we understand as carrying our hand (say) through a certain amount of what then we call 'space.' [4]

Space, then, Grote concludes is more prominent at the center of the scale. Yet he admits that space is a form of the understanding and hence is present at the top of the scale.

It seems that he should, also, have given space a much larger place at the bottom of the scale. For in order to have 'things' act on each other space is required. It is, of course, also required in order that 'things' may have *position* in place (that is, in order that 'things' may be in place). In the realistic philosophy of Aristotle, 'things' have

[1] Kant, CPR, 67.
[2] Grote, EP, I, 110.
[3] Cf. pp. 91–92, below.
[4] Grote, *op. cit.*, 108.

position, and position is an Aristotelian category. It would seem, there-force, that space (also a category for Bowne [1]) is a phenomenal word (in Grote's meaning of phenomenal) and should also appear at the bottom of 'the scale of sensation.' The only foundation for Grote's view that space is more pronounced at the center is that here (at the center) both thought and phenomenal reality are emphasized equally, and space is characteristic of both. Whereas he is trying to point out that it is not exclusively characteristic of either thought or phenomenal reality, and hence its place is not so prominent at either end of the scale.

Why Grote does not hold that time could be considered as having its place in the center also, is not clear. It seems that it is here (at the center) that it should be placed. Yet Grote seems to regard it as more fittingly placed at the top of the scale.

Grote makes many thoughtful reflections on both space and time, for example, such as, to point out that *we* could not be without time, but it is possible that we could exist without having space. "We could not have been otherwise than in time, we might have been otherwise than in space." [2]

There are certain broad perspectives that one looks for in Grote, regarding time and space, and does not find. He does not dwell on Plato's view of time as the moving image of eternity. Aristotle also could have been discussed through his definition of time as the number of motion, with respect to before and after. Plotinus said that time was the productive life of the soul. This comes close to Grote's view where the latter places time on the thought, or conscious end of the scale. Without time, Grote held, *we* cannot be. It is necessary for the life of the soul therefore.

In Plato, the 'receptacle,' though wholly indeterminate, "must be rather construed as the potency of matter, and of space, and of physical motion." [3] And it is of motion (whether physical or psychical) that time is the number. Both time and space, then, are the actualizing of the potency of the receptacle.

Again space and time may be regarded as space-time [4] or reality. Grote is attempting to see reality as separate entirely from space (when he asserts that it is possible that *we* might be even though space might not be). He does not consider certain ancient views of space and time,

[1] Bowne, TTK, 66–116.
[2] Grote, EP, II, 200.
[3] Demos, POP, 31.
[4] Alexander, STD.

such as Plato's or Aristotle's. He seems concerned, in Part II of *Exploratio Philosophica*, in making general comments on both time and space. In Part I he tries to show the relation of each to the scale of sensation. In attempting to show this relation there are various questions left unanswered, such as: Why does space belong more to the center of the scale rather than to the top? How much place does time have at the center of the scale? What is the relation of space to time? Are space and time inseparable?

Let us look at these questions to see what Grote could have said in reply to them, if he had given one. What he could say regarding the problem of whether space belongs more at the center of the scale than at the top is that in a sense space is found equally prominent with time at the center of the scale. And both space and time are at *both* ends of the scale. At the top of the scale, space and time are (somewhat as Kant regarded them) pure concepts of the understanding. At the bottom of the scale space and time are empirical. Grote has, all along, been speaking of the consciousness and the phenomenal sides of reality. It seems that he could have included space and time in dealing with these two aspects.

This view of what Grote could have said about space and time would seem also to settle the several other questions noted above. Let us look briefly at the several other answers. Time would appear to have as much place at the center of the scale as space has, since there are two ways of looking at time as there are two ways of regarding space, namely, from the side of consciousness and from the side of phenomena.

The relation of space to time is a very intimate one, both being required in order that a 'thing' may be known (or, to speak more generally, in order that we may have knowledge). In the light of this intimate relation between space and time, it seems incorrect for Grote to remark that, "We could not have been otherwise than in time, we might have been otherwise than in space: space might not have been at all, and yet *we* might have been." [1]

Part of his meaning, however, in this passage is evident. He means that thought requires time but, *as thought*, thought does not require space. Yet, he admits, thought requires a body of some sort in order to be what it is, and a body requires space. Grote would seem to be ready to admit that in this way thought requires space indirectly, though he does not say so. He is emphasizing the fact that the 'we' or thought side of us can *be* without space being assigned to it. However,

[1] Grote, EP, II, 200.

it must be admitted that this is a rather odd way of expressing oneself.

However, there is one basic and underlying fact that Grote does answer in regard to space and time. The communication of 'things' with our bodies requires both space and time; hence, phenomena require both (even though Grote's conception of phenomena does not require that we are conscious of them). Also, consciousness requires time and is related to our bodies which are spatial.

Grote attempts to picture this basic fact regarding space and time in the scale of sensation which must remain unclear to the extent to which it leaves many questions unresolved. So we must conjecture, or figure out just what the answers to these questions are. One important point must be continually kept in mind, however, namely, the meaning Grote gives to 'philosophy' and phenomena.[1] Almost everything he writes hinges on this basic distinction.

In human knowing we must use either the philosophical or the phenomenal assumption. In the former subjectivity is the test of truth, in the latter objectivity is the test. In the one, the philosophical assumption, knowledge is having reason, or having meaning, concerning that which, but for the knowledge, would be characterless and confused. In the phenomenal assumption "we begin with supposed existence independent of us," [2] with which we coexist, and take for granted just what knowledge is – even though, actually, knowledge can never be investigated on this view, due to the phenomenal nature of the view.

Grote believes that space is a 'simple' notion that does not bear much analysis.

All discussions about space are in one point of view unprofitable, namely, because space, so far as it is an idea or notion at all, is preeminently what Locke would call a 'simple' one, and these simple ideas of Locke will not bear much talking about. They cannot be defined, and for their reality in any way Locke has to appeal to the individual consciousness of each one.[3]

Concerning space, Grote states that T. K. Abbott argues against Alexander Bain that we get our notion of space from sight. Bain contended that we get it from movement of the arms, etc. Grote believes that the matter is not thus to be settled. For, to arbitrate between Abbott and Bain one should have a notion of space by which to judge Abbott's and Bain's views. This notion of space would reveal

[1] Grote, EP, I, Chapters I and II.
[2] Grote, op. cit., 109.
[3] Grote, EP, II, 195.

to us what space is, rather than the other views would, between which views it would pose as arbitrator.

However space may be explained, Grote states, we cannot well avoid two main strands in its constitution, namely, the notion we have of space so that we 'think spatially.' And to say that we 'think spatially' is to emphasize the thought side of space. We also have locomotion in space, and this locomation is phenomenal. This indicates, then, what Grote means when he states that space dominates *neither* end of the scale of sensation but its proper place is, better, at the center of the scale. In support of his view that we conceive of space through consciousness Grote makes the following remark:

We cannot at all find out and be sure that when different people use the term 'space,' even thinkingly, they mean the same thing by it; that is, in other words, we cannot tell whether there is any one meaning of 'space' for us to find out.[1]

Yet space is an important part of our notion of the phenomenal universe. We must conceive space as we conceive the phenomenal universe.

The notion of space is an important ingredient or part of our notion of the phenomenal universe or external world, and we mean by space a supposed something which (speaking from the objective point of view) enables us to unite in one conception our heterogeneous experiences, or (speaking from the objective point of view) which gives a basis or bond of connexion to our heterogeneous sensations (or occasions of sentience); which experience or sensations are what make us aware of the *so-called* qualities of matter. According as we conceive the phenomenal universe, so we must conceive space.[2]

Now, just how do we conceive the phenomenal universe is a basic question. For, evidently, the way we conceive it, is the way we must conceive space. The briefest reply is that, actually, we do not conceive the phenomenal universe at all, that is, at least, as phenomenal. 'Conception' is a thought (or consciousness, or 'philosophical') word. To say that we conceive what is *phenomenal* is a mixing of the two ways of looking at reality. What we actually do is to conceive of the phenomenal insofar as it is consciousness or 'philosophy.' We must conceive the phenomenal universe, therefore, as 'philosophical' and not as phenomenal.

In the passage quoted immediately above Grote is evidently looking at reality from the phenomenal point of view. What he means by saying, "according as we conceive the phenomenal universe, so we must conceive space," is what we have said, immediately above, about

[1] Grote, EP, II, 195.
[2] *Op. cit.*, 196, 197.

phenomena. For space, considered from the side of the phenomenal is itself phenomenal, while considered from the side of 'philosophy' space is 'philosophical' or conceptual. We may look at space either *subjectively* or *objectively* depending upon which end of the scale of sensation we are emphasizing.

We must assign to it a *subjective* or *objective* existence according to our general view of the phenomenal universe. We may regard it as that by which we create to ourselves the phenomenal universe: or we may regard it as that which contains, holds, gives a frame or canvas for, the various sensal objects which we come to know – their 'continent' as I have elsewhere called it: were it not for this these objects would not be a universe to us.[1]

One cannot say that space is 'internal' or 'external' as Grote intimates.

The reason why I do not here make use of what might be thought the easier expressions, 'external world,' is because the word 'external,' in the proper use of it, *supposes* space, and is therefore better avoided in trying to come at this true notion of space.[2]

Externality to our bodies will not represent space, because our bodies themselves have magnitude or occupy space: and externality to our minds can only mean independence of them, which does not represent anything like what we want to mean by space.[3]

Space seems more objectively real than time.

Space has the appearance to us of being the more objectively real and necessary, time of being the more intimate to us. If we could conceivably get *out of ourselves* for a moment, and look at immediateness as immediateness, it would involve space, but not necessarily time.[4]

"We could not have been otherwise than in time, we might have been otherwise than in space: space might not have been at all, and yet *we* might have been." [5] Just what Grote meant by this statement we have already considered.[6]

Another main issue dealt with in this chapter is consciousness as 'philosophy' in relation to the scale of sensation. To clarify his own views Grote examines Hamilton's view that we are equally conscious both of our own selves and of matter. Grote is very clear on this issue, pointing out that we are immediately conscious of our own selves but that we are only mediately aware of matter – we are not conscious of it. This criticism of Grote conforms with his view of phenomenal reality in communication with our bodies through our senses, and yet –

---

[1] Grote, EP, II, 197.
[2] *Loc. cit.*
[3] *Op. cit.*, 198.
[4] *Op. cit.*, 200.
[5] *Loc. cit.*
[6] Cf. p. 92.

this communication may take place even though we are not *conscious* of it.

Hamilton begins, by affirming matter as though it were already known to us and then speaks of our consciousness of it. But the object is not a sort of *given* irrespective of a mind to which it is given, which then has an immediate consciousness of it. It is all right, to say with Hamilton, that we are conscious of matter *if* we are careful to note that this is a different kind of knowing than when we say we are conscious of our own selves, i.e., of ourselves as thinking (not of ourselves as extended in a certain portion of space).

Professor C. I. Lewis presents a somewhat similar view of the given which cannot be regarded as something *external* which we are conscious of. But rather it is a given that is given to consciousness.

This given element is never, presumably, to be discovered in isolation. If the content of perception is first given and then, in a later moment, interpreted, we have no consciousness of such a first state of intuition unqualified by thought.[1]

"The given is admittedly an excised element or abstraction; all that is here claimed is that it is not an 'unreal' abstraction, but an identifiable constituent in experience." [2]

Hamilton's error in speaking of consciousness of matter and consciousness of mind as the same kind of consciousness is an attempt to bridge the gap between thought and what we ordinarily speak of as 'objects' or as the 'external world.' His attempt was no more successful than Locke's where the primary qualities of an object are regarded as in the object as in our perception of the object.

Grote holds that Mill is involved in error similar to that of Hamilton. When Mill refers to 'phenomena of mind' as well as 'phenomena of matter' he is asserting, in a sense opposite to Hamilton, that both are alike phenomena. But without a consideration of the consciousness of mind the 'phenomena of mind' would make no *sense*. Whereas Hamilton overemphasized consciousness, Mill overemphasized phenomena. But Mill is justified in writing on the 'phenomenalist logic' whereas Hamilton's position, emphasizing the top of the scale of sensation, scarcely allows him to write on phenomenalist logic at all. To a consideration of phenomenalist logic, and its relation to knowledge (and to the growth of knowledge), we now turn our attention.

[1] Lewis, MWO, 66.
[2] *Loc. cit.*

CHAPTER VI

PHENOMENALIST LOGIC AND KNOWLEDGE

1. INTRODUCTORY

In the last chapter the chief point presented was the relationship of 'philosophy' to what Grote calls the 'scale of sensation.' Let us briefly survey what was presented in that chapter, and then show its relation to 'phenomenalist logic and knowledge,' before dealing specifically with the latter – the subject of the present chapter.

i. Brief résumé

'Sensation,' as this term is used in the phrase 'scale of sensation,' refers to all of our consciousness. It covers the most lively and agitated feelings of pleasure and pain where the body is in contact, or in touch, with things – as at the bottom of the scale. It is also used in a sense wide enough to include thought, as much abstracted from what we call 'things' as possible. The logical, or thought, end of the scale is at the top. The 'philosophical' (or logical) aspect of reality is mostly concerned with the very top of the scale, and in proceeding downwards, regards what it confronts as of progressively less *intellectual* importance. Finally the lowest part is virtually altogether neglected by the logical view. It is treated as 'unreason' or 'nonsense' – which it is the business of thought in the higher part of the scale to convert into knowledge. Each higher part is a sort of form to what is below it.

The lower part of the scale, as one descends, becomes wholly phenomenal. Here thought is as much as possible abstracted and absent from phenomenal reality. This reality is not interpreted in the usual sense of the objective as it appears to the senses. Grote is very careful to exclude from phenomenal reality any *meaning*. For *meaning* belongs to the thought end of the scale. It pertains to the 'philosophical' view. The essential characteristic of phenomena is that they be devoid of *all meaning whatsoever* – when there is *no* admixture of intellect with them. We can never be *aware* of such utter abstract phenomena, for should we be aware of them, they would not be pure 'phenomena.'

Yet these phenomena must not be confused with things in themselves. The latter cannot be thought. It might be better to call things in themselves figments of the imagination. The only trouble with calling them this is that once they become such, they are no longer things in themselves but things related to imagination. However phenomenal reality affects us, it communicates with our bodies through our senses and so acts even when we are not aware of its acting. That is, utter phenomenal reality devoid of any consciousness whatsoever is an abstraction, because it cannot *mean* anything without *some* degree of awareness being present.

In relation to us phenomenal reality is essentially communication – communication with the bodily organs. Any meaning that is given to it is not due to its character of phenomena *qua* phenomena, but phenomena *qua* 'philosophy.' Just how much awareness is present in the communication between ourselves and 'things' is what Grote tries to illustrate in the 'scale of sensation.'

ii. Relation of the 'scale of sensation' to phenomenalist logic

Let us now link the last chapter, through the foregoing résumé, with the main content of the present one dealing with phenomenalist logic and knowledge.

When the lower end of the scale is emphasized the view is phenomenal. Here 'things' are stressed with as little of intellect involved as possible. The thought side of 'things' cannot be neglected if 'things' are going to mean anything at all. But here it is the phenomenal emphasis that is of chief concern. It is not a case of complete phenomenal reality that is under consideration. In the phenomenal sense things can affect us even when we are *unaware* of them. The essential concern we have with phenomena is that they fulfill the role of communication, not that they are 'things.' For 'things' carry meaning along with them. Hence we cannot regard 'things' as though they had a sort of 'out-thereness' about them, in contrast to an 'in-hereness' of thought.

The 'out-thereness' of things is dependent upon thought to which they are in the contrast of 'out-thereness.' To speak of things,' therefore, in contrast to thought is to regard them as 'things-as-thought' and hence not as bare 'things' at all.

The above is a free rendering of Grote regarding thought and phenomena. Now, the point at which Grote differs from Mill is in regard to what he thinks is over-emphasized in Mill, namely, phenomenal reality as almost altogether separated from consciousness. Mill approaches epistemology, Grote holds, through emphasis on the lower part of the scale of sensation.

2. GROTE'S OWN POSITION REVEALED THROUGH CRITICISM OF HAMILTON AND MILL

i. Mill and Hamilton – their consistency compared

In this chapter it will be shown that Mill is peculiarly qualified to write on phenomenalist logic because of the strong emphasis which he placed on the phenomenal view. It will also be shown that Hamilton is not justified in writing on phenomenalist logic because he places 'phenemena of matter' side by side with 'phenomena of mind' and regards both as established on the same basis, namely, the logical or the 'philosophical.' We are, Hamilton holds,[1] immediately aware of matter as well as mind. Sufficient has already been said, on this error of Hamilton's, to show that matter is exactly what we are not immediately aware of.[2] Hamilton's position, then, should prevent him from writing on *phenomenalist* logic. He could have written on a logic which dealt with concepts, and he could have called such logic, *formal* logic, but not *phenomenal* logic. His metaphysics was such that it did not warrant his writing on phenomenalist logic at all.

The two sets of Lectures of Sir William Hamilton which have been published are one on Metaphysics, and the other on Logic, the two courses having some introductory Lectures in common. The Lectures on Metaphysics I have to a certain degree examined, because,... the subject is called Metaphysics, and the point of view, the purpose assigned being the analysis of conscious ness.[3]

ii. Basis of Hamilton's error

Hamilton wrote on both logic and metaphysics. Grote calls attention to the fact that students of Hamilton wondered why it was necessary to write two large volumes on logic when an equal amount (or less) of writing on metaphysics would have been sufficient, and could have avoided confusion between the 'philosophical' and the phenomenal

---

[1] Cf., above, pp. 80–81.
[2] *Loc. cit.*
[3] Grote, EP, I, 154.

points of view. The type of error which is so evident in Hamilton may be seen in his first dealing with 'perceiving' things and then with the 'forming concepts' of these things. He should not have dealt with the perception of 'things,' as though things somehow existed as 'things' apart from their relation to us. For those 'things' are things for us, only because they are known through concepts.

Sir William Hamilton speaks, as we have seen, of matter being the object of consciousness. It seems odd that he should do this, when, in a different set of Lectures, those on Logic, we have the real objects of consciousness, which he calls 'concepts,' [1] treated truly and properly as such: we seem to have here, all along, that difficulty which I spoke of, and the student of Sir William Hamilton's Lectures on Metaphysics is astonished to find that, when he has got through them, there are two volumes, as big as the others, treating knowledge and the processes of the human understanding in an entirely different manner and with different languages – after all, he asks, have I only got half the subject, and now I know what 'perceiving' things is have I got to learn all about the 'forming concepts' of them, and is it a different thing or the same? [2]

That irreconcilable bifurcation clouds the clarity which otherwise could be brought out by showing that the emphasis was meant to be particularly on the side of 'things.' Hamilton precluded any possibility of doing this by dealing with 'perception' of things as well as with 'things' out of relation to (perceiving) mind. Grote states that the obscurity becomes more pronounced when Hamilton deals in the second place, in his logic, with *concepts* of things. The result is a confusion together of the phenomenal and logical approaches.

iii. Mill is justified in writing on phenomenalist logic

Hamilton cannot justifiably write on Phenomenalist Logic, Grote contends, because his approach is at one time 'philosophical' or 'logical,' and at another, phenomenal. Mill, on the other hand, takes his starting-point from Aristotelian or Formal Logic. "Mr. Mill's book is what I call a Phenomenalist Logic with a starting point from the Aristotelian or Formal Logic." [3]

Mr. Mill's phenomenalist logic is in effect a description of the facts of nature, the heads of this description being suggested by the relations and processes of

---

[1] It is possible that Hamilton was influenced by Hegel. It seems that this infleunce can be seen in such statements as the following: "The objective Mind is the absolute Idea." Loewenberg, HEG, 218. "The real objects of consciousness" of which Hamilton speaks could be analogous to "the objective mind" of Hegel which includes morality and all social institutions (according to Professor E. S. Brightman, in a class lecture, February, 1947). The concepts of Hamilton are also analogous to "the absolute Idea" of Hegel.

[2] Grote, EP, I, 155, 156.

[3] Grote, *op. cit.*, 157.

logic, as these have been previously understood. Our knowledge is then, in his view, a following or tracing in one direction or another, a keeping close to, these facts.

Thus in respect of propositions, what Mr. Mill considers is, that where the proposition is important for the advance of knowledge, what we are doing in it is not the assertion of anything as to the applicability of the terms or names (which is the same thing as the reference of things to classes), nor the making a judgment, in the sense that the result of the proposition is something in or having reference to our own mind (a view, a change of view, a notion &c.) but the *assisting*, as it were, the standing by or looking on at, an (imagined or actual) natural fact, which the terms of the proposition, indicate.

The proposition in this phenomenalist logic, is not the reference by us of a thing to a class, nor is a judgment, or opinion, on our part, about a thing, but is an expression of a natural fact or relation of things. What is important about the proposition is not the goodness and good employment of a classification of things which it may imply, nor the correctness of thought on our part which it may imply, but its trueness to the phenomenal fact... The object of the previous logic has been correctness of thought: that of Mr. Mill's logic is true following and rendering phenomena.[1]

It seems that Grote is impressed in Mill's logic by what he refers to as the notion of 'adstance,' or the view that might be regarded as one where there is a 'presence at' the 'things' being considered.[2] He explains this notion of 'adstance' by pointing out that there are three possible positions that may be taken regarding reality, and that one of these is characteristic of Mill's logic. Let us note these positions: (1) Here we view things by saying that "they exist." (2) Or, referring to 'things' we assert "we believe them." (3) And, the third possibility is a sort of mixing of both (1) and (2), such as appears in the statement, "we have learnt them."

It seems to Grote that the first position is characteristic of Mill's logic. By saying that Mill's Phenomenalist Logic has its "starting point from the Aristotelian or Formal Logic," he seems to mean that there is something realistic in the sense of being 'out there,' about Aristotelian logic and that Mill has continued this 'Real Logic' of Aristotle.

However, there appears to be less justification for taking this approach either to the logic of Aristotle or of Mill than Grote appears to allow. It is possible that Grote was impressed with the assumption that, because Aristotelian philosophy is ordinarily classed as 'realistic' that Aristotelian logic is 'Real' or 'Phenomenalist Logic.' Taking this attitude toward the logic of Aristotle it seemed fair enough to regard Mill's logic as also Phenomenal. But the fact that the logic of both is

[1] Grote, EP, I, 157n, 158n.
[2] Grote, *op. cit.*, 157.

conceptual, rational, and judgmental, there appears less reason for calling this logic Real than for calling it 'Philosophical.' However, we will continue to follow the analysis of Grote in dealing with Mill's logic, in what follows.

iv. Formal and Real Logic contrasted

Grote contrasts Formal Logic with what he calls Real Logic. Real Logic deals with the growth of knowledge because it has to do with actual experience.

I shall call a supposed method of Logic, of any kind, which so far incorporates into itself the notion of actual experience as to be able to take into account *the growth* of knowledge, whether in the individual or the race, a *Real* Logic, in contrast with such as the Aristotelian, which we may call if we like, when pure and by itself, Formal, and which may have various valuable applications, besides this, if we consider it one: as to verification, to grammar, or to digestion of argument.[1]

The reason why Mill may deal with Phenomenalist Logic and Hamilton should not is because fundamentally the opposite approach is taken by each to metaphysics. The basis for Hamilton might be regarded as consciousness, or Formal Logic, and from this he deals with perception of the external world. The starting point for Mill is the 'external world,' or phenomena. Hence Mill's Logic is consistent with his metaphysics, whereas Hamilton's is not.

v. Mill's phenomenalism and Hamilton's 'philosophy'

There appears to be good reason for the treatment of Mill's phenomenal approach by the side of Hamilton's 'philosophical' view. Since the contrast between both is rather sharp, Mill's phenomenalist logic shows up even more clearly than it would if considered without the strongly contrasted position of Hamilton. It is interesting to observe that Herbert Spencer compares Mill and Hamilton also. Spencer takes the side of the empirical in defence of Mill, but sees that one must go beyond empiricism. Spencer criticizes the position with which Hamilton identifies himself.

Metaphysical reasoning is usually vitiated by some covert 'petitio principii.' Either the thing to be proved or the thing to be disproved, is tacitly assumed to be true in the course of the proof or disproof. It is thus with the argument of Idealism. Though the conclusion reached is that Mind and Ideas are the only existences; yet the steps by which this conclusion is reached, take for granted that external objects have just the kind of independent existence which is eventually denied.[2]

[1] Grote, EP, I, 153.
[2] Spencer, EMP, 396.

Though Empiricism, as at present understood, is not thus suicidal, it is open to... criticism on its method, similarly telling against the validity of its inference. It proposes to account for our so-called necessary beliefs, as well as all our other beliefs; and to do this without postulating any one belief as necessary. Bringing forward abundant evidence that the connections among our states of consciousness are determined by our experiences – that two experiences frequently recurring together in consciousness, become so coherent that one strongly suggests the other, and than when their joint recurrence is perpetual and invariable, the connection between them becomes indissoluble; it argues that the indissolubility, so produced, is all that we mean by necessity. And then it seeks to explain each of our so-called necessary beliefs as thus originated. Now could pure Empiricism reach this analysis and its subsequent synthesis without taking any thing for granted, its arguments would be unobjectionable... Empiricism, starting from an uncertainty and progressing through a series of uncertainties, cannot claim much certainty for its conclusion.[1]

vi. Spencer's reflections support Grote

Spencer seems to be saying that the conclusions of Idealism claim to be much more unobjectionable, and with considerable justification. Whereas, empiricism cannot claim certainty for itself, for certainty is not essentially empirical. He could have said, in terms used by Grote, that empirical certainty is founded upon the 'philosophical' view. Moreover, he could have added that 'certainty' is a 'logical' term rather than a phenomenal one. In the passage before us, it is not clear that Spencer wishes to commend Hamilton through a comparison of his position with that of Mill. Moreover, whether he wishes to do that or not, does not particularly concern us here. But it is significant to note that Spencer contrasted Mill with Hamilton because he saw that the one tended toward empiricism and the other toward idealism. Grote seems to go even further than Spencer in contrasting these two philosophers. Grote's additional contribution is to note that Hamilton is not unwaveringly faithful to a sort of idealistic position even though he states that we are *immediately* aware both of our own selves and also have 'consciousness of matter.' Grote notes further, too, that Hamilton even writes on phenomenalistic logic. Hamilton – if he tends toward idealism, as Spencer implies, and as Grote realizes in identifying Hamilton with a 'philosophical' view – is in error, in writing on phenomenalist logic, whereas Mill – not professing (or practicing) other than the phenomenal approach – is correct (or much closer to being so) in writing on phenomenalist logic which Grote refers to as Real Logic.

---

[1] Spencer, *op. cit.*, 397, 399.

vii. Mill is faithful to phenomenalist logic

a. *General comment*

Grote deals with the metaphysics of Hamilton, and his view of 'consciousness of matter' as immediate, in order to show his inconsistency and to contrast him with Mill. He does this not to show inconsistency in the Phenomenalist Logic of Mill, but rather to illustrate, still further from the outstanding philosophical thought of the period, a fundamental confusion between the phenomenal and the philosophical points of view. This is not to say that Mill is guilty of the error of mistaking the difference between the two but rather he is contrasted with Hamilton whose position is not so strictly philosophical as Mill's is phenomenal. Mill remains generally true to phenomenalism; Hamilton (whether influenced in this by two incompatible currents – one from Reid and the other from Kant is at least very possibly influenced) in his attempt to be consistent with both phenomenalism and philosophy ultimately ends by being true to neither.

I suppose that Sir William Hamilton, in his attempt to unite logic, Reidian psychology, and Kantian criticism, really did confuse together the logical view of knowledge as a forming proper notions of what (no matter to logic *what*) in virtue of the notions thus formed, we call *things*, and the view of knowledge as a communication or presence with something supposed existent.[1]

Mill attempts to be faithful to what Grote called 'Phenomenalist Logic,' by using the methods of traditional logic in dealing with 'things.' He takes "care to preserve the old logical methods and language, while altering their application and utilizing them." [2] That is, Mill deals only with names which are expressions for things instead of dealing with concepts or ideas. Taking exception to Hobbes, Mill states,

Are names more properly said to be the names of things, or of our ideas of things? The first is the expression in common use; the last is that of some metaphysicians, who conceived that in adopting it they were introducing a highly important distinction. The eminent thinker seems to countenance the latter opinion.[3]

In dealing with concepts or ideas one remains within the 'logical' point of view, according to Grote. Mill, if he is to remain within the field of phenomenal logic, cannot make ideas and concepts his chief

[1] Grote, EP, I, 189.
[2] *Op. cit.*, 160.
[3] Mill, SOL, I, 23.

concern. Mill classified things under four heads, namely, minds, bodies, attributes of mind or feelings, and attributes of bodies with their subcategories. For the basis of this classification Mill goes back to the categories of Aristotle, Grote states. These categories, though included in a *realistic* philosophy (that of Aristotle) may be regarded either as 'logical' or phenomenal, depending upon the specific emphasis involved. In regarding them as applicable to phenomenal reality they form the chief constituents of almost all conceivable universes.

I mentioned previously about the Aristotelian categories, that though they proceed from a logical point of view, yet they might be turned round to a sort of quasi-phenomenalist one, in which view they will represent the main constituents, so to speak, of almost any possible universe. Mr. Mill finds, reasonably enough, that they are a very poor catalogue of the constituents of *this* universe and proceeds to utilize the notion by substituting others for them.[1]

The imperfections of this classification are too obvious to require, and its merits are not sufficient to reward, a minute examination. It is a mere catalogue of the distinctions rudely marked out by the language of familiar life, with little or no attempt to penetrate, by philosophic analysis, to the *rationale* even of those common distinctions. Such an analysis, however superficially conducted, would have shown the enumeration to be both redundant and defective. Some objects are omitted, and others repeated several times under different heads. It is like a division of animals into men, quadrupeds, horses, asses, and ponies. That, for instance, could not be a very comprehensive view of the nature of Relation which could exclude action, passivity, and local situation from that category. The same observation applies to the categories Quando (or position in time), and Ubi (for position in space); while the distinction between the latter and Situs is merely verbal. The incongruity of erecting into a *summum genus* the class which forms the tenth category is manifest. On the other hand, the enumeration takes no notice of anything besides substances and attributes. In what category are we to place sensations, or any other feelings and states of mind; as hope, joy, fear; sound, smell, taste; pain, pleasure; thought, judgment, conception, and the like? Probably all these would have been placed by the Aristotelian school in the categories of *actio* and *passio*; and the relation of such of them as are active, to their objects, and of such of them as are passive, to their causes, would rightly be so placed; but the things themselves, the feelings or states of mind, wrongly. Feelings, or states of consciousness, are assuredly to be accounted among realities, but they cannot be reckoned either among substances or attributes.[2]

It should be noted that Grote frequently employs the terms 'logical,' 'rational,' 'mental,' 'consciousness,' and several others as synonymous for 'philosophy,' or 'philosophical.' Just which word he uses is sometimes arbitrary and sometimes dependent upon the view he is discussing. In dealing with Mill's philosophy he is likely to use the term

[1] Grote, EP, I, 160.
[2] Mill, SOL, 29, 30.

'logical.' And by his use of it he means to imply the conceptual or thought side of reality.

Mill found the Aristotelian categories as not entirely practicable for this universe and hence suggests ways in which a list of categories might be drawn up to include, for example, feelings, and states of consciousness. For Mill the substratum for the attributes of mind was mind, and of bodies was bodies or things. Grote believes that Mill was in error in placing these categories side by side because categories should be selected from either one or the other but not from both, if faithfulness to phenomenalist logic is to be maintained. To be clear as to which should be made the starting point for a system of philosophy is the chief point.

Apparently, then, two steps were open to Mill: 1. He could have started from the phenomenalist point of view where the logic of our knowing about things, as body and its attributes (in Mill's classification), could be traced. 2. He, then, could have considered it as probably possible in the future history of physiology to bring into relation with things such unassimilated, unappropriated or incommensurable matter which are not yet *things* and which are *known* to exist. Mill seems to have gone only so far as the end of the first step. At least, he professed to going only this far. But he did not altogether avoid mixing the 'philosophical' and the phenomenalist views together in a sort of combination of Formal and Real (or Phenomenalist) Logic. He could not speak of 'notions' with ease because of the implied non-phenomenalistic connotation. He placed 'mind and its attributes' by the side of 'matter and its attributes,' and looked at both phenomenally, which was the opposite to the method of Hamilton who placed 'matter and its attributes' by the side of 'mind and its attributes,' and looked at both 'philosophically.'

b. 'Names' and 'notions'

Mill has taken great care to avoid 'notions' because of their 'philosophical' or 'logical' implications and has dealt with 'names' instead. What he really means by names is difficult to see. Grote asserts that 'names' could be more easily replaced by 'notions' or 'concepts' but if Mill used either 'notions' or 'concepts' in his system of logic he might readily be accused of departing from his main thesis which is Real Logic, and is essentially phenomenal. Mill appears to recognize that there is difficulty here but has not been able to see exactly what it is.

Grote believes that Mill has been misled by the logical view, more so because he has partially rather than wholly made use of it.

c. Syllogistic logic

Grote holds that the three main parts of syllogistic logic will probably always continue unmodified; he designates these parts as, perception (or conception), judgment, and reasoning.

The old logicians had then these processes, 'simple apprehension' (perception, conception), 'judgment,' and 'reasoning,' and one way or another this triplicity must always exist. Thought or language naturally divides itself into notions or words, judgments or propositions, and syllogisms or arguments.[1]

In the first, 'names' rather than 'notions' are the expressions of 'things' in nature. In the second, 'propositions' are the expressions of 'phenomena' or 'facts.' Just as Mill made great efforts to classify things in the first process he now takes great pains to classify 'facts' (in the second process) which he regards as five in number, namely, coexistences, sequences, existence, causation, and resemblance.

Mr. Mill gives five great heads of natural fact, just as he gives, with whatever success, four great heads or categories of *things*. The facts are facts about the things, or what the things enter into, in the same manner as propositions are about the terms, or what *they* enter into. These categories or kinds of fact are Coexistences, Sequences, Existence, Causation, Resemblance.[2]

3. PHENOMENALISM INADEQUATE FOR A PERFECT SCHEME OF KNOWLEDGE

i. Reasoning not an element in phenomenal reality

Just as the term 'names' is used by Mill for 'things' so may 'assertables, or 'asseribles' (though the terms are not employed by Mill, but *both* are used by Grote) be used for propositions. Both names and propositions must have behind them 'things' and 'facts.' But Mill passes over to the logical (or philosophical) point of view illegitimately inasmuch as a perfect scheme of knowledge (which must include propositions) requires something more than what can be supplied by phenomenalism alone. And in the third and most important process of logic, viz, reasoning, Mill appears to be even more dependent upon the 'logical' point of view. He is concerned not only with the existence of things but also with reasoning *about* things.

[1] Grote, EP, I, 159.
[2] *Op. cit.*, 165n.

ii. Time and space, and phenomenal reality

Further, what Mill considers in nature has to do more with time than with space for what he considers is not so much what *exists* as what *goes on*. 'Order' occupies many pages in his logic but is not as important as 'function' which appears to be characteristic of practically all the 'things' with which he deals. 'Sequences' or 'simultaneities' are of more importance than spatial considerations, and within sequences 'uniformities' are of great moment. Grote shows the importance of action in comparison with the lack of importance of existence in regard to what Mill is dealing with in nature.

It may be noted that Mill had what might be called a theory of time. For he held that geometry and arithmetic were concerned with physical things, and that these occupy both space and time.[1] Alexander felt that Mill fell victim to a mistaken conception of empirical method when he maintained that mathematical propositions are simply generalizations from experience. Alexander also held that Mill tried to place geometry and arithmetic on the plane of inductive sciences by holding that they are concerned with physical things and not with space and time in which physical things exist. There seems to be affinity between Alexander and Grote regarding Mill at this point. For both regard Mill as empirical in his approach to reality, at least on this issue of space and time. Grote would say that Mill is *phenomenal* in his approach, and this would give some credence to Grote's view of Mill's logic as Real or Phenomenal.

iii. Belief and phenomena

In dealing with fact (within the second process of logic) Mill speaks of 'belief.' This word suggests that there appears to be for Mill something existing in the phenomenal realm which is there independently of whether or not anyone is present to know. That is, phenomena are what they are, for Mill, quite independent of their being known. When he speaks of 'belief' he is inconsistent with *Phenomenalist Logic*.

iv. Mis-psychology

Grote states that if there is anyone who should be regarded as not guilty of 'mis-psychology' it is Mill because Mill distinguishes very clearly between 'sensation' considered as 'bodily affection' and 'sensation' considered as 'consciousness.' The lack of making this dis-

[1] Alexander, STD, I, 232.

tinction is, what Grote calls, 'mis-psychology.' Yet Mill identifies him-self definitely with phenomenalism and hence his 'philosophical' (or 'logical') point of view remains part of his unprofessed position. Mill says, in effect, that the truth about objects must be considered as knowledge if the truth is to become truth *for us*. This is practically to state that the phenomenalist point of view is an abstraction from the 'logical' and never can be considered apart from the point of view of consciousness. Moreover, according to this phenomenal view, facts of mind should never be regarded as objects themselves and reduced to the logic of phenomenalism, for they can in that case never be regarded as facts of consciousness. To strengthen his theory Grote makes the statement that it appears impossible to regard our conscious-ness of activity or will as reduced to the phemomenal realm unless we consider it as mere delusion. And there is no more reason why we should consider consciousness of activity or will as delusion than there is to consider our supposition of the existence of the 'external' world to be delusion.

4. CRITICAL OBSERVATIONS AND ANALYSES

i. Why Grote deals with Hamilton and Mill at all

Now, there is no reason why Grote should deal with either Mill or Hamilton *except* that in so doing he tries to show that a phenomenalist logic is impossible, *qua* phenomenal. Grote believes that Mill provides an excellent example of Real or Phenomenalist Logic. Mill is much more correct than some others who do not remain faithful to what Grote calls Real Logic, the 'real' nature of which is dependent upon phenomena abstracted from consciousness.

That there can be such Real Logic should be admitted as impossible. Mill does not admit this in any sort of testimonial. But there is evi-dence of his definitely phenomenalist position far stronger than any verbal admission can present. This evidence is found in his use of 'names' instead of 'notions,' 'concepts,' and the like. Somehow, Mill felt that by the use of 'names' he could refer to 'facts,' or 'things denoted by names,' [1] and avoid language foreign to Real or Phenome-nalist Logic.

Instead, if Mill had used such terms as 'notions,' 'concepts,' etc., he would have gone beyond a *phenomenalist* logic. The point is, that

[1] Mill, SOL, bk. I, chap. III.

Grote wants to show the impossibility of avoiding a mixing of the 'philosophical' and the phenomenal approaches in epistemology. And that *any* system professedly (or otherwise) based on phenomena alone is foredoomed to disaster. In order to show this he must deal, he feels, with those who have been guilty of this. Mill and Hamilton are good examples. He deals with each, showing their merits and demerits. Mill, he believes, has not been a great offender since he has much more success in keeping the 'philosophical' and phenomenalist views separate. He does not waver back and forth, one time writing in conceptual language and again in phenomenal language. Nevertheless, neither Mill nor anyone else can avoid dealing in conceptual language, because a language which will present phenomenal reality *qua* phenomenal does not nor cannot exist.

Mill is the least guilty of mixing the two possible epistemological emphases, the 'philosophical' and the phenomenal. One of the greatest contemporary offenders, living in Grote's time, was Sir William Hamilton. Hamilton's grievous fault seemed evident to Grote at almost every turn. Grote deals with him again and again since he seems to be the most glaring offender of all. He sees no justification for Hamilton's writing on metaphysics and later on logic in order to make a contribution to philosophy with almost similar content, in each work. One, metaphysics, dealt mainly with perception of 'things' – with an emphasis on both the 'philosophical' and the phenomenal views in a way that left the epistemological situation hopelessly confused.

This confusion arises from the basic error that Hamilton makes when he does not distinguish between consciousness of things and consciousness of self. In the former case, regarding consciousness of things, Hamilton is asserting that we are conscious of 'things,' or of what is already in a definite relation to mind, and without which relation the 'things' (which Hamilton is concerned with in his metaphysics) would not be 'things' for us. In the latter case, Grote asserts, and apparently correctly so, that consciousness in such a phrase as, 'consciousness of self,' is the only place in which the term 'consciousness' is correctly applied.

The other work of Hamilton, on logic, dealt with the nature of 'perceiving,' 'notions,' etc. – with emphasis on the 'philosophical' view. Thus, when both his metaphysics and logic are considered, Hamilton leaves the reader in extraordinary perplexity, as to how we know and what we know. Grote is concerned in showing that much

clarity is possible through regard for two basic views in epistemology –
to which he continually called attention in dealing with Hamilton and
Mill – that should always be kept in mind, namely, the two based upon
whether one's approach is 'philosophical' or phenomenal.

ii. Things in themselves and phenomena

We have seen that Grote dealt with Hamilton and Mill in order to
make his own fundamental epistemological position clear. Both
Hamilton and Mill provide good illustrations of Grote's distinction
between 'philosophy' and phenomena. Grote claimed that Mill is
basically 'realistic' in his approach to reality. This realism is referred
to under the terms 'Phenomenalist Logic' or 'Real Logic.' Grote
frequently employs the term 'logic,' instead of the term 'philosophy,'
as referring to the 'thought' or 'consciousness' aspect of reality. But
by the terms 'Phenomenalist Logic' and 'Real Logic' he is referring to
Mill's *A System of Logic*, which, Grote believes, presents the phenomenalist (in contrast to the 'philosophical') approach to reality.

Hamilton, Grote affirms, mixed the two aspects of reality together,
the 'philosophical' and the phenomenal; he did not distinguish between
these. He uses phrases such as 'consciousness of self' and 'consciousness of matter,' and, terms such as 'perception,' 'conception,' 'matter,'
'sensation,' 'thing,' and 'object,' in such a way that one cannot discern
whether he is referring to thinking, or that which is thought about, or
that which is thought about in relation to consciousness – the given for
consciousness. Grote's point is that we *must* distinguish between the
two views of reality, the 'philosophical' and the phenomenal, if we are
going to have any semblance of clarity in what we say in epistemology.

There is another question which may be regarded as arising out of
Grote's concern with Hamilton. Or it may be considered even apart
from Hamilton and Mill altogether. This question is in regard to the
relation between things in themselves and phenomena. It may be
examined wholly apart from any philosopher with whom Grote deals.
But first let us note the dissatisfaction which Grote finds in Hamilton's
use of the term 'things in themselves.'

Of things absolutely and in themselves, be they external, be they internal, we
know nothing, or know them only as incognizable; and become aware of their
incomprehensible existence, only as this is indirectly and accidentally revealed
to us, through certain qualities related to our faculties of knowledge, and which
qualities, again, we cannot think as unconditional, irrelative, existent in and of
themselves. All that we know is therefore phaenomenal – phaenomenal of the
unknown.[1]

[1] Hamilton, IOM, 65.

'Phaenomenal' for Hamilton is not clearly separated into conscious-ness on the one hand and 'things' on the other. From Hamilton's use of the term, one does not know how much consciousness he is going to admit into his 'phaenomena.' Nor does one know some of the time whether he is going to speak of phaenomena as 'things.' Also, he admits that the unknown may be spoken about, as though there were something non-phaenomenal which *is* the unknown. This unknown is the thing in itself, for Hamilton. But one may ask, what is this un-known which is unknown? If it is known in *any* respect it is not the unknown. And if it is unknown then it is clearly unknown, especially since Hamilton is treating the 'unknown' as 'things absolutely and in themselves.' To speak, as Hamilton does, therefore, in language like 'phaenomenal of the unknown,' doesn't make sense, in Grote's meaning of phenomena. For, as soon as anything is known to us in any way it is phenomena. And to speak of what is known to us in some way as also unknown is meaningless. This meaninglessness is significant, therefore, considering what phenomena mean for Grote. But for Kant to refer to *phenomena of the unknown* does make sense, for phenomena considered as the objects as they appear to the senses can very well be objects that are somehow related to the unknown. Or, again, phe-nomena of the unknown could refer to unknown objects which might, under suitable circumstances, appear to the senses.

Grote feels that he has to illustrate his epistemology by reference to some of those who did considerable research in the field. Hence he is considerably occupied by several of his contemporaries. Before con-sidering Grote's distinction between 'philosophy' and phenomenal reality further, it should be pointed out that he is not using the term 'phenomenal' as a synonym for Hamilton's 'phaenomenal.' Hamilton's 'phaenomenal' is 'all that we know'; it is 'phaenomenal of the unknown.' Now, Grote has no place for the 'unknown' as a sort of thing in itself. As Grote uses the term 'phenomena' it may seem that he has in mind things in themselves, and that 'phenomena' *are* things in themselves. This resemblance is only on the surface. Things in themselves cannot exist – probably this remark gives more information than one should entertain about what things in themselves are. But we can speak of what Grote calls 'phenomena.' These are influential; they are not *in themselves*. They produce effects. But the phenomenal effects they produce, *qua* phenomenal, are not conscious effects. The phenomenal may also be looked at *qua* 'philosophical' where there *are* conscious, or at least, 'philosophical,' effects. Consciousness is the mental, logical, or 'philosophical' element which contributes to the knowing process.

Phenomena are 'things' inasmuch as they have some relation *to us*. Phenomena are of utmost importance in the knowing process, but their specific role stops short with the making of impressions on the physical constitution of the body. They are not psychical in the sense of 'mind,' 'awareness,' or 'consciousness.' This consideration takes 'phenomena,' as Grote uses this term, out of any basic similarity with things in themselves. Phenomena are not *in themselves* at all, but they *are* in relation *to us*. But the relation in which they are to us is not a *conscious* relation *until* consciousness is present. The essential role of phenomena is to communicate rather than to make aware. If phenomena produce effects upon us, even though we are not conscious of these effects, we are justified, in Grotian language, in referring to them as 'phenomena.'

Justification for our speaking of phenomena at all must rest upon *qualities* of 'objects' and *faculties* of comprehension, according to Grote. He refers to the qualities of an object as fitted to our faculties of knowledge. "We know the object through certain qualities fitted to our faculties of knowledge – these, in language I have used, fit each other." [1] This is a peculiar manner of expressing what he means, but peculiarity of expression is not uncommon in Grote.[2] But the meaning is fairly clear. He states that 'qualities and faculties of knowledge go together.' Grote should admit that the term 'qualities' had a double (or triple) meaning in the senses present in Locke's use of the word, as primary and secondary (and tertiary). He seems guilty here of the error which he points out in others, namely, of using a term in two senses, one 'philosophical' and the other phenomenal. Along with the two (or three) implicit senses in which the word is used he speaks of 'faculties' which is a term clearly 'philosophical' – not phenomenal. But Grote puts 'qualities and faculties of knowledge' together in order to show that no object can be known that has no qualities.

Suppose one single universal faculty of knowledge, in place of various special and particular ones, what the mind having this must know is – one universal quality of the object and no more. *Who* then knows the object *itself*, if even omniscience does not and cannot go beyond quality? Here we have doubtless got at an unknowableness of the 'thing in itself,' but it is an unknowableness I think of *my* sort, viz. because there is nothing to know.[3]

[1] Grote, EP, I, 187.
[2] Peculiarity of expression may be traced to Grote's awareness that *Exploratio Philosophica* should be revised. For he gives this work the sub-title, *Rough Notes on Modern Intellectual Science*.
[3] Grote, *loc. cit.*

Grote affirms, that minds such as ours know objects through qualities, and it seems unlikely, he holds, that there are minds that know objects independent of all qualities, namely, as things in themselves.

It seems of the nature of knowledge to have qualities 'fitted to' faculties. The impossibility of severing 'reality' from faculties operating by 'concepts,' 'notions,' etc., is exemplified in the case of J. S. Mill. Mill works out a Phenomenalist or Real Logic fairly successfully, Grote believes. But Mill is not *altogether* successful. It is not that Mill lacked the ingenuity to be highly successful in working out a Real Logic. The lack of success that Mill experienced is due to the nature of knowledge. One seems safe in concluding the following from what Grote has inferred about Mill. It is not *essential* (though very helpful) to have illustration from Mill's philosophy or from any other, to reach the conclusion that if there were minds that could know objects otherwise than through their qualities, then Phenomenalist or Real Logic is wholly possible. One might go further and say that if this type of logic is possible, then things can be known other than through their qualities (which seem inseparably connected with our faculties). The consequent of what, in the foregoing statement, thus masquerades as an implication, is equivalent to maintaining that we can know things in themselves!

iii. Further reflections on 'phenomenon'

The term 'phenomenon' is used to designate a reality that *may* exist independent of *being known* by any knowing mind. If it makes any effect on us at all, conscious or unconscious, it is phenomenon. Of course, for Plato and Kant the phenomenal is that which somehow appears to our senses. For Plato, the phenomenal world is the world of appearances. "The phenomenal assumption is that the world of reality exists quite independently of being known by any knowing beings in it." [1] That means that a Phenomenalist Logic is a logic which exists independent of any knowing mind. Such a logic, of course, is impossible.

Mr. Mill gives us what I have called a thoroughly phenomenalist logic or method, i.e., treats of things in the first instance, for science and life, – with careful putting aside all mention of our conceptions of them, – as if they were reality to us. The consideration of their 'seeming' or being conceived by us he will not allow to disturb the science of them. [2]

The strictly non-conscious nature of phenomenal reality is an abstraction from consciousness:

[1] Grote, EP, I, 4.
[2] *Op. cit.*, II, 243.

The great rule of phenomenalism is to be sure that we do not do that which, as we shall see, we always naturally *do* do, humanize the universe, recognize intelligence in it, have preliminary faith, persuasion, suppositions about it, find ourselves, if I may so speak, at all at home in it, think it has any concern with us.[1]

To me there is something in the simply phenomenalist spirit, so far as one has a tendency to sink (as I should say) into it, inexpressibly depressing and desolate.[2]

The depressing and desolate nature of phenomenal reality is the absence of 'spirit' or 'mind' in it. The term 'phenomenalist spirit' seems a somewhat unfortunate choice of words in Grote, since he means by the term, simply phenomenal reality (not abstracted from 'philosophy') 'Phenomenal reality' regarded as abstracted from 'spirit' or 'mind' is phenomenal reality of a depressing and desolate nature. It is like Aristotle's matter in the sense that it is never wholly devoid of all 'philosophy' as Aristotle's matter is never completely lacking in some form.

This reality is markedly different from 'phaenomena' as used by Lotze:

In our varied and complex civilisation there are many thoughts which seem to have a stamp of intellectuality and a certain striking elegance and simplicity, because they detach from the soil of common experience and transplant as it were into empty space, apart from all explanatory surroundings, ideas familiar to us in everyday life, where we observe, patiently and minutely, all the conditions on which their validity depends. This fate has overtaken the idea of *phaenomenon* or *appearance* among others. It is plain that in order to be intelligible this idea must presuppose not only a being or thing which appears, but also, and quite as indispensably, a second being by whom this appearance is perceived.[3]

Lotze's meaning is present in current usage, whereas Grote's is not. If Grote were discussing Lotze's use of the term he would say that 'phaenomenon' as 'appearance' (as Lotze uses the term 'phaenomenon') must be regarded as possessing two elements the 'thing which appears, and the one to whom this 'thing' appears. But this analysis does not go far enough, Grote would maintain. Grote is concerned about showing that the 'thing which appears' [4] is not a 'thing' until it is related to consciousness, or if not to *consciousness*, then related to us in some other way, as, for example, productive of certain effects on us. However, for Grote the 'thing which appears' is 'phenomenon' (if in 'appears' consciousness is absent – supposing this were possible) even

---

[1] Grote, EP, I, 14, 15.
[2] *Op. cit.*, 15.
[3] Lotze, MIC, II, 159, 160.
[4] *Op. cit.*, 160.

without the presence of consciousness. That phenomena fulfill the role of communication with the bodily organs is enough, but such communication does not necessarily involve consciousness. This phenomenon does not have the difficulty involved in the Ding-an-sich, for we cannot say anything about the latter or it will turn into phenomenon. But we can speak and act in regard to the phenomenon. In fact the phenomenon is *already* related to us.

Moreover, phenomena, of course, could not be *known* without consciousness. Probably it is better to say, 'phenomena' *qua* 'phenomena' do not necessitate consciousness. And these 'phenomena' *qua* 'phenomena' are what 'phenomena' are essentially. Yet if we are conscious of 'phenomena' this consciousness does not affect phenomena so that they become other than phenomena.

In no case are we justified, according to Grote, in calling 'phenomenon' 'appearance,' for appearance means appearance to some mind when Grote's meaning of 'phenomenon' is such that we do not need to be aware of it, nor does it need to *appear* to us, and yet it may affect us. Phenomenalist Logic in Grote's sense of Real Logic would not have any place in Lotze's thinking, and he does not seem to mention or allude to such logic anywhere. The meaning that Lotze gives to 'phaenomena' precludes having any place for Real Logic at all.

For Lotze the *real* is what is affirmed, is actualized, or occurs:

We call a thing Real which is, in contradistinction to another which is not; an event Real which occurs or has occurred, in contradistinction to that which does not occur; a relation Real which obtains, as opposed to one which does not obtain; lastly we call a proposition Really true which holds or is valid as opposed to one of which the validity is still doubtful. This use of language is intelligible; it shows that when we call anything Real, we mean always to *affirm* it, though in different senses according to the different forms which it assumes, but one or other of which it must necessarily assume, and of which no one is reducible to or contained in the other. For we never can get an Event out of simple Being, the reality which belongs to Things, namely Being or Existence, never belongs to Events – they do not exist but occur.[1]

The meaning that he gives to reality does not lead him to consider the possibility of Real logic. Yet Lotze does refer to the *real* which cannot have its being in the form of concepts, judgments, and syllogism.

It is out of the question that... Reality should move and have its being in the forms of the Concept, of the judgment or of the Syllogism, which our thought assumes in its own subjective efforts towards the knowledge of that reality.[2]

[1] Lotze, LSP, 439.
[2] *Op. cit.*, 493, 494.

Lotze does not seem to develop this view of the real into a Real, or what Grote would call a Phenomenalist, Logic. If he did so develop it, his grounds for so doing would be open to the same criticism as we have already found in Grote's view, of Mill. It is interesting to note that Dewey also does not consider the possibility of phenomena as real, for he states that there is "true reality in contrast with the merely phenomenal." [1]

That there are *existential phenomena* is asserted by Hartmann. Yet Hartmann does not dwell unduly on the existential nature of phenomena, but states that there are mental phenomena.

Thus also in the problem of Being, certain existential and cognitive phenomena are indices which point to real self-existence... Certain phenomena of the moral consciousness indicate the existence of moral freedom. [2]

Hartmann also states that the basis of phenomenon may be illusory. "The phenomena may always rest ultimately upon an illusion." [3] This sharply contrasts with the *real* nature of phenomena in Grote.

Hartmann appears to regard phenomena as indicative of something else which substantiates or supports the phenomena. This is supported, for example, by his contention that moral phenomena indicate moral freedom. Now these phenomena are different than the phenomena of Grote. Hartmann asserts that there are entities beyond phenomena. But Grote does not allow that there is anything at all beyond his phenomena. Phenomena, for Grote, do not seem to be illusory at all. They *are* reality. They cannot rest upon illusion. The only illusion that is possible in Grote's theory is another sort of phenomena that seems to be the same as something that we are thinking about. Hartmann seems to hold that beyond phenomena there may be nothing to substantiate them.

It may be briefly noted here that in the phenomenology of Husserl the nature of the *real*, or of *being*, is always the *real as known*, or *being as known*.

It cannot be emphasized too strongly that the phenomenological method deals with *phenomena*, and that all the questions it raises are significant only in respect to a knower. When 'being' is spoken of, *known being* is meant. [4]

---

[1] Dewey, EAN, 66.
[2] Hartmann, ETH, III, 139.
[3] *Op. cit.*, 144.
[4] Farber, "Phenomenology," in Runes, TCP, 363.

iv. Personalism

Let us look now at the phenomena of Grote which are essentially 'philosophical' on their 'inner' or thought side. For Grote 'being' means 'known being.'

Grote acknowledged that in all knowing there must be a knower. And when being is spoken of, it is *known being* that is meant. In this respect Grote resembles Husserl. Husserl states that

I am the ego which invests the being of the world which I so constantly speak about with existential validity, as an existence which wins for me from my own life's pure essence meaning and substantial validity.[1]

Grote's analysis leads him to the position of maintaining that being may be considered independent of any knower, only as an abstraction – what he calls 'phenomena' which may affect us even when we are not aware of them, and when we do not philosophize about them.

But that phenomena require a knower to be phenomena *to us*, Grote does not deny. For *phenomena* are *always* phenomena *to us*. He even emphasizes this point very strongly to the extent of calling it "idealism, personalism, or whatever it may be called."[2] This, he states, "which lies at the root of all that I have said, is not simply a doctrine or opinion, but seems to me to have been my earliest philosophical feeling, and to have continued, if not so vivid, yet not less strong, ever since."[3]

Philosophy is, essentially, individual, Grote maintains. Our tendency is to sink our individuality into the phenomenalism so that the world is too much with us in the sense that we overlook the personal element in it. Grote means that we can never regard phenomenal reality correctly as a sort of reality for a social group, or reality that is characterized by 'out-thereness.' Reality is *always* phenomenal reality for him. This reality is for each individual, fundamentally. Reality for a particular person is not reality for a second person on the basis of it being a reality for the first. Just what reality for another person may be, will always remain fundamentally unknown to us.

Sinking our individuality into phenomenalism means, for Grote, the obliteration of individual meanings of 'things' where there is a tendency to regard the world as essentially 'out-there' for all, rather than phenomenal reality for each individual – a phenomenal reality always with its 'philosophical' side. Hence, Grote says that we are inclined to have 'the world' too much with us.

[1] Runes, TCP, 365.
[2] Grote, EP, I, 146.
[3] *Loc. cit.*

In earlier years, there is a disposition in us to be struck with what I may call our personal or conscious difference from it, or independence of it, or however else we may style the *individual* feeling: this is what is with me the root of philosophy.[1]

I suppose there is more of what may be called personal or individual philosophy in the world than one readily hears of, but it is not a thing which seems much in people's mind that any real philosophy... is something that they must see for themselves, and that they must value any chance or early glimpses they may get about it, because the course of life and study will in many respects make it more difficult for them to get such.[2]

This personalist view, which Grote professes, is not at all surprising since he holds that 'philosophy' is an indispensable element in all knowledge. By 'philosophy' he means a sort of idealism which he feels is very appropriately called 'personalism' since all experience is basically individual. There appears to be a close relationship between Grote's personalism here, and Professor Brightman's. Personalism is the "theory that only *persons* are *real*; that all *true* being is personal."[3] For Grote, all being is phenomenal reality. And outside of persons there is no being of any sort. We are justified in speaking about being at all only on the basis of being related to us.

But there appears in conjunction with his discussion of personalism a most arresting remark which seems out of harmony with Grote's epistemology: "A belief in a real *substance*, or thing in itself, is what I have always had, and have most strongly."[4] This remark seems to belie much of what Grote has already affirmed. It seems that he should not have admitted any place whatsoever for the thing in itself for he has been saying all along that phenomenon *qua* phenomenon is an abstraction and is nothing *for us* consciously (though it may affect us even when we are unaware of it, and when we do not 'philosophize'). Now, he brings in the thing in itself which by its nature has no relation to us whatsoever, and does not allow us strictly to refer to 'its nature' or to 'it,' as an *it* at all. If he means by 'substance' the *self*, then this statement would seem in harmony with the rest of his epistemology. But this statement appears, rather, to be plainly an inconsistent one which would be excusable only on the recognition that *Exploratio Philosophica* claims to be only 'rough notes.' That 'real *substance*' is a thing in itself is a view that is evident nowhere else in Grote's writings.

Moreover, Grote does not appear to qualify his professed belief in

---

[1] Grote, EP, I, 146.
[2] *Op. cit.*, 147.
[3] Brightman, ITP, 389.
[4] Grote, *loc. cit.*

a thing in itself in the passage immediately following his affirmation of a belief in its existence:

It is this very belief which makes me revolt against the philosophy which would disjoin from the substance or reality of the thing every thing, it appears to me, which we do or can come to know about it: it is the assigning a character of unknowableness to the substance which is repugnant to me.[1]

Here he speaks of revolting against any philosophy which seeks to abstract from the substance all that we know about it, and thus "assigning a character of unknowableness to the substance." And yet this is what Grote has done in stating belief in a thing in itself, namely, assigning a character of unknowableness to this thing in itself, and yet stating a belief in it! This position of Grote's is hopelessly confused. If he had stated that he believed strongly in the possibility of the *unknown* in substance, his position would be allowable. He seems to admit easy entrance to the critic here by the following statement, also:

Of the unknown there is no reason for us to suppose either that it is unknowable, or that it is (necessarily) more important to the thinghood of the thing about which the knowledge is than the qualities which we *do* know about it.[2]

Already Grote has given us to understand that the thing in itself is both unknown and unknowable, because it is the thing in itself.

It may be said that Grote believes in a real substance, but real substance is *always* phenomenal reality or phenomenal (substance). It is correct to say that phenomenal reality can be known, for it has an 'inner' or consciousness side that gives meaning to it. Phenomenal reality, however, does not need to be *known* to be knowable, for it may act upon us and hence be real *for us* even when we are actually unaware of it (yet could be aware of it).

Moreover, to affirm belief in the unknowable thing in itself is to deny personalism in the sense of all experience being fundamentally individual. It is difficult to see how this fundamentally individualistic character of reality which Grote calls 'idealism,' as 'personalism,' relates to what is *in itself*. To hold with Grote that personalism is idealism is to overlook dualists who were also personalists:

It would be a terminological blunder to identify personalism with... idealism (since most scholastics and many religious realists are dualists, yet are also personalists in the sense of holding that personality is either the only ultimate creative reality, or else is the controlling reality, in the universe).[3]

---

[1] Grote, EP, I, 147.
[2] *Loc. cit.*
[3] Brightman, POR, 314n.

It should also be noted that, not only is it true, as Grote states, that personalism is idealism, but idealism also may be personalism.

It is interesting to observe that a personalistic philosophy is not a distinctly American development since Grote presented a philosophy of personalism. There are elements of personalism in Greek philosophy as early as Heraclitus, and Anaxagoras:

The trend toward naming the qualities of personality as the ultimate reality began at least as early as Heraclitus... who affirmed mind as the fundamentally real because it alone had the power to differentiate itself from the objective world and from its own experiences.[1]

Personalistic elements may also be observed in the philosophy of Anaxagoras for whom there was a special kind of matter, self-named, animate or psychical. The fact that Grote presented a personalistic philosophy supports the statement:

It has been quite the custom among American Personalists to assume that Personalism is a distinctly and original American development in philosophy. Except in a superficial way, nothing could be farther from the truth.[2]

Inasmuch as there will be a fuller account of personalism in a later chapter (Chapter IX), further discussion on the subject may be left in abeyance. Suffice it to have shown that personalism cannot entertain the possibility of a Real or Phenomenalist Logic, in the sense in which Grote uses these terms as well as the term 'phenomenon.'

v. Transition

Regarding the nature of Grote's professed idealism, or personalism, we will consider in the following chapter the introspective method as exemplified in Locke and others. An attempt will be made to understand the basis which led Locke to declare that certain qualities were present in the mind and others present in objects. The analysis and criticism which this discussion involves will be followed in Chapter VIII by a consideration of the issues to which this introspective method in knowledge leads, namely, immediateness and reflection. Following this topic it seems appropriate to devote Chapter IX to the significance of personalism in Grote's writings. The next step, however, is to analyze the introspective method in knowledge, and to this subject we will now proceed.

---

[1] Flewelling, "Personalism," in Runes, TCP, 327.
[2] Op. cit., 323.

CHAPTER VII

THE INTROSPECTIVE METHOD IN KNOWLEDGE

1. INTRODUCTION

i. Introspection concerned both with
'knowing' and 'the known'

Let us turn from a consideration of Phenomenalist Logic where the basis for knowledge is erroneously, according to Grote, regarded as real independent of us, to a consideration of the introspectionist method in knowledge. For without that which is introspected there can be no knowledge. That is, the field of the introspective is necessary to all knowledge, and without this field, or, more specifically, without 'philosophy' or consciousness there could be phenomena. Since the thought side of reality is so significant it seems appropriate to devote a special chapter to it.

It may be stated, at the outset, that the examination of what goes on in the human mind during any process of knowing is an application of the introspective method in knowledge. Knowledge, with which the introspective method deals, concerns both knowing and the known. Specifically, introspection should confine itself to 'knowing,'[1] but since all knowing is inseparably connected with what 'knowing' knows, or at least the reference to the known – it is fundamental, in the introspective method as employed by anyone, to consider 'the known,' the object, or the datum, only as this is necessarily and inseparably related to knowing. We are not here concerned with a description of physics, chemistry, biology, etc. Introspection, then, is specifically an epistemological issue and is not clearly bound to idealistic monism where the self is all-important, nor to dualism where

---

[1] For introspection is "observation directed upon the self or its mental states and operations. The term is the modern equivalent of 'reflection' and 'inner sense' as employed by Locke and Kant." Runes, DOP, 149.

there is what we may call 'introspecting' and 'the introspected.'

It is important to notice this vast area over which introspection may spread – now into a field whose universe of discourse is thinking, and again pointing to a field of 'objective' reality, or of things thought of. However hard we may work to keep introspection in the field of thinking, the attempt will meet with inevitable disaster, for it will overflow the boundaries of this enclosure and flood the adjoining area.

ii. Ideas not innate but of empirical origin

Locke attempted to curtail introspection and found himself at one time denying innate ideas when he advocated a 'tabula rasa' theory, and professed knowledge to be of empirical origin. At another time he accepts the view that there are ideas of various sorts though he is never clear as to whether these ideas are wholly self originated or an inevitable result of our experience with objects in everyday life.

He does say, however, that our senses convey into the mind distinct perceptions of things according to the way that objects affect the senses. This is the professed empirical character of Locke's philosophy. The introspection side is also evident in Locke's thinking. Both the mental and the empirical emphases appear in the following:

The object of sensation one source of ideas. – First. Our senses, conversant about particular sensible objects, do convey into the mind several distinct perceptions of things, according to those various ways wherein those objects do affect them.[1]

The operations of our minds the other source of them. – Secondly. The other fountain, from which experience furnisheth the understanding with ideas, is the perception of the operations of our own minds within us, as it is employed about the ideas it has got.[2]

The mind can neither make nor destroy them. – These simple ideas, the materials of all our knowledge, are suggested and furnished to the mind only by those two ways above mentioned, viz., sensation and reflection. When the understanding is once stored with these simple ideas, it has the power to repeat, compare, and unite them, even to an almost infinite variety, and so can make at pleasure new complex ideas. But it is not in the power of the most exalted wit or enlarged understanding, by any quickness or variety of thoughts, to invent or frame one new simple idea in the mind, not taken in by the ways before mentioned; nor can any force of the understanding destroy those that are there.[3]

Locke states that the mind "can make at pleasure new complex ideas" and that "the mind can neither make nor destroy" simple ideas. This shows the active and the passive characteristics of the mind which account for the ideas that we have.

[1] Locke, EHU, in Frost, MOP, 378.
[2] *Op. cit.*, 379.
[3] *Op. cit.*, 380, 381.

iii. Reflection has both active and passive elements

Before dealing specifically with Grote's examination of Locke, let us still further, consider some basic reflections on Locke's introspective method. The introspective method, professedly dealing, in Locke's *Essay*, with reflection, does not confine itself to *reflecting*, merely. Reflecting is always a reflecting upon something. It is as though introspection has both active and passive elements in it, the part that introspects and the part that is introspected. This question has to do with the reflective capacity of the human mind, which is dealt with in considerable detail in Chapter VIII of this dissertation under the heading, "Immediateness and Reflection."

The reflective character of the introspective method is justifiably restricting in its emphasis as it confines attention to the self. Introspection tends toward being more and more solipsistic as it leaves reflection behind and approaches immediateness; it becomes less and less solipsistic as it leaves immediateness behind and approaches reflection. Complete immediateness where there is no reflection at all, is never reached, Grote means to point out. Introspection in this sense of an utmost solipsistic extreme is impossible. It can be regarded as a limit no more capable of comprehension than an infinite magnitude. Introspection, then, may be regarded as more and more solipsistic when it approaches this limit, and less and less solipsistic as it progressively moves away from it. Solipsism characterized, thus, by degrees, shares this character with introspection.

Introspection is necessarily solipsistic, but it cannot be so extremely solipsistic that its confines would be infinitely small – so much so that the momentary states of the very psychic self would be so infinitesimally minute that they would scarcely allow of being considered at all. This introspecting is of an 'introspected,' but the introspected are better described as our own past and future experiences rather than 'objects.'

But we must distinguish further. The introspecting mind is surrounded by objects either of a psychic or physical nature. The active phase of introspection requires that other phase upon which it acts. Aristotle affirmed an inescapable fact when he presented 'action' and 'passion' as categories.[1]

---

[1] "Expressions which are in no way composite signify substance, quantity, quality, relation, place, time, position, state, action, or affection." Aristotle, BWA, 8.

iv. Two questions faced in this chapter

With these general remarks on the introspective method we are ready to introduce Grote into the scene of the introspective method and knowledge. In this chapter we must face two questions, namely, first, the nature of our problem, and second, the method employed in dealing with it. The first question has already been presented. It is to consider the chief issues involved in the introspective method, which issues are especially concerned with 'thinking' and its 'objects.' The second question, regarding methodology, has not yet been dealt with; we will consider in turn the issues as they arise from the specific epistemological positions of Locke, Berkeley, Hume, Spencer, and (to some small extent) Morell. Let us now turn to the second question, regarding method, which also commits us to dealing with the issues involved in introspection as these arise in connection with the various philosophers on whom we now center attention.

2. LOCKE'S PSYCHOLOGY

i. Error in the introspective method

The introspective method as Locke uses it involves what Grote refers to as 'mis-psychology' or 'bad psychology' where things perceived are considered apart from (or even before) our perceiving of them. What is involved here is "the mis-psychological supposition of the independence, first, of the things perceived, and of our then, as such, perceiving them." [1]

ii. Mis-psychology

To see the source of the fundamental confusion in the introspective method, for example, of Locke, let us consider 'mis-psychology' more fully. Since this psychological approach to epistemology is evident in the introspective methods of the British Empiricists [2] we will do well to analyze it further to see its significance in the whole noetic process.

Sometimes Grote refers to "the mis-psychological supposition" as attaching itself to what he calls "'the Philosophy of the Human Mind' or Psychology." 'Mis-psychology' is 'wrong psychology' which consists, substantially, in the attempt to analyze our consciousness while nevertheless we suppose ourselves, who have the consciousness, to be particular

---

[1] Grote, EP, I, 242.
[2] We will consider chiefly Locke, Berkeley, and Hume.

local beings in the midst of an universe of things or objects similar to what we ourselves are.[1]

'Mis-psychology' may be traced as originating in the relation of the individual to the human race, and may be illustrated by our mode of speech as in the remark, 'A stone lies before me: I see it.'

The great mass of 'the Philosophy of the Human Mind' is in its details an attempt at a Real Logic of individual knowledge; an attempt vitiated in various ways. For this Real Logic of the individual is of more complicated and difficult consideration than the Real Logic of the knowledge of the race, unless we may say that this, to counterbalance, has difficulties of a different kind. The greater difficulty is in this: that we are considering the growth of the knowledge of *one* mind in the midst of a quantity of others where the knowledge exists. This I believe, at bottom, is the origin of the mis-psychological error on which I comment so abundantly. 'A stone lies before me: I see it.' We put this down quite naturally in the account of the growth of individual knowledge, not apparently thinking that the *first* clause is *other* people's knowledge: the second is the step of *mine*: and, *now*, that the step is taken, I say the stone lies before *me*.[2]

Let us look at 'mis-psychology' and see if it can be defined more explicitly than it is defined or explained above. Mis-psychology is an approach to reality in which there is the supposition of the independence of the 'things' perceived, and second, our perceiving of them. Leaving this definition, let us now look at a brief explanation or illustration. Take the sentence, "We see things, touch them, and thus know that they exist." Mis-psychology (otherwise also called 'bad psychology,' or 'wrong psychology') would analyze this sentence into three steps: (1) The 'things' are there for us to see. (2) We see and touch them. (3) We infer from this seeing and touching that the things exist.

It is important to consider the generic distinction which is made between the idea and the fact involved in the case of seeing an object, for example, a stone. It is not fact, *as fact*, which requires an idea to complete it, but it is rather, the fact that is not accounted for:

For the notion of the generic distinction of the idea from the fact, there needs to be substituted the notion which I gave above, that it is not the fact, qua fact, which wants the ideas as something to complete it, but the fact as unaccounted for. "We see two trees of different kinds; but we cannot know that they are so, except by applying to them our idea of the resemblance and difference which makes kinds." The superinduction of the idea upon the fact as fact is just that same relativism and wrong psychology united which makes us suppose the existing universe first, and then speculate how we know it... When we first see the trees, how do they seem to us? of the same kind? then what leads us to apply to them the idea which makes us change our mind about them and think them

---

[1] Grote, EP, I, ix.
[2] *Op. cit.*, 153.

of different kinds? Or, on the other hand, do we see them of different kinds? then we *do* know their difference already before the idea is applied. Or, again, do we see them of *no* kind? but then we do not see them as trees: they cannot be trees to us without the thought on our part of kind.[1]

What Grote is concerned about pointing out here is that, in the case, for example, of seeing, there is no actual seeing *until* there is the idea. And after the seeing takes place, the idea is not needed for that seeing, but may be needed very much for what that particular seeing suggests. We should notice the distinction, and also the relation, between the idea and the fact here, Grote would seem to say. And it is not the fact, *as fact* that requires the idea to complete it. For the fact, *as fact*, must somehow have an idea already or *it could not be fact*. But what does need an idea to complete it is the fact that is unaccounted for. By a statement like this last one Grote implies that there are many 'things' yet that we do not know. These are the 'things' that are unaccounted for. And before we can actually know these things there must be an idea (or ideas) to complete them.

iii. The mind as a tabula rasa

'Mis-psychology' comes in when we regard fact *qua* fact before we have an idea of the fact. It is all right to refer to fact *qua* fact if we already have an idea of the fact, that is, if the fact is a *known* fact, and has relation to us. Otherwise to refer to fact without idea, or thought of the fact, is meaningless. Grote is implying that mis-psychology is evident in much of Locke's *Essay*. Quite independently of Grote's statements we may fairly assert that Locke's affirmation concerning the mind as a *tabula rasa* at birth and that all knowledge comes to us from experience is knowledge resulting from the 'experiencing' of the 'experienced.'

An uncompromising and decisive dualism in which we have ideas on the one hand, and facts on the other, in abstraction from each other is simply fictional. Because all facts already have ideas connected with them, Grote seems to be saying that Locke sometimes expresses himself in this type of dualistic language, where the 'perceived' is abstracted from that which perceives it. That is, if the mind is a *tabula rasa* at birth then there are no ideas but simply those *facts* in isolation (from ideas). This is what is meant above when we said that, "all knowledge comes to us from experience is knowledge resulting from the 'experiencing' of the 'experienced.'" That is, quite evidently, we cannot have

[1] Grote, EP, I, 236, 237.

the 'experienced' except in necessary relation to that which is 'experiencing' (the 'experienced'). It would be presumptuous to state that Locke engages in fictional demarcations. Yet there is a close resemblance between Locke's introspective method and such abstractions as the two above, namely, of mind from objects, and objects from mind.

iv. All experience requires ideas

Locke obliterates the view which he presents for consideration, to the effect that the mind has ideas at birth. Without some sort of a semblance of ideas nothing even of the vaguest sort could ever be experienced. For the 'experienced' must *be* to someone. Even to speak of the empirical world for a *tabula rasa* mind is to give that mind an empirical world that has no meaning at all! We are therefore forced to the conclusion that with a postulate of a *tabula rasa* mind must go necessarily, a *tabula rasa* empirical world as far as that mind is concerned. This is equivalent to saying that if there are no ideas at all, not even very poorly or partially developed ones, then neither is there for that mind an empirical world.

The preceding paragraph is an attempt to give a free rendering of Grote's criticism of Locke. Grote seems to have an important point in mind here. In language fundamental for the whole of his *Exploratio Philosophica*, it can be said that Locke sometimes makes the mistake of considering what Grote calls phenomenal reality, as simply phenomena *qua* phenomena without any regard for phenomena *qua* 'philosophy.' Phenomena are *never* wholly abstracted *from us*, according to Grote. If they were, then there would be nothing to give them any meaning either noetically or as effects upon us in some other way.

Now, it seems to Grote, in terms of his fundamental epistemological thesis regarding the essential connection between phenomena and 'philosophy' that Locke has sometimes written as though phenomena *could* be wholly abstracted from 'philosophy.' And one of the places where Locke seems to do this is where he speaks of that which is *absolutely essential* for 'philosophy' (namely, a mind that is *not tabula rasa*), as non-existent.

v. Ideas give the 'external world' meaning

These propositions, although not specific statements of Grote, seem to be supported by him. Now, let us come a bit closer to the specific critical analysis which Grote contributes to the introspective method in knowledge, and also see at the same time how he supports the argument presented above. In his explanation of what takes place in the human mind when we think, Locke denied what he needed for the explanation in his rejection of 'innate ideas.' Only through experience and contact with external objects can ideas come, according to Locke. The external world waits, he says, for mind to come into contact with it. But he might just as well have said that mind waits for the external world to come into contact with it. To speak of an external world (and therefore a world abstracted from mind) at all, is superfluous, one must conclude. There isn't in the *tabula rasa* mind anything that would give the 'external world' meaning and hence the perceived would have no meaning. To speak of an external world is already taking for granted what already has been denied, namely, an external world for the *tabula rasa* 'mind.' In his introspection, then, Locke was not justified in stating that mind has no ideas even partially formed; he might as well have said that for that mind there is no external world either. And if there is no external world for that mind there can be no growth of knowledge, for such growth depends upon the existence of the empirical world in relation to it.

vi. Phenomenal reality cannot produce thought

Now, there does appear to be a better solution for this difficulty than the one which Locke offers. The prerequisites in this solution seem to be offered by Grote if we consider his distinction between 'philosophy' and phenomenalism. Briefly, it may be paraphrased as follows: Phenomenal reality, as Grote uses this term, which is essentially communication between the 'world' and the sense organs, nerves, and other essentially non-sensible parts of the body, affects us even though we may be wholly unaware of this action. (We must always keep in mind that phenomena *qua* phenomena do not involve consciousness, for Grote. This fact is embraced in the peculiar and unusual sense in which he uses the term.) No amount of such stimulation, affection, or action can ever produce any ideas whatsoever unless the mind makes some sort of contribution, through consciousness, awareness, activity, or however we may describe this essentially conscious part of life. Now if the mind is a *tabula rasa*, how does knowing ever begin in the first place, to say nothing of a knowing process going on which increases so that we have a right to refer to the mind as having ideas?

In his method of introspection, which is essentially a consideration of what it is that the mind knows, Locke virtually says that first the mind knows nothing. This is the view he professes, *but* the view he does *not* profess has already boldly entered the scene through his assertion that there is an external world for the mind that *has no ideas*! For the external world is already – since Locke speaks of it as existing – a sort of partially formed, more than potential (in Aristotle's sense of potency), idea.[1] Locke supports this last statement himself when he refers to the concurrence of the idea and the thing:

When Locke says, an idea is right if it agrees with the thing, what purpose is served by the language? For what is the *thing* to us except the idea which we have of it...? If we can know the facts in any independent way, so as to be able to test the notions which we form of them by the facts themselves, what is the good of forming the notions, if the facts are already known?" [2]

vii. Primary and secondary qualities

The concurrence of the idea with the thing (which strangely enough is regarded by Locke as a 'thing' before we even have an idea of it) is a situation presented by Locke as legitimate which nevertheless is classed by Grote as 'mis-psychology.' This criticism of Grote's, which seems to be well made, applies also to Locke's classification of qualities into primary and secondary. Let us, then, look at this classification. 'Mis-psychology' repeatedly has appeared in Locke's writings sometimes in a subtle and intricate form. The primary qualities as Locke enunciated them were figure, number, situation, bulk, etc., and rest or motion, which *are in* the object as well as in our perception of it. The secondary qualities, as color, taste, and sound, are really modes of perception brought about by the characteristics of the objects which do not, however, coincide with the perception.

In general, then, when the senses come into contact with the external world we receive, passively, general or elementary ideas. Here, Locke is assuming the external world as such even before we have ideas of it. But the external world is such only because we already have an idea (however vague or undeveloped) of it. That is, it is no more true that the mind is passively awaiting the 'external world' to affect it – thus giving it ideas, than that the external world is awaiting the mind to come along with ideas of it – thus giving to it, its nature as the 'external world.' This is partly what Grote's division in epistemology into 'philosophical' and phenomenal aspects, amounts to. Grote is virtually saying that you cannot separate knowledge into ideas and what the ideas are of, and say that the latter affects us so that we have ideas.

---

[1] Substance is, for Locke, "something I know not what."
[2] Grote, EP, II, 90.

That is, conscious states exemplified in the nature of ideas simply cannot be brought about by the phenomenal reality of the 'external world.' The most that phenomenal reality can do is to communicate with our bodily organs and senses. The *awareness* must be left up to the non-phenomenal factors which are the only ones that can give meaning to anything.

So, to say that the primary qualities of objects affect us so that ideas are produced implies that the phenomenal world (*qua* phenomenal) is creative of ideas. The point is that phenomenal reality does not create anything at all on the thought side of any epistemological issue. If this is so, as there seems excellent reason to believe, (on the basis of what has already been presented many times throughout this book, in distinguishing 'philosophy' from phenomena) then the mind is not a *tabula rasa* at all, but is activated by ideas in a sort of medium of consciousness, or awareness, which assumes a necessary 'philosophical' approach in questions concerning introspection and reality. Then to speak of powers in objects capable of bringing about the secondary qualities in us is erroneous. In fact to speak at all, of primary qualities as in the object is to assume that we already have ideas of these qualities and hence to say that they produce ideas in us is superfluous.

viii. Interrelations among ideas

Now, let us look at the introspective method as it deals with interrelations of ideas. According to Locke we are aware, however it happens, of external things (such as objects, qualities in them, etc.) to begin with, and these give rise to ideas. The ideas in some virtually mysterious manner become interwoven and related so that the objects are then created for the mind just as though they did not exist before this.

It is to be observed that all those ideas which either sensation or reflection imprints upon the understanding are all pure and unblended, and therefore I call Simple Ideas; as are those of whiteness, blackness, heat, cold, softness, length, or extension, unity, and all the particular tastes and smells, and other sensible qualities for which we have no names, and also thinking in all the several modes of it; which the understanding, when it is stored with, has the power and faculty to join together, enlarge, compare one with another, and consider them with reference to others, which is all a sort of comparing, and unite even to an almost infinite variety and so make at pleasure new complex ideas.[1]

The mystery involved in the interrelating of ideas is no mystery for Locke for he plainly states that when the mind is stored with simple

[1] Rand, EHU, 66.

ideas it has the power of joining together, enlarging, and comparing them with each other in an infinite variety so that complex ideas are possible. One might state that this is a capacity that one would scarcely expect to find in a mind that, previous to the possession of simple ideas, had to wait for impressions to be made by 'objects' so that ideas were formed. That the mystery is not so easily explained may be illustrated in the following:

Locke betrays considerable perplexity in his attempt to give an account of ideas of relation and the manner of their formation in accordance with his preconceived theory of complex ideas.[1]

Now it seems that Locke, in stating how complex ideas are formed, is emphasizing the 'philosophical' approach to epistemology, and that he is doing this as though there were, for the time being at least, no phenomenal reality to which this 'philosophical' approach applies.

ix. Locke emphasizes the 'philosophical' and the phenomenal approaches to epistemology, interchangeably

That Locke emphasizes now one point of view, that of consciousness, and again the other point of view, that of phenomena, is recognized by another English philosopher.

The confusion of the two points of view usually appears (as in Locke's philosophy, and again in Hamilton's) in the twin assumptions of a material world existing independently of being known and a mind or consciousness which knows this independently existing world.[2]

Hence one may conclude that the Lockian introspective method in knowledge is confused by a mixing of two fundamental approaches that may be taken in epistemology. The basis of this criticism of the introspective method is the same as that employed in dealing with Sir William Hamilton who took a double point of view, namely, that of consciousness of mental states on the one hand, and – what was a much different kind of consciousness – consciousness of matter on the other.

x. Grote's suggested improvement for Locke's introspective method

a. Locke should have recognized the 'purely mental experience' in our mental history

Grote holds that Locke, true to his professed empirical starting-point, should have asserted that there is 'purely mental experience' in

[1] Gibson, JL, 21.
[2] Forsyth, EP, 140.

our mental history, and that would have removed the view that the mind was originally a blank tablet – and it would have been in conformity with Locke's empiricism. This 'purely mental experience' would cause us to infer that there is fact outside of us, so that we could say there is experience analyzable into 'experiencing' and 'experienced.' Thus we might conclude that the fact of the external world would gradually become known to us. This is, at least, the general procedure that Locke's epistemology could have followed. And this procedure would be an advance from consciousness where 'purely mental experience' resides, to phenomenal reality which is none the less real even when we are not conscious of it though it does not become real until it is *real for us* (through awareness). This procedure seems to be advocated by Grote as more consistent in the sense that there would not be an assumption of 'the external world' even before we have any idea of it where the mind is a *tabula rasa*.

b. Appraisal of Grote's suggestion

Whether Grote's suggested procedure would have been as fruitful for Locke as the one Locke himself followed is open to speculation. There might have been much less likelihood of 'mis-psychology' (noö-psychology, or 'bad psychology') but it might have so restricted Locke that he would eventually decide to sacrifice the contribution that he made in order to be consistent and so, probably, would never have given us *An Essay Concerning Human Understanding* at all.

3. HUME'S RATIONALISM

i. 'Mis-psychology'

Like Locke, Hume seems guilty of a 'mis-psychological' approach to knowledge. Grote is going to try to explode the skeptical basis from which Hume views rationalistic theories since Hume affirmed that reality has primarily an empirical basis. It will be noted throughout this discussion of Hume that there is a strong strain of rationalism in Hume and that Grote, generally, tends to overlook this rationalism. In overlooking Hume's rationalism Grote tends to look upon Hume as more of a phenomenalist than he is justified in doing.

Yet, Grote maintains that Hume, in referring to the creative power of mind and the activity of the senses when we have 'impressions,' is correct. Let us look at the following statement by Hume:

This creative power of the mind amounts to no more than the faculty of compounding, transposing, augmenting, or diminishing the materials afforded us
by the senses and experience. When we think of a golden mountain, we only
join two consistent ideas, gold, and mountain, with which we were formerly
acquainted. A virtuous horse we can conceive; because, from our own feeling,
we can conceive virtue; and this we may unite to the figure and shape of a horse,
which is an animal familiar to us. In short, all the materials of thinking are
derived either from our outward or inward sentiment: the mixture and composition of these belongs alone to the mind and will. Or, to express myself in
philosophical language, all our ideas or more feeble perceptions are copies of
our impressions or more lively ones.[1]

But there is much evidence of elements of 'bad psychology' in this
passage. This error is especially evident where the

creative power of the mind amounts to no more than the faculty of compounding,
transposing, augmenting, or diminishing the materials afforded us by the senses
and experience.[2]

Here, Hume assumes that there are 'materials afforded us by the
senses.' These materials are not materials at all for the mind if the
mind is not allowed as being present in order that 'materials' would
have meaning. Now, 'materials' are in the same position in Hume's
writing here, as phenomena are in Grote's *Exploratio Philosophica*.
But, for Grote, phenomena *for us* always require awareness. One might
comment on Grote's position here to the effect that Hume cannot
regard 'materials' as such apart from mind, as though they have no
relationship with mind and yet are related to mind so that we can
know them! Grote observes too that Hume shifts emphasis back and
forth between the 'philosophical' and the phenomenal as though there
were at times a definite distinction between – to put it generally – the
'subjective' or the thought side in epistemology, and the 'objective'
or the 'external world' side. Hume speaks at times as though reality
is reality *without us*, that is, without any relation to self, and again he
refers to it as a *reality for self*. Hume inclined to confuse perceiving
with the object perceived.

That Hume is inclined to be confused here, is supported by the
following observation:

What Hume really did in his work on the external perception, was to shift his
attention from the objects generally perceived, on to the conscious experience
of perception itself. This is not to say that he always realized what was involved
in this change of attitude. He was often inclined to confuse the 'perception'
with the object perceived, and to argue, – that because space, time and matter,
and all that they involved, were not themselves to be found in the 'perception,'

[1] Hume, EHU, 16.
[2] *Loc. cit.*

although they were undoubtedly 'perceived,' that space, time, and matter, did not really exist.[1]

To say that space, time, matter, and all that they involved are not to be found in the 'perception' "although they are undoubtedly 'perceived'" is to make the error of 'bad psychology' to which Grote calls attention. For Grote contends that we cannot say that anything is 'perceived' without also being "found in the 'perception.'" What Grote is actually saying here is that there is one reality, and two aspects or ways of looking at this reality, that is, from the point of view of consciousness and the point of view of phenomena.

ii. Strong tendency toward rationalism

It is interesting to note that Mill, contending for what Grote calls, a Real or Phenomenalist Logic, implies that Hume should have regarded matter as an original fact of consciousness. But that Hume had this in mind is evident from what he says about 'unknown causes,' or as it is otherwise expressed: "Substance is the unknown, indescribable support of the known contents of ideas." [2] That is, Mill implies that matter can be postulated as *real* even apart from consciousness, and that we can then be conscious of what we have postulated without any consciousness being present at all. Mill doesn't quite say that the presence of consciousness is not required. This position would be too glaringly defective. But, the point is that Mill tends to develop a Real Logic, as the last chapter indicated. Differing with Grote and agreeing with Salmon, I contend that Hume is much more rationalistic than Grote makes him out to be. Moreover, Hume's rationalism does not allow him to be identified with the generally phenomenal position presented in a considerable portion of Mill's logic. The justification for mentioning the subjectivistic and objectivistic strains in Hume at all is to show that at one time he follows the phenomenal approach and at another time the 'philosophical.' Ideas, Hume holds, are pale copies of impressions; and impressions are received from experience. Ideas should be regarded as pale copies of what is received from experience. But Hume is assuming experience corresponding to which there are no ideas, and having made this step he is ready to say that there are ideas of what he has already accepted without ideas. This is the 'bad psychology' to which Grote refers.

[1] Salmon, CPH, 14.
[2] Windelband, HOP, 473.

Let us subject the following passage to sufficient analysis to present the point that Grote is trying to make here:

Suppose... a person to have enjoyed his sight for thirty years, and to have become perfectly acquainted with colours of all kinds except one particular shade of blue, for instance, which it never has been his fortune to meet with. Let all the different shades of that colour, except that single one, be placed before him, descending gradually from the deepest to the lightest; it is plain that he will perceive a blank, where that shade is wanting, and will be sensible that there is a greater distance in that place between the contiguous colours than in any other. Now I ask, whether it be possible for him, from his own imagination, to supply this deficiency, and raise up to himself the idea of that particular shade, though it had never been conveyed to him by his senses? I believe there are few but will be of opinion that he can: and this may serve as a proof that the simple ideas are not always, in every instance, derived from the correspondent impressions; though this instance is so singular, that it is scarcely worth our observing, and does not merit that for it alone we should alter our general maxim.[1]

Hume clearly means to imply that ideas are "derived from the correspondent impressions," when he says that "the simple ideas are not always, in every instance, derived from the correspondent impression."

Now this means, in the language of Grote, that Hume is using 'bad psychology' in asserting that there are impressions from which ideas are derived. For, Grote would say here that if an impression *means* something then we must have an idea of it already. In that case, Grote would remark that, we have ideas of impressions even before ideas are derived from 'the correspondent impressions'!

Again, it is evident, according to Hume, that impressions *do mean* something, for: "By the term *impression*... I mean all our more lively perceptions, when we hear, or see, or feel, or love, or hate, or desire, or will." [2] Already, then, Grote would assert, there are ideas of the impressions, even before the ideas are "derived from" them. That is, wherever we have Grote's phenomena there is an 'inside' to them which may be designated variously as 'philosophy,' 'consciousness,' or even 'ideas.'

iii. 'The creative power of the mind'

Grote appears to criticize Hume somewhat too severely, for Hume regarded 'the creative power of the mind' as an important factor in knowledge. Now, if Hume were completely empirical his strictly objective approach in epistemology would be as glaringly evident as

---

[1] Hume, EHU, 18, 19.
[2] *Op. cit.*, 15.

Grote makes it out to be. The view that he was *not* an outright empiricist is supported in the following:

It is seriously misleading to say that Hume was an empiricist 'pure and simple'; such a view arises by neglecting the more or less tacit assumptions that lie in the background of Hume's philosophy but none the less effectively determine the nature of his conclusions. So far as his ideal of what ought to constitute true knowledge is concerned, Hume is almost if not quite as much a rationalist as Locke; his extension of empirical principles consists largely in irrefutable proofs that the rationalist ideal is unattainable, a suspicion which Locke shared, though with only the most confused perception of its consequences.[1]

Yet Grote's view of the very great significance to be attached to Hume's empiricism is not an isolated one. A sharing of this view by others is evidenced in the following statement:

It is in virtue of the relentless faithfulness with which he follows out the logical consequences of the empirical point of view that we are compelled to admit that in the 'Treatise of Human Nature,' the logic of empiricism works itself out to its inevitable conclusions... We cannot describe the sceptical philosophy of Hume as the complete logical development of the Lockian and Berkeleian philosophy, but only as the logical completion of the empirical element in the philosophy of his predecessors. That which had for them been a part becomes for Hume the whole; he is an empiricist pure and simple, and he shows us with singular insight the ultimate meaning and consequences of pure empiricism.[2]

iv. Place of mind in 'impression'

Hume, however, does not disregard the important place that mind has in what he calls 'impression,' particularly when he holds that ideas (as mental entities) are pale *copies* of impressions. It is scarcely possible to give mind as subordinate a place as Grote does in considering Hume as an empiricist. That there are rationalistic elements evident in Hume is manifest from the following:

Now I ask, whether it be possible for him, (that is, a person who enjoyed his sight for thirty years) from his own imagination, to supply this deficiency, and raise up to himself the idea of that particular shade, though it had never been conveyed to him by his senses? I believe there are few but will be of opinion that he can: and this may serve as a proof that the simple ideas are not always, in every instance, derived from the correspondent impressions.[3]

Here Hume makes provision for the mind to form an idea *without* a "correspondent impression."

However, Grote seems unjustified in taking a particular passage from Hume, and in dwelling at length on this extract in order to exhibit the possible imperfection in Hume's argument. It is quite possible that

---

[1] Sabine, PE, 43, 44.
[2] Seth, EPS, 150.
[3] Hume, EHU, 18, 19.

this unfairness is due to the fact that Grote, after a study of Kant's *Critique of Pure Reason* (especially in regard to the categories), became fully convinced of the weakness of Hume in giving less place than he should have to the mind in considering a problem like that of causality.

v. Relations

Actually, Hume in the sections dealing with the association of ideas [1] and skeptical doubts concerning the operations of the understanding [2] deals with various types of relations. Relations amongst ideas include resemblance, contrariety, and cause and effect. Relations depending upon matters of fact include identity, time and place relations, and again cause and effect. At first sight it would seem presumptuous to criticize this distinction of Hume's. But a second look enables us to see that the distinction seems somewhat arbitrarily made. For example, Hume doesn't seem quite sure where to place cause and effect relations and settles the question for himself fairly satisfactorily by holding that these relations have to do with 'Matters of Fact.' "All reasonings concerning matter of fact seem to be founded on the relation of *Cause and Effect*." [3]

Matters of fact, then, depend upon relations of cause and effect.

If you were to ask a man, why he believes any matter of fact, which is absent; for instance, that his friend is in the country, or in France; he would give you a reason; and this reason would be some other fact; as a letter received from him, or the knowledge of his former resolutions and promises. A man finding a watch or any other machine in a desert island, would conclude that there once had been men in that island.[4]

But that there is a clear affirmation of 'thought' or 'thing' relations is a tantalizing hope that turns out to be illusion. It seems that Kant was awakened from his dogmatic slumber by observing Hume wrestling with this problem in an arena of relations. Grote, too, surmised that all was not well and began searching for a defect. He found one which assured him still more that his hypothesis of a basic distinction in epistemology, between the phenomenal and 'philosophical' approaches, was correct.

vi. Are cause and effect relations concerned with ideas or with matters or fact?

Grote could well ask, Are cause and effect relations concerned with ideas or with matters of fact? Grote seems to conclude that Hume,

[1] Hume, EHU, sec. III.
[2] *Op. cit.*, sec. IV.
[3] *Op. cit.*, 24.
[4] *Op. cit.*, 24, 25.

true to his professed empiricism, holds that these relations deal with matters of fact. Then Grote is ready to show that cause and effect relations are already accepted as matters of fact, even previous to any corresponding relations amongst cause and effect as ideas. And he is ready to point out that this is the defect of the phenomenal approach where 'things' are accepted as existing even before they are connected with mind, and that 'things' can only be considered as such *to a mind* which regards them as things. Grote could have gone further and said that the same thing holds true of the other matters of fact, namely, identity, and time and place relations, as held true (as we just pointed out) in the case of relations of cause and effect.[1]

vii. Idea, impression, and 'impressioning'

Now, what is said about matters of fact being considered apart from ideas can also be said about Hume's whole discussion of 'impression' and 'idea.' "By the term 'impression,' then, I mean all our more lively perceptions, when we hear or see or feel or love or hate or desire or will." [2] Here the term 'perception' is vague. It may mean something perceived, or the act of perceiving, and we are left uncertain what Hume meant. It seems quite possible that the reason for this uncertainty is founded on the possibility that Hume himself was not too clear whether he should be emphasizing the subjective or the objective phases of the question. If he meant to imply that *ideas* are involved, in emphasizing the *subjective* side of 'impression' he could have used some such term as 'impressioning.' If he meant to imply that *things* are involved, in stressing the *objective* side of 'impression' then 'things' are considered apart from any mind to which they are 'things'! Also, such a term as 'impressioning' is hardly a good substitute for 'idea.'

---

[1] It will clarify remarks made on relations to note specifically how Hume classifies these relations.

There are seven different kinds of philosophical relation, *viz. resemblance, identity, relations of time and place, proportion in quantity or number, degrees in any quality, contrariety, and causation.* These relations may be divided into two classes; into such as depend entirely on the ideas, which we compare together, and such as may be chang'd without any change in the ideas. Hume, THN, 185.

It appears ... that of these seven philosophical relations, there remain only four, which depending solely upon ideas, can be the objects of knowledge and certainty. These four are *resemblance, contrariety, degrees in quality, and proportions in quantity or number.* Hume, THN, 186.

This is all I think necessary to observe concerning those four relations, which are the foundation of science; but as to the other three, which depend not upon the idea, and may be absent or present even while *that* remains the same, 'twill be proper to explain them more particularly. These three relations are *identity, the situations in time and place, and causation.* Hume, THN, 190.

[2] Hume, EHU, 15.

And yet this term 'impressioning' seems to express what Hume meant when he used the term 'impression,' for 'impressionings' are clearly more lively and vivid 'ideas.' "The less forcible and lively are commonly denominated *Thoughts* or *Ideas.*" [1]

4. BERKELEY'S SUBJECTIVISM

i. Berkeley's approach wholly 'philosophical'

Berkeley may be contrasted with Hume. Instead of assuming the external world previous to 'impressions' (or 'impressionings') Berkeley did not regard the universe of 'things' as existing at all. Ideas are the only reality. Berkeley's approach in epistemology is wholly 'philosophical.' Berkeley, a subjective idealist, possesses the virtue of consistency.

ii. Importance of judgment

In his *Theory of Vision*, Berkeley holds that people are generally biased since they regard the 'things' that they see as real external objects, whereas the true account, according to Berkeley, is that the judgment intercedes on behalf of sight in order that the seen may be real to the mind. Taking the case of a blind man who recovered his sight, Berkeley indicates the importance of judgment:

For, we have shown that to the immediate objects of sight, considered in themselves, he would not attribute the terms high and low... Without this motion of the eye, this turning it up and down in order to discern different objects, doubtless 'erect,' 'inverse,' and other the like terms relating to the position of tangible objects, would never have been transferred, or in any degree apprehended to belong to the ideas of sight – the mere act of seeing including nothing in it to that purpose; whereas the different situations of the eye naturally *direct the mind to make a suitable judgment* [2] of the situation of objects intromitted by it. [3]

Berkeley states that we see 'perspectively' when what we see is sometimes regarded as in association with things. In order that the real may be *seen*, judgment must be present. The basis for this judgment may be seen in the following remark by Philonous:

Whatever opinion we father on Him, it must be either because He has discovered it to us by supernatural revelation; or because it is so evident to our natural faculties, which were framed and given us by God. [4]

[1] Hume, EHU, 15.
[2] Italics mine.
[3] Berkeley, WOR, I, 81.
[4] *Op. cit.*, 339.

Berkeley's use of judgment in reference to distance is significant. Distance may be 'seen' but cannot be calculated without judgment acting on behalf of what is seen. In other words it is simply nervous affection that is responsible for what is 'seen,' and then through experience (the important part of which for Berkeley is judgment) the distance is calculated.

iii. Vision at the eye

Berkeley believed that one's vision of the so-called 'external' world is all *at* one's eye.

An account of some observations made by a young gentleman, who was born blind,... When he first saw, he was so far from making any judgment about distances, that he thought all objects whatever touched his eyes (as he express'd it) as what he felt did his skin.[1]

Grote attempts to refute this view by showing that a person just recovering from blindness would really not see things *at* the eye.

We have only to affect the eye: there might be imagined medicaments for the optic nerve which might enable us to live in a visible world of our own, perpetually varying and of whatever beauty we pleased and could pre-imagine. But all this gives us no reason to consider that a person beginning to see will see things as at the eye. What is in the eye is nervous agitation, and corresponding to this in the world of consciousness is true sensation or thought, and according to the nervous agitation this thought creates the visual object and projects it into space which it has created likewise, and this is its locality as a part of the visual scene. It is at the eye in quite a different sense from the sense in which it has this locality, and no experiences can make a bridge between one and the other.[2]

Neither would one be inclined to think, Grote continues, that, if cured of deafness in the midst of an instrumental concert, one were a victim of head noises! Grote holds that the eye, in the case of the blind receiving sight, is an organ of nervous agitation corresponding to which, in the mind, is thought. But to say that it is 'an organ of nervous agitation' is to become phenomenalistic in one's approach. Berkeley illustrates his view in the following, concerning a "most intelligent boy, nine years of age, who had congenital cataracts of both eyes."[3]

He gradually became more correct in his perception, but it was only after several days that he could or would tell by the eyes alone, which was the sphere and which the cube; when asked, he always, before answering, wished to take both into his hands; even when this was allowed, when immediately afterwards the objects were placed before the eyes, he was not certain of the figure. Of distance he had not the least conception. He said everything touched his eyes,

[1] Berkeley, WOR, I, 444, 445.
[2] Grote, EP, II, 123, 124.
[3] Berkeley, *op. cit.*, II, 413n.

and walked most carefully about, with his hands held out before him, to prevent things hurting his eyes by touching them.[1]

iv. Phenomenalism evident in Berkeley

Grote disagrees with Berkeley, for he does not believe that 'everything touched his eyes.' Grote contends that Berkeley's view commits him to the 'philosophical' approach in knowledge, and (that) the phenomenal approach is simply avoided, or professedly non-existent. Grote is obviously attempting to enrich his hypothesis of the possibility of a division into two possible approaches to the problem of knowledge, namely, the 'philosophical' or 'logical,' and the phenomenal. Grote holds that with equal justification Berkeley could have affirmed that there are phenomena which affects us even when we are not aware of them, and that these phenomena are *real* even though we are not always aware of them. Yet it may be maintained in Berkeley's defence that spirits affect us, especially the divine spirit. Nature (regarded by Grote as phenomenal reality), for Berkeley, is divine language.

Phenomena, in the sense in which Grote uses this term, have no *meaning* apart from some consciousness. It seems, then, that Grote does not differ so greatly from Berkeley as he professes. For Grote virtually holds that in order to have meaning (or 'sense') in anything we must be 'philosophical' in our attitude. It seems that Berkeley would not dispute this and is simply carrying the 'philosophical' lead to knowledge, to its (logical) conclusion, namely, that nothing can mean anything 'without the mind.' Grote seems to be saying somewhat the same thing in another way and by use of different terms, namely, by saying that there are two ways of approaching reality, that is, from the point of view of consciousness, and again from the aspect of phenomena. Whereas, Berkeley approaches reality from one side only, from the *mind*.

But there is an important point in Grote's criticism of Berkeley that should not be overlooked. It is a point that partly concerns the unfortunate way in which it is sometimes necessary to express ourselves. This point is where Grote criticizes Berkeley for stating that in the case of the person recovering his sight all things would be seen *at* the eyes. Now, Berkeley seems to have meant to illustrate that things are *real* on the basis of mind alone. His illustration regarding objects seen *at* the eyes appears unfortunate. For the eyes are *not* mental and are safely classed as 'external' (in the sense

[1] Berkeley, WOR, II, 414, 415.

of external to the mind). So Berkeley still is not showing that 'objects' are mental, at least through the use of this illustration, any more than if he held that 'objects' are somewhere 'out there.' Grote does not seem to have mentioned this point anywhere, nor is there any intimation that he had it in mind. But he could have mentioned it, and shown that Berkeley sometimes mixed phenomena with 'philosophy.'

v. Fundamental agreement between Grote and Berkeley

However, Berkeley's meaning of reality as mental (or spiritual) is prominent. If any illustration is not altogether acceptable it seems to be due to the refractory nature of the problem with which he is dealing. Thus, there is revealed the difficulty of always expressing oneself in 'philosophical' language when to do so seems to overlook the facts of phenomena which affect us even when we are not aware of their so doing. To account for those phenomena by an affirmation of the existence of deity is to admit the existence of such phenomena – though never giving them meaning apart from some mind, either human or divine. In short, that anything can have *meaning* wholly apart from any mind (considered as consciousness) is a view held neither by Berkeley nor Grote. The introspective analysis which each makes of the human mind seems to make such a conclusion legitimate, despite the fact that their main contention is reached by different roads where the respective emphases do not always coincide. It seems to have been the denial of 'a material world' that inspired Mansel to write:

Like Malebranche, Berkeley maintains that the ideas which we perceive are imprinted on our minds by the Author of Nature, to whom they are ever present; and in denying the existence of a material world corresponding to these ideas he merely discarded an assumption which, as far as philosophy was concerned, his predecessor had already dispensed with.[1]

But in the case of Mansel as well as Malebranche there seems no readiness to make the legitimate contention that Grote makes for phenomena which are always for some mind (either God's or our's). These phenomena are an excellent substitute for 'objects' or an 'external world.'

vi. Berkeley's illustration valuable to
Grote's interpretation

Grote's contention that phenomena must be somehow accounted for appears in the following:

[1] Mansel, LLR, 390.

We should have no notion of the wide prospects of earth or the vast spaces of the heavens without sight; but there would be no meaning in the notion of them as wide or vast, without the humble experiences of our own individual handling and walking.[1]

Grote would say to Berkeley that in stating that the blind person sees things *at* the eyes is an affirmation that bears out his hypothesis regarding the *existence* of phenomenal reality. T. K. Abbott very strongly emphasizes sight rather than touch for the truth of the tangible. The basis for this emphasis is 'common sense' or 'the evidence of consciousness.' He seems to have overlooked the fact that the sense of sight is also a sort of sense of touch or contact, inasmuch as the eye, physically, adjusts itself as it makes contact with the atmosphere and with so-called physical objects. One of Abbott's purposes in writing his book is

to assail the theory in its foundation – the assumption that Touch is the sense pre-eminently perceptive of extension and distance. And here, again, we have no really philosophical theory to combat; nothing is opposed to us but vague and popular impressions. Touch proper gives us nothing but a series of sensations which have of themselves no more connection with extension than with colour.[2]

Now, sight contrary to Abbott's view, is only *apparently* free from phenomenal interpretation. Abbott seems to have been wholly unaware that the eye through the special organ of sight is also a sort of organ of touch or physical contact, as is evident in the fact that the mind through sight judges distances. Abbott is mentioned here as a glaring example of the necessary recognition of the fact that phenomenal reality affect us even in the case of sight – sight which is so *apparently*, to Abbott and even to Berkeley, free from non-phenomenal entities.

5. SPENCER'S AND MORELL'S EVOLUTIONISM

i. Spencer repeats the error of the Lockian psychology

Grote asserts that the error, or 'mis-psychology' of which Locke is guilty is one into which Spencer also falls. Yet the *Principles of Psychology* "contains... a more correct account of the process of perception and understanding than any other I know." [3] Grote appears to have seen the error in Spencer's *First Principles* not by the reading of Spencer first, but by coming upon the idea of there being a mis-psychology and then turning to Spencer to find out if he is guilty of

[1] Grote, EP, II, 128.
[2] Abbott, SAT, 60.
[3] Grote, *op. cit.*, 91.

this error. For this error is frequently mentioned as the error of the Lockian psychology. Apparently, then, when Grote discovered mis-psychology in Locke he turned his attention to various philosophers, including Spencer and Morell, to see if they like Locke stumbled into the same pitfall.

ii. Identity of consciousness of facts with the facts themselves

Spencer believed that the clearer our consciousness of facts are the nearer we are to the truth. He would identify clear consciousness of facts with the facts themselves! Spencer asserted that experience explained the origin of our powers of thinking, or (the origin of) the features of our knowledge. Grote asserts that experience is sufficient to show to us phenomena but not the features of our knowledge.

iii. Perfect success of the attempt to harmonize thought with things reveals truth

Grote borrows the term 'pre-established harmony' in clarifying Spencer's position. This harmony may be conceived as existing between intelligence and things and it is from this standpoint that Spencer discusses the *growth* characteristic of his system. Truth is nothing more than the goal of the effort to make thought and things harmonize. As consciousness grows the truth becomes clearer and clearer. Spencer virtually asserts that "things correspond with consciousness and consciousness with things." [1] If this is so, Grote asks, then is there any difference between thought and things, or are they identical? Spencer's answer is that the truth is that which cannot be conceived otherwise. Truth for Spencer is innate and therefore logically necessary.

As against the associational psychology he admits that there are for the individual immediately evident principles, and truths which are innate in the sense that they cannot be explained by the experience of the individual.[2]

Moreover, he states that the truth as proper conception is identical with "the independent existence of sensible things." [3]

iv. Spencer compared with Spinoza

It is Grote's contention that it is impossible to establish this identity if a confusion between the two views, 'philosophy' and phenomena,

[1] Grote, EP, II, 92.
[2] Windelband, HOP, 658, 659.
[3] Grote, *loc. cit.*

is to be avoided. What Spencer's position really is, seems to be more correctly stated by Frederick Pollock than by Grote, though Grote centers attention upon the way in which Spencer expresses himself. Pollock compares Spencer with Spinoza, in showing what he regards as Spencer's correct view:

Spinoza does not say, be it observed, that every apparent certainty is true knowledge, but that there is no true knowledge without certainty, and the certainty is given in the knowledge itself. In other words, there is ultimately no external test of truth; we must be content in the last resort with the clear and persistent witness of consciousness. This doctrine is not necessarily transcendental or dogmatic. It is compatible with a purely empirical account of the origin of all our knowledge, and indeed is adopted in that connection by one of the leading philosophical authors of our own time and country. Mr. Herbert Spencer's view of the final test of truth, though he puts it in the negative form as the inconceivableness of the contrary, is substantially not distinguishable from Spinoza's. Rightly understood, the doctrine is not an assumption of infallibility, but a warning against any such assumption.[1]

Truth for Spencer is inconceivableness of the contrary; Pollock remarks that this means the same as the basis accepted for truth by Spinoza, namely, "the clear and persistent witness of consciousness." This seems to harmonize with the comment, above, that, for Spinoza truth is innate, or what is logically necessary. This extract is based upon a study of Spinoza's *Ethics* and is especially dependent upon the following passage:

No man who has a true idea is unaware that a true idea involves the utmost degree of certitude. For to have a true idea signifies nothing else than to know the thing perfectly or as well as possible; nor can any one possibly doubt of this unless he thinks an idea to be a lifeless thing like a picture on a panel, and not a mode of thought, to wit the very act of understanding.[2]

The congruence between Spencer and Spinoza on this point is rather remarkable in view of Spencer's statement:

I obtained... books which bore in one way or other on my set purpose – books, however, which did not bear upon it in the most obvious way. For I paid little attention to what had been written upon either ethics or politics... The books I did read were those which promised to furnish illustrative materials.[3]

That Spencer was less interested in the psychological aspects of epistemology is supported in the following:

As regards his philosophical equipment, it is to be remarked that there continues the same singular absence of the metaphysical, and even of the psychological interest.[4]

---

[1] Pollock, SLP, 129, 130.
[2] Spinoza, ETH, prop. 43.
[3] Spencer, AUT, I, 304.
[4] Pringle-Pattison, PR, 119.

v. Not necessary to trace the growth of knowledge to reveal truth

The question which Grote raises in the light of the foregoing is, How far is such a fundamental view a proper account of the beginning of knowledge? If it is merely an intuition or innate idea it is not necessarily knowledge, and because it exists in the realm of consciousness it will have nothing to do with what one might call 'independent reality.'

But if this view of Spencer's, that it is necessary to trace the growth of knowledge to exhibit truth, is left out entirely – that is, if the hypothesis – that knowledge is partly made up of potentially innate ideas – is cast aside, then it is useless to trace the development of knowledge. This is one of the reasons why much of Spencer's writings have become obsolete. Yet this critical analysis, by reason of its limitations, does not entirely discount the significance of his philosophy. A well-deserved tribute to Spencer has been expressed thus:

We must admire the grandeur of the outline he has sketched, acknowledge the greater breadth of view he has given to human speculation, and appreciate the abounding wealth of suggestion displayed throughout the work, which not only enriches human knowledge, but it is sure to give rise to further earnest, bold, and penetrating research into the mysteries of nature.[1]

Nevertheless, this appreciation is expressed in conjunction with the view that "with regard to Mr. Spencer's system of philosophy taken as a whole, we come to the conclusion that, ... he fails in his vast attempt." [2] The failure is based upon Spencer's own admission that "the conception of mental evolution as a part of Evolution in general, remains incomplete." [3]

vi. Spencer compared with Locke

Grote sees a close similarity between Spencer and Locke:

Mr. Spencer's opening chapters may be considered an expansion of Locke's 'when our senses are conversant with external objects,' and then he traces, as Locke does, but in a wider field, how intelligence becomes possessed of (or by) its ideas or consciousness... I think then, that in spite of the care with which he lays down the position which he wishes to take, Mr. Spencer is still not able to escape the kind of 'circularity' which belongs to all that I have called the wrong psychology. His proceeding is a very bold application of the positivist or historical method, in this way: truth *to us* is, with him, what I have ventured to call 'incounterconceivableness': this incounterconceivableness of certain

---

[1] Guthrie, SUK, 476.
[2] *Op. cit.*, 475.
[3] *Op. cit.*, 157.

things to us is a fact of our present nature, a fact which has had a historical origin.[1]

Spencer's method is to trace out how intelligence came by consciousness or idea. His method is one of process, while that of Locke is more concerned with mental activity. While Locke deals with thought (or ideas) and things, Spencer regards things as an hypothesis to which mind or the criterion of that which cannot be conceived otherwise is the *truth*. It should be noted, however, that

Spencer's ultimate interest in the systematic treatment of all problems from the point of view of Evolution was, according to his own account, practical rather than theoretical. 'The whole system,' he says in the 'Autobiography,' [2] 'was at the outset, and has ever continued to be, a basis for a right rule of life, individual and social.' [3]

vii. Explanation by considering the genesis of thoughts
is inadequate

Spencer makes a vast underlying assumption that Grote considers in the following way: The race believes, Spencer states, that the earth moves round the sun and not *vice versa*. The physicist could come to this conclusion very readily in comparison to the speed with which the philosopher would arrive at it. And the reason is this. The philosopher cannot make the assumption to begin with that he exists and that there is an external world about him while the physicist can. Spencer has taken the physicist's approach on this point and waived the approach of 'philosophy.' Or, to vary the statement, if we know that an experience is *things* then we know that knowledge is of *things* in the first place – apart from experience.

Hence, thought is independent of experience and does not need experience to test its truth for the experience is assumed to exist (in the form of 'things' above) apart from the thought. That is, Spencer's method of dealing with the genesis of thought as related to experience is invalid. For at one time he takes the approach of physics, and at another of 'philosophy.' Then he assumes the correspondence theory of truth, in his view that truth is that which cannot be conceived otherwise. And to affirm, as Spencer does, that the thought of the most advanced thinker of the race is *truth*, is a different standard from the coherence theory of truth which is implicit in this view and explicit in the view of truth as inconceivability of the contrary. Through

---

[1] Grote, EP, II, 94, 95.
[2] Spencer, AUT, II, 314.
[3] Seth, EPS, 292, 293.

consciousness we are on the side of thought, but cannot be on the side of phenomena unless we speak of 'consciousness of matter' and then we make the error already indicated in the philosophy of William Hamilton.[1]

viii. 'The experience-hypothesis'

Grote illustrates the 'bad psychology' in Spencer's writings by centering attention upon what Spencer calls 'the experience-hypothesis.' Here, the assumption is made that experience of things, or notions of them, is assurance that there is an outside world and this is the groundwork and root of all knowledge. 'The experience-hypothesis' simply means that experience is fundamental for the beginning of all knowledge and growth of knowledge is attained by the adding of new knowledge to the former. Grote could have criticized Spencer here by pointing out that there is a curious mixture of 'thought' and 'things' involved. For, taking the physicist's point of view, as Spencer is inclined to do, experience is the 'experienced' or the 'things' side of the epistemological issue. He holds the view that such 'knowledge' can be increased by adding new knowledge to this 'experience.'

There is no objection to the view that there is an adding of new knowledge to the experience one has already attained. Grote's point is that if Spencer takes the physicist's attitude toward experience, then the adding of knowledge, which can be analyzed into 'knowing' and the 'known' is hardly a good way of expressing what is meant. It seems that the reason Grote objects to Spencer's view of how 'knowledge' is increased is that, for example, one can hardly say that to the 'experienced' as the physicist would regard it, a number of thoughts are added – which is a contribution from a 'universe of discourse' quite different from the one in which Spencer, considered as a 'physicist,' operates.

ix. Criticism of the use of the term 'experience'

Grote criticizes the word 'experience' as used in this connection; he illustrates from the experience that nettles sting. Suppose the sentence, 'I know by experience that nettles sting.' [2] This might be considered in the light of the following sentence employed by Grote:[3] "A stone lies before me: I see it." In the case of the stone we have seen that it is useless to say that we see it after asserting that it lies before

[1] Cf. pp. 83–84, above.
[2] Grote, EP, II, 99.
[3] Grote, op. cit., I, 153.

us, for the only reason why one can say that it lies before is that one sees it.

"A stone lies before me," and "I see it," are taken as meaning the same thing for Grote. He holds that "I see a stone" does not add anything to what is given in the sentence, "a stone lies before me." Now, it may be questioned whether these two statements mean exactly the same thing. But this question does not vitiate Grote's point, namely, that when we see an 'object' it is an 'object which we already see.' Hence there is no purpose served by saying, "I see what I already see."

Likewise in sentence, 'I know by experience that nettles sting,' one would have to know the nature of nettles before a statement could be made concerning experience of nettles stinging. 'That nettles sting' must be contemporaneous or anterior to the experience and not posterior to it, hence 'experience' is unnecessary or useless as well as misleading when employed in this connection. For to say, virtually, as Spencer does, that we know by experience with 'things' assumes that there are things which we know even before we actually have experience of them.

x. Much evidence of 'bad psychology' in Spencer

Grote examines a number of passages from *The Principles of Psychology* one of which may be cited here in order to indicate the confusion between logic and phenomenalism.

The multiplied phenomena of heat are resolvable into dynamical ones, on holding a thermometer near the fire; the same agent which causes in the hand a sensation of warmth causes motion in the mercury.[1]

The fault which Grote finds with this passage is that in the case of the agent and warmth there is an inanimate object *producing* warmth. *Producing* is also caused in the case of 'motion in the mercury.' The question is as to the meaning of *producing* in both cases. Spencer does not distinguish between the meaning of the word in each. To say that the agent *produces* the sensation of warmth in the hand is to give to the agent what does not rightfully belong to it.

Activity of consciousness is as important a factor as is the agent in the production. Here both phenomena and consciousness are involved. Yet Spencer does not appear to be at all aware of this for if he were he would not make a comparison where the agent 'causes motion in the mercury.'

[1] Spencer, POP, 192.

In the one case, where fire heats the hand to give a sensation of warmth, the sensation has a 'philosophical' side which gives *meaning* to the sensation. What is produced in this action is quite different from what is produced in the motion of the mercury when heat is applied. In tha latter case, there is no 'sensation' and hence no *meaning* involved in the reaction. That is, what is produced in the former case involves meaning, in the latter case there is no meaning involved in the reaction.

That is, in the former case the 'philosophical' aspect of reality is prominent, in the latter it is absent. Yet Spencer makes a comparison between these two cases that are, for the reasons given, not parallel. There are many cases of this confusion throughout *The Principles of Psychology*. Grote calls attention to a few of them and indicates where the confusion has arisen. This we have pointed out.

xi. Explanation of the origin of 'consciousness' is unsatisfactory

In his comparative psychology Spencer has left himself open to criticism. His method of approach here is to study forms of life from the very lowest up to the highest, man. He believes that man is self-conscious but denies self-consciousness to the lower animals. But self-consciousness cannot be denied to the lower animals because one does not know directly about the self-consciousness of other people, let alone animals. All we can say about other people we can say also of animals, namely, that they act as though they were self-conscious. Spencer has erred in saying that what animals *feel* we *know*. Contrary to this, what animals actually feel we do *not know*.

Grote seems to contend, here, that only knowledge that is immediate can be relied upon entirely, for when we speak of consciousness of an 'object' for example, we are speaking of a consciousness of 'something' which already has a relationship with consciousness. Now, to say that we are aware of what animals know is to make a statement that cannot be supported. For what animals feel (or know) is not related to our consciousness already, and there is no way for us to know (or be conscious of) what they feel (or know). The best we can do is to be reasonably sure from the actions of animals (as also of human beings) as to what is going on in their minds. Just what is taking place, exactly, we can never know.

That is, we cannot deny self-consciousness to the lower animals because of our incapacity for knowing whether they actually have self-consciousness or not. And *since this is the case* the explanation of the origin of 'consciousness' is unsatisfactory. For Spencer says, unjustifiably, that the lower animals do not have it and that we do.

And since this is so, how can we proceed from a 'materiality' or an unconsciousness, postulated about non-human forms of life, to postulate consciousness in a human being? The main point to notice is that there is a confusion between phenomena on the one hand, and consciousness on the other. Spencer proceeds from a synthetic study of the lower living forms, which he regards in the same way as Grote regards phenomenal reality, except that, in the case of the phenomenal reality Grote holds that we can be conscious of it. He, also, does not deny consciousness of phenomenal reality to non-rational animals, whereas Spencer does deny self-consciousness to the lower animals. Spencer, then, in dealing with lower animals regards them in the same way as he would regard inorganic objects. Coming further along in the evolutionary process he has to admit consciousness or leave it out altogether. If Spencer leaves consciousness out completely then there are no things *for us*. If he admits it he admits the 'bad psychology' referred to by Grote where 'objects' are admitted as *objects for us* which *then* act on us, when, in actuality they acted on us already in being *objects for us*. Spencer proceeds from a synthetic study of the lower living forms, and then rises for no adequate reason to belief in consciousness in the individual which cannot be spoken of as phenomenal. And, besides, it does not seem certain that there is no consciousness in the lower forms even though we may be unaware of it.

If the lower forms of life are entirely void of consciousness then there must be some stage in the organic development toward higher forms at which consciousness begins. If this were not so it would seem entirely justifiable to speak of the lower forms under the term, positivism – that is, if consciousness were not even represented in any form either as 'potential' or sub-conscious. If the lowest forms of life, as Spencer represents them, are devoid of any consciousness whatsoever then one may refer to them as phenomenal. If they are therefore, purely phenomenal, there appears to be no justification for supposing consciousness in the higher forms. And, again, if in the lower forms there is something more than 'materiality' then this cannot rightly be referred to as phenomenal.

xii. Morell's 'bad psychology'

a. Morell resembles Spencer in repeating the error of the Lockian psychology

John Daniel Morell is in some respects alike Herbert Spencer and may be considered here.[2] Morell uses the term 'zoocosm' frequently.[1] This term may refer to a graduation of forms of life which are co-existent, and hence form the present zoocosm, or to a succession of zoocosms in the past. Morell's starting-point in comparative psychology is with a view of the zoocosm which is necessarily *man's* (or Morell's) view. From this he creates a scale of sensation at the bottom of which is the animal world and at the top is man. However, in this scale Morell appears to have made an illegitimate jump from what is phenomenal to what is consciousness.

For the jump that he makes is from a consideration of the 'inferior animals' as having 'knowledges' which 'we appreciate by observation' to the position that we have knowledge (in the sense of consciousness, or 'philosophy'). But the question that Morell does not answer adequately is whether we can say that the lower animals have knowledge that we can be sure of, by our simple observation of them. Grote states that this question cannot be answered in the affirmative. All that we can be sure of is that animals have phenomenal reality only, and not consciousness. Or, that they do have consciousness cannot be ascertained by observation. We can say only, that they *act* as though they are conscious. There is no immediate knowledge of animal consciousness.

If we cannot be sure that animals have consciousness then it cannot be said that there are gradations in consciousness from the animal to the human consciousness. Hence the illigitimate jump Morell makes from phenomena to consciousness.

b. Concerning the origin of consciousness

Where did consciousness commence and how?, Grote asks. The difficulty in Morell's philosophy, with which this question is concerned, is the same as that in Herbert Spencer's.

The great point as to comparative psychology is, whether we can really hang on human knowledge,[3] as we appreciate it by consciousness, to the various,

---

[1] Let us consider, briefly, the following works by Morell: 1. *Historical and Critical View of the Speculative Philosophy of Europe in the Nineteenth Century*; 2. *The Elements of Psychology*.

[2] Morell, EOP.

[3] Grote seems to mean, "hang human knowledge (as we appreciate it by consciousness) on to."

and, we will suppose, graduated, knowledges of the inferior animals, as we appreciate them by observation.[1]

Grote's criticism is that this *hanging on* appears unjustified. It is unjustified in Morell as it was unjustified in Descartes. In fact, Descartes held that animals were unconscious machines and the only argument which can be put up against this conviction is one which may be employed in dealing with Morell, namely, that animals act as though they had consciousness. Moreover, this is the only 'proof' that each person has concerning belief that his fellowman possesses consciousness. Just how the step can be made from proof of the existence of our own consciousness to proof of the existence of consciousness in others is the problem, for Grote, exactly as the problem for Morell is, How can we be certain that there is any consciousness in the race anywhere outside of ourselves? Since we cannot be certain that there is, then we cannot be sure that there is a growth of consciousness in the race which corresponds to growth of the same in the individual in the succession from what Morell describes as, sensation to intuition, etc.

c. Morell compared with Spencer

In other words Morell ends at the same place as he starts. His starting-point, from *man*, is essentially philosophical and from here he proceeds to phenomena. He may be contrasted with Spencer, therefore, who started from phenomena and proceeded toward consciousness.

Mr. Herbert Spencer begins with an analysis of the action of the human mind, from its most complicated processes to its most simple: and having arrived at these latter, he recommences with an exceedingly elaborate and valuable *synthesis*, as he calls it, or examination of the zoocosm from the bottom (i.e. from the simplest organizations) in conjunction with the circumstances of the universe belonging to it at each stage, or in other words, an examination of the relations of life, in its successive steps, to its environment, till we come to the relation of human life to *its* environment, a part of which relation is human knowledge.[2]

6. RETROSPECT AND PROSPECT

i. Retrospect

a. Purpose

Let us now return to survey the present chapter and consider briefly its content. A chapter, such as this one, which purports to act

[1] Grote, EP, II, 107.
[2] *Op. cit.*, 106.

as a fitting prelude to one on Grote's professed idealisn, or personalism, should be introspective in nature, namely, dealing with what goes on in the human mind when we think.[1] The purpose of this introspective chapter is to examine the bases upon which several of the best known British Empiricists take their stand. This purpose involves showing that it is extremely difficult, yes, impossible, to consider reality as 'out there' and separate *from us* entirely. For, to so consider 'reality' is to consider it in relation to us, as though it were in no relation to us at all!

b. Locke

It seems best, then, to start with the foremost introspectionist among the British Empiricists, namely, John Locke, and see if he is always consistent in holding the view that all knowledge comes from experience considered as 'objects' making their effect upon the mind. Locke found himself considering 'things' with their primary qualities as 'things' apart from the mind altogether, which at birth is a *tabula rasa*. This is clearly what Grote would call a phenomenal approach to reality. That Locke also gives much place to the mind in recollecting, combining, etc., must not be denied. When he does so he is emphasizing the 'philosophical' or 'logical' approach to reality. Advance made from either viewpoint is quite all right so long as it is implied that such advance is made with an awareness that abstractions of one from the other are for the sake of clarity. That Locke is not always aware of the change in emphasis is evident, for example, in his distinction of primary qualities as located in 'things,' or that there are 'things' for a *tabula rasa* mind.

c. Hume

Let us next consider the introspectionist, Hume, leaving Berkeley to be considered later because of his specifically subjectivist position.[2] In Hume we see a tendency toward rationalism, especially in his treatment of ideas, and impressions. We can see this tendency toward rationalism in his assumption that, for example, the mind *can* have ideas that are *not* "derived from correspondent impressions." Also

---

[1] Introspection, according to Ledger Wood, has to do with "observation directed upon the self or its mental states and operations." Runes, DOP, 149.

[2] The reasons for implying that Hume is less subjectivist than Berkeley are at least two: (1) Hume accepts 'impressions' as a fundamental postulate for his epistemology. (2) In dealing with relations he assumes that there are relations of 'matters of fact.' Berkeley, on the other hand, seems to be specifically subjectivist in postulating that there is no reality 'without the mind.'

there are 'philosophical relations' that depend *solely* upon ideas, namely, "resemblance, contrariety, degrees in quality, and proportions in quantity or number." [1] Now, if these relations are dependent solely upon ideas, it would seem that this emphasis upon mind (pre-eminently as rational) as the origin of these ideas would justify referring to Hume as having a tendency to rationalism.

Let us now look, further, at ideas and impressions. Ideas are pale copies of impressions, and are clearly mental in character. It is not so clear that impressions are mental. In fact 'impressions' is a term which lends itself to analysis into active and passive elements. 'Things' are treated as active in relation to mind as passive. But the mind is also active in generating ideas. And the ideas generated correspond to impressions. The question naturally arises whether impressions are mental or physical? If they are mental then what is it that correspond tothem as physical? Clearly they must have some sort of mental nature to be impressions of which we are *conscious*.

Again, if impressions are physical, then one may ask if this physical nature (of impressions) is somehow known independently of its (physical nature) being known! Grote is aiming at a point on which Hume does not seem to be altogether clear. For Hume *does* say that ideas are "derived from the correspondent impressions." Now, one may ask, What are these impressions *before* ideas are derived from them? If they *mean* anything then there must be ideas of them already. But Hume says that the ideas are derived from them. That is, first there are the impressions, *then* the ideas are derived from them. If the ideas are mental entities it would seem that 'impressions' are *non-mental* entities from which these ideas are derived.

At least, then, impressions must be partly physical. This view of the essential physical nature of impressions is supported also by Hume's definition of impression: By impression "I mean all our more lively perceptions, when we hear, or see, or feel, or love, or hate, or desire, or will." Now, these 'more lively impressions' take place when we, for example, 'see,' or 'feel.' Seeing and feeling must be of physical things as Hume seems to imply. This appears to be what Grote would have in mind if he were called upon to support the view that 'impressions' are physical. He would contend, on the basis of his meaning of phenomenal reality, that they are *at least partly* physical. Also, Hume's division of relations, into relations of ideas and relations of matters of fact, falls into the same error. For example, Are the matters

[1] Hume, THN, 186.

of fact such, apart from a mind that regards them as matters of fact? If this is so, we know them before they are related to the mind in any way! Hence, Grote points out the mistake in professing an empiricism devoid of any idealistic or personalistic elements.

d. Berkeley

Of the three British Empiricists so far studies, Berkeley is the one least open to criticism. There are some points on which Grote seems justified in passing critical reflections. For example, in speaking of vision as *at* the eyes, a view that Berkeley variously illustrates, the error of 'mis-psychology' seems to be evident. The eye is physical. Even though things touch the eyes, this touching is not *vision*, and the touching is external to the consciousness that is aware of the touching. To say, then, that *there is* a touching that somehow affects us is to say that there is something already in relation to us. Then Berkeley goes on to show that that which is granted in relation to us, then affects us! This is a sort of double consideration of what affects us, which Berkeley has accepted as already mental – namely, a touching *at* our eyes.

Grote criticizes Berkeley on this issue of vision, but there seems to be more agreement between Grote and Berkeley than between Grote and either of the other two introspectionists, Locke and Hume. Both are obsessed with the view that there is no reality but *reality in relation to us*. There is then a basic epistemological idealism evident in both Berkeley and Grote.

The reason for maintaining that Grote is an epistemological idealist is that, in a certain sense his idealism derives the metaphysical idealism with which it is inseparably involved from the identification of 'objects' with ideas. Now rationalism argues that there cannot be an object without a subject. Hence, one may refer to Grote as both an epistemological and metaphysical idealist, and a rationalist.

Grote's epistemological idealism derived from metaphysical idealism is based on the fact that 'objects' are identified with the ideas we have of those 'objects.' However, Grote seems to depart from this traditionally accepted definition of metaphysical idealism sufficiently to reveal his own peculiar position. We have said that, for him, 'objects' are identified with ideas. It seems even better to say that, for Grote, reality is one. This oneness has two aspects, the 'philosophical,' or 'idea,' aspect, and the 'object' or phenomenon aspect. He asserts that we can never have phenomena apart from ideas though we can have ideas apart from phenomena.

Again, phenomena *qua* phenomena are only one way of looking at reality. But in order to look at it from this aspect we must have ideas which correspond with these phenomena as the opposite side of reality from phenomena. In other words, phenomenal reality is identified, partly at least, with thought, or the 'philosophical' side of reality.

With regard to Grote's rationalism, it is very evident throughout all his writing. For Grote there cannot be an 'object' without a subject. *All* phenomena have their 'philosophical' side. In fact, without the subject, as representing 'philosophy,' there could be no reality at all. Phenomenal reality is essentially dependent upon 'philosophy,' and it is inseparably bound up with it.

e. Spencer (and Morell)

We turn away from the several outstanding introspectionists to consider the evolutionist, Herbert Spencer. Spencer traces the growth of knowledge from early beginnings. But if the hypothesis that the growth of knowledge can take place without a consideration of what are actually or potentially innate ideas, and on the basis of experience alone, then it seems useless to trace the growth of knowledge at all. And it should be noted that, by 'experience' Spencer implies an 'out-thereness' considered as external before it is considered as affecting us! Grote seems to have a suspicion that he may be over-critical of Spencer in concluding that Spencer lacks an idealistic approach to reality. Hence he illustrates his critical view of Spencer by showing more evident discrepancy in Morell and then showing how Spencer and Morell are considerably similar. Morell in tracing evolutionary development makes an illegitimate jump from phenomenal reality in early animal life to phenomenal reality in conjunction with consciousness. The error in Morell is his regarding phenomenal reality in early organic life as something 'existing' even apart from consciousness of it, that is, apart from any mind.

Phenomenal reality *qua* phenomenal is not knowledge at all and cannot be spoken of as such. It only becomes knowledge when the 'knowing' element is present. To speak of any knowledge at all before consciousness or awareness, is to characterize one's reflections as 'mis-psychological.' We cannot speak, then, of a growth of knowledge by the addition of knowledge to what is not knowledge without implying that what is not knowledge is somehow knowledge! This error is very evident in Morell; it appears less overtly in Spencer but is present for the same reason in him as it is in Morell.

ii. Prospect

The chief introspectionists in British empirical philosophy have now been considered, along with Spencer and Morell. Grote's purpose in considering these is to show that reality must always be considered as related to mind, either human or divine, The term 'phenomena' or 'phenomenal reality' is reality *for us* inasmuch as the reality signified by these terms, to be spoken of or thought of at all, implies consciousness. But there is reality which affects us even though we are not aware of it. We refer to this reality as 'phenomena' or 'phenomenal reality,' but we can never *refer* to it without having it in relation *to us* as conscious beings; hence Grote asserts that phenomenal reality is an abstraction from 'philosophy,' or, as we might say, abstraction from 'mind.'

Phenomenal reality implies immediacy or reflection, if it has any *meaning*. It is this characteristic of phenomenal reality that prompted Grote to refer to his fundamental belief in idealism, or personalism. It is important, then, to consider more fully the personalistic nature of Grote's philosophy. This consideration will comprise a complete chapter.[1] But before dealing with the personalism of Grote, we will turn to the important and kindred topic of "Immediateness and Reflection."

Having dealt, in the present chapter, with the most outstanding introspectionists to show the fundamentally, though frequently non-professed, 'subjective' character of their approach, it seems well to deal with immediateness and reflection [2] previous to the chapter immediately following it, on the significance of personalism in Grote's writings.

---

[1] Chapter IX.
[2] In Chapter VIII.

IMMEDIATENESS AND REFLECTION

1. INTRODUCTION

Introspectionists cannot overlook the significance of what Grote refers to as phenomenal reality. Toward the latter part of the last chapter it was stated that phenomenal reality implies immediateness and reflection. It may be said, also, that introspection implies immediateness and reflection with equal reason. Introspection implies immediateness first and reflection afterwards. Introspection, as pointed out in the previous chapter must take into account both the 'philosophical' and the phenomenal approaches to epistemology. Both of these approaches and introspection – as we use this last term in referring to the British Empiricists – involve both immediateness and reflection to be considered in the present chapter. Let us now look more closely at these two terms, immediateness and reflection, and the purpose of the chapter in introducing them. Let us also consider their meanings and significance in Grote's philosophy. Last of all critical comments applicable to these terms will be made.[1]

2. PURPOSE OF THE CHAPTER IN INTRODUCING THESE TERMS

The purpose of the chapter in introducing these terms is to analyze more fully the nature of the 'philosophical' approach in the epistemology of Grote. Both terms, having to do with thinking, deal with the nature of consciousness in its very beginnings, as becoming aware (for example, upon awaking from sleep), at any stage in the life of the individual. Immediateness also is concerned with consciousness, in the early life of the child. But Grote is concerned with consciousness as

---

[1] It should be noted that mention is made of Grote's use of terms that do not mean what they seem to say. Cf. below, pp. 182–185.

immediateness, in adult life. Consciousness as reflection is also analyzed and a commitment made regarding the earliest beginnings of reflection, that is, regarding the point at which reflection takes leave of immediateness sufficiently in order to be referred to, distinctly, as reflection at all. The purpose, then, of considering immediateness and reflection is to analyze the nature of consciousness and to indicate just how much, if at all, phenomenal reality is involved.

3. MEANING OF IMMEDIATENESS AND REFLECTION

i. No reality without mind

Now if immediateness and reflection are concerned in any way with phenomenal reality, this fact would seem to make Grote a metaphysical idealist for whom no reality can exist 'without the mind.' [1] Already, in various places throughout the foregoing part of this book this conclusion (that all reality is personal) was reached, and further consideration of the content of this conclusion will be dealt with in the next chapter on personalism. If immediateness and reflection are so 'mental' as we shall see them to be, and yet involve phenomenal reality, then it seems necessarily clearer than ever that no reality exists except in relation to the mind, consciousness, or thought. But let us turn more specifically to the meaning of these terms.

Immediateness, or "immediate thought may be described as the *feeling* of being, in contradistinction to the realizing (or presenting to ourselves) ourselves or anything else, as being or existing." [2] What Grote means here, is that immediate thought has no object to which this thought stands as subject. Immediate thought is simply "the *feeling* of being" in distinction from a thinking upon ourselves as in reflectiveness or a thinking upon anything else whatsoever (on which we may reflect).

ii. 'Immediate' and 'mediate' thought

'Immediateness' has to do with thought which is not reflective but immediate. Consciousness consists of immediateness, but self-consciousness does not. 'Immediateness' refers to what Grote calls the 'self-self' in contradistinction from the 'thought-self.'

[1] Berkeley, TDH, in Fraser, WOR.
[2] Grote, EP, II, 148, 149.

By the 'self-self' I mean that which cannot really be thought of, [1] i.e. which cannot be made an object of thought, but which is *with-thought* (mitgedacht), thought along with, or included in, our *immediate* thought and feeling, or which, in other words, is one of the essential elements of such thought or feeling. There is a sort of contradiction here, for by attempting to make the reader understand what it is, I am making it an object of thought: it is therefore to be remembered, that when we talk of it we are making a supposition only, which requires accompanying correction in our mind, or the accompanying thought that, for the purpose of talking about it, we are obliged to make a supposition about it, which is for the occasion only. [2]

In the 'self-self,' thought is immediate or unreflective, while with the 'thought-self' thought is 'mediate' or reflective.

The 'thought-self' is that, more or less distinctly conceived, which I have been obliged inevitably to foreshadow and suppose in trying to describe or set in view the 'self-self.' As soon as we in any degree distinctly conceive of ourselves thinking, it is evident that thought is no longer simple or immediate. We are ourselves then *double*. And we are this as soon as ever we set the object of thought out before us as a separate object to contemplate. Concurrently with this, we necessarily separate (bisect or double) ourselves. [3]

The ambiguity of 'I think, therefore I am' is somewhat evident in the light of the above distinction. According to Grote, Descartes's state of mind was 'I am thinking that I think, therefore I am.' That is Descartes's thought is reflective rather than immediate. But Descartes's words, 'I think,' carry both the meaning of 'I think,' that is immediate thought, and 'I think,' that is, reflective thought ('I am thinking that I think.').

Grote simply means, in analyzing 'I think,' that when one says 'I think,' that the self, thinking, is an object for thought. That is, I am reflecting when I say, 'I think.' But, there is a larger question with which one should deal, namely, 'Do I always reflect?' Grote's answer to this question is that in *strict immediateness* we do not reflect. Our concern is only with the *feeling* of being as wholly unreflective.

If one were to ask Grote, 'Do we ever experience strict immediateness?' his answer would be: Immediateness is a sort of impractical and theoretical extreme such as we designate by the term 'self-self.' And, he would say, the further we go away from the 'self-self' the more we become the reflective self. The question, then, regarding whether we always reflect, is answered. In the *extreme of immediateness* there is *no reflection*. In all variations of thinking where there is no strict immediateness, there is *always reflection*.

[1] Grote realizes that, strictly, the 'self-self' cannot even be mentioned or even thought of, else it becomes an object of thought which means in that case that it no longer can be the 'self-self.'

[2] Grote, EP, II, 145.

[3] Grote, *op. cit.*, 146.

If we apply what I have just been saying to the Cartesian 'Cogito, ergo sum,' it will appear more strongly than before that such truths as it has must have reference to that primary indistinction of knowing and being which exists in immediateness. If we explain it, *Cogito, ergo sum conscius*, we have not advanced a step: if we interpret it, *Cogito, ergo vivo*, we have advanced too far. And I cannot understand what the absolute notion of being, here apparently involved in 'sum' is. *Being* is being *something*: being something is looking in some way, or, in grander language, possessing some character presentable to intelligence. It may be more than this, for it may be intelligence itself as well: but this is what is contained in the 'cogito,' or what the 'cogito' means. In order to get a step beyond the 'cogito,' we want the addition of some property, some character, something for us to be: and it is quite impossible for us to proceed from the bare 'cogito' to this. I do not understand the seeming predication of this absolute 'being' to carry any meaning... The primary fact is not 'cogito,' but is what I have called immediateness.[1]

Grote regards immediate thought as resultless in that we can conclude nothing at all from it until the elements in it are distinguished and the object developed, and when this is done it is no longer immediate thought. Immediate thought may be said to *be being* rather than to *imply* it. Mediate thought is something more than this. Descartes did not appear to distinguish between immediate and mediate thought in his 'cogito.'

Let us now, briefly, consider a question involved in the whole of this discussion on immediateness. Grote's view regarding the necessity for immediateness and reflection to be considered as inseparable finds kinship in Hegel's *Der Geist*. Hegel is pointing out that people are frequently too concerned with experience, for example, when the getting of technical education is considered as of supreme importance. Over-emphasis on empirical requirements may well lead to the disregard of metaphysics and theology.

Reasoning (and rationalizing!) may go on in the immediate; there may be grave doubt of the objective truth of results of these processess, but in so far as they are actual processes there can be no doubt that they are going on. This infallibility of the immediate causes it to exercise a fascination over the mind. Not only is the immediate the necessary starting point of all thought and the point at which all eventual empirical verification occurs; it seems also to be the point at which objective reality is revealed, free from all distortions.[2]

Grot e would agree that 'objective' reality is revealed in immediateness. R evelation is only possible in the 'self-self.' This "immediacy is the truth about the real." [3] Here we see a coherence theory of truth; all is coherent and true as immediateness.

---

[1] Grote, EP, II, 178, 179.
[2] Brightman, "Immediacy?" in *Idealismus*, I (1934), 88, 89.
[3] *Loc. cit.*

For Grote, there is no immediate 'knowledge.' 'Immediateness' is a term employed to show the extreme where all reflection would be absent – granting that such abstraction could be carried out. Let us note the following:

There is no immediate knowledge. "Immediate knowledge" is that in which we do not have the consciousness of meditation, but it is mediated. We have feeling, and it seems immediate. We have intuition, and it appears under the form of immediacy.[1]

We may note that "here Hegel concedes that feeling and intuition may be immediate, although thought is not." [2] This is very reminiscent of Grote in speaking of immediate 'thought' as the *feeling* of being. This *feeling* for Grote is intuition in the sense of immediateness. But it is never wholly abstracted from thought. Thought is regarded, by Grote, as reflective and is therefore mediate. Grote would seem to reject the relationless immediate as Hegel did. There is no possible escape, both would agree, from relational thought which seeks after a reality that is both true and whole.

W. R. Sorley makes the following statement in which he acknowledges Grote's contribution to a doctrine of knowledge:

From the first self-consciousness is implied in every conscious state, because it can be brought to light by reflexion. But it is not explicit there, because reflective examination may show that it did not appear in that past state. Its appearance means the raising of mental life to a higher level.[3]

This higher level is the level of immediateness. "Grote suggests that in such a state there is acquaintance with self as knowing but not knowledge that one knows." [4]

The point here is that in immediateness, according to Grote, and as Sorley acknowledges, there is knowledge of the self. This knowledge is knowledge of acquaintance, where the self knows itself, giving us the term which Grote uses in connection with immediateness, namely, the 'self-self.' This is what Sorley is referring to in his remark that "in such a state there is acquaintance with self."

The "knowledge that one knows" is "knowledge about," or reflective knowledge. Grote distinguishes between these two types of knowledge, namely, of immediateness and reflection, and Sorley here is recognizing this distinction. It should be noted that the two kinds of 'knowledge' distinguished as 'knowledge of acquaintance' and 'knowledge about'

---

[1] Hegel, *Philosophie der Religion*, XII, 92.
[2] Brightman, "Immediacy?" in *Idealismus*, I (1934), 90.
[3] Grote, EP, I, 60, 61.
[4] Sorley, MVI, 206.

have had their origin in Grote's distinction between immediateness and reflection.[1] But the former has long since come to mean immediate knowledge of a thing or person, and the latter to mean only mediate knowledge as conveyed, for example, by statements of others who had first-hand or immediate knowledge.

iii. The 'self-self' and the 'thought-self'

The 'self-self' or the self with which immediate thought is concerned has little to do with the 'thought-self'; and when it has then the 'self-self' is no longer the 'self-self' but the 'thought-self.' That is, when the self-self passes over into the thought-self, thought is reflective. This distinction between the self-self and the thought-self are not so separate from each other as an attempt to distinguish them here would seem to indicate. The self-self cannot be thought of, though it may be regarded as 'with-thought.' It is not an object of thought, though for purposes of explanation it may appear at first to be so; at most it may be supposed to exist.

In general, the very close relationship existing between the self-self and the thought-self cannot be completely broken down. Reflection has at its basis immediateness. All thought that is concerned not solely with consciousness has this basis. Grote asserts that as soon as we conceive ourselves as thinking we are ourselves 'double.' There is an analogy to this co-existence in contemporary philosophy:

An actual entity is at once the subject experiencing and the superject of its experiences. It is subject-superject, and neither half of this description can for a moment be lost sight of. The term 'subject' will be mostly employed when the actual entity is considered in respect to its own real internal constitution. But 'subject' is always, to be construed as an abbreviation of 'subject-superject.' [2]

To say that an actual entity is a subject-superject is to clothe the self in terms similar to that of the 'self-self' hyphenated with the 'thought-self,' giving " 'self-self'-'thought-self'." There is one general difference, however, namely that this latter term does not include objects beyond the thought-self.

But the 'thought-self' is an 'object' and hence a 'superject.' Yet as the term 'superject' cannot *be* by itself, without the 'subject,' neither can the 'thought-self' be regarded as an 'object' or 'superject' unless the 'philosophical' side of it is also kept in sight. And the 'thought-self' is, again, a sort of 'object' for the 'self-self' which Grote seems to regard after the nature of the *self to itself*.

[1] Grote, EP, II, bk. II.
[2] Whitehead, PR, 39.

What, then, is this term that we may call the " 'self-self'-'thought-self' " which Grote does not actually use but which seems to be implicit in his writing on immediateness and reflection? The answer is that the 'self-self' is the self *thinking*, or the subject. The 'thought-self' is the *self thought of*. One is the 'subject' and the other is the 'superject," in Whitehead's terms. Now the 'self-self' is pure immediateness. There is no distinction into 'philosophy' and phenomenon here. All is 'philosophy' or consciousness. On Grote's own basis, then, namely, that consciousness and phenomenon are each necessary to the other, Grote would have to admit that the 'self-self' is fictional.

Probably Grote recognized the fictional nature of the 'self-self.' There is no evidence that he thought the 'self-self' could actually *be*. But, there seems to be implicit, in Grote, the recognition that the 'self-self' is the extreme toward which we would advance (but never reach), the more we became non-reflective.

Now we must look briefly also at the 'thought-self.' There is not so much difficulty involved in this term. Here there are the two parts which Whitehead would admonish us should never be lost sight of, namely, the 'subject' and the 'superject,' or 'thought' and the 'self thought of' (or 'philosophy' and phenomenon). Again, the 'self-self' and the 'thought-self' stand in relation of 'subject' and 'superject,' also. For the 'thought-self' requires the 'self-self' as pure immediateness (or as close to this immediateness as it is possible to go). And the 'thought-self' is phenomenon, and the 'self-self' is 'thinking' or 'philosophy.' On Grote's terms, then, each of these, the 'self-self' and the 'thought-self' are as necessary to each other as are consciousness and phenomena. Consciousness and phenomena are of crucial importance to the whole of Grote's epistemology.

iv. Where reflective thought departs from immediateness

As soon as we are aware or think of objects, thought is reflective thought, for we cannot conceive of objects existing without conceiving ourselves in some way as co-existing with them. That is, we have, Grote states, a 'co-conception' of ourselves in counter-distinction from other objects. This reflectiveness is evident even as we think of such entities as 4004 B.C., or the twenty-first century. We think of them in conjunction with ourselves who do the thinking.

Reflectional intelligence appears to be somewhere about half-way between, on the one hand, an infinite universe or creature, conscious, but not active and with no desire to be, and on the other hand, an universe of activity. Grote believes that in order to explain reflectional intelligence we must begin either with the supposed universe of activity or the infinite universe of consciousness. If we begin with the former we could imagine, for example, the sun warming a leaf and causing movement; if we begin with the latter, we might imagine a person seeing an apple, putting out his hand and taking it.

The wide region of reflectional intelligence is a region intermediate between, – if we can conceive such – an infinite creature or universe on the one side, conscious, but actionless and without change or desire for it, and neither self-conscious nor distinguishingly perceptive, and, on the other side, a universe full of movement of regular actions, interactions, and reactions. In order to present to ourselves the reflectional or the developed human intelligence, we must begin with immediateness, either of thought or of action. If of action: let us imagine the interaction between the light or air and the leaf of a plant causing the movement of the latter or the opening of its pores, and let us follow upward interaction of this kind, if we may still call it so, to the long and complicated process which takes place when an apple strikes the eye of a man, leading him to put out his hand and take it and eat it. We have no means of knowing *within* the plant, further than we can trace the movements: perhaps there is nothing but the movements; and then the action is reflex or immediate. What passes within the *man* is the complicated process of reflectional intelligence: but there is not much more that we can say about it except so to name it, when we proceed in this way of investigation from immediate action.[1]

v. *Reflectional intelligence*

Even though we may know that reflectional intelligence is a possession of the human we have no reason to conjecture that there is anything more than immediate action in the plant. In the former case, that of the universe of activity, there may be supposed an immediate action with the reflectional factor abstracted, in the latter, that of the universe of consciousness, there may be supposed immediate thought with the reflectional factor abstracted. Now, whether we are dealing with the universe of activity or the universe of consciousness there is actually at least a small amount of reflection involved.

vi. *Immediate knowledge possesses a minimum of reflection*

Grote speaks of immediate knowledge as immediate thought with a small portion of reflection attaching to it. However, according to the way in which he distinguishes between immediateness and reflection, *immediate* 'knowledge' does not seem possible. Reflection would imply knowledge but immediateness would not. To join both terms and say that there is immediate knowledge does not appear admissible. Just how small a portion of reflection is necessary to make immediate

[1] Grote, EP, II, 149, 150.

thought immediate knowledge appears very indefinite. Grote states that it should be only large enough so that a distinct judgment is not formed. What appears so indefinite is that this small portion apparently may range from nothing to something *just* less than enough for a distinct judgment. Grote has referred to such immediate knowledge as 'knowledge of acquaintance.' [1]

vii. *Immediate thought develops into knowledge*

In stating that there is immediate 'knowledge,' which is derivable from immediateness with a minimum of reflection, Grote is simply stating that knowledge develops from immediateness as a basis. To immediateness much reflection may be added; the more reflection we have, the more knowledge. Knowledge is a combination of 'distinction' and 'indistinction' of thought. The former, 'distinction,' corresponds somewhat to reflection so characteristic of self-consciousness or of the 'thought-self,' and the latter to immediateness of the 'self-self' which cannot be thought but which is, rather, immediately felt.

Perhaps the best way in which we can describe knowledge is that it is an union of *indistinction* and *distinction* of thought, the indistinction giving the reality or trueness of knowledge, the distinction its point or particularity. Knowledge is thought, with a particular kind of value, which we call trueness, understood to attach to the thought. This value, it seems to me, is the carrying on of immediateness into reflection, while reflection on *its* side supplies another kind of value, that namely of distinction among objects, enabling us to know their relations one to another. [2]

There are two kinds of value furnished. First, from immediateness, the value has nothing to do with the 'thought-self,' while, second, from reflection, it has everything to do with the 'thought-self' and also the 'self-self' which forms the intuitive basis for the former.

viii. *'Pre-distinctional' immediateness*

In the case of immediate knowledge Grote states there is a sort of 'pre-distinctional' immediateness. J. Loewenberg uses the term 'pre-analytic' instead of 'pre-distinctional.' But by preanalytic Loewenberg refers to what "consists of a tentative intuition of the general field of facts to be studied." [3] 'Pre-distinctional' refers to immediateness where 'facts' are not yet recognized. The facts arise when reflection

---

[1] Grote, EP, I, 60, and II, 201–208.
[2] Grote, *op. cit.*, II, 153.
[3] Brightman, POR, 117.

takes place. It is true that this grasp of reality is most inadequate and *conveys* little meaning. Loewenberg's 'preanalytic stage' is more informative. Both terms, 'pre-distinctional' and 'preanalytic,' are synoptic in character.

What Grote means by pre-distinctional immediateness may be observed in the following. In immediateness there is a oneness of the thinker and the thought which makes the thought or immediate knowledge true; this is not the case with reflection as in the 'thought-self' for in the latter there is a distinction between subject and object, and since there is, the trueness vanishes. Grote, very evidently does not believe in a correspondence theory of truth. The closer, he says, that knowledge can remain to immediateness the more likelihood is there that truth obtains. 'Distinction' has to do with reflection rather than with immediateness but not wholly so because of the element of reflection which enters into immediate knowledge. If, then, 'distinction' is in any way a characteristic of immediate knowledge one may be justified in saying that there is 'pre-distinctional' (that is, before reflection makes 'distinction') immediateness. This involves trueness which is a characteristic of immediateness.

Yet it is not the distinction which gives the character of *trueness* to the thought, and in *that* way marks it as knowledge, but it is the *pre-distinctional* immediateness which involved the trueness, and on which, for foundation, the trueness rests and must always rest. The oneness of subject and object, thinker and thought, in immediate thought, is the germ of all after knowledge: it is this which constitutes the life, essence, special character of knowledge, *the trueness* in one word, though it cannot be called knowledge till it is developed.[1]

ix. Intuition

a. Meaning of 'intuition'

The word 'intuition' in all this discussion should not be passed over without examination. It is concerned with immediateness but not with reflection primarily. For reflection implies 'distinction' which is no direct concern of intuition in its character as immediateness, as contrasted with its character of distinction bound up as it is with 'indistinction' and merged with the thinker and thought (when no distinction is made between the two), or with subject and object. Intuitive 'knowledge,' as Grote speaks of it, is concerned with only a minimum of reflection (not enough for a judgment). We may have an intuitive knowledge of an object, say a tree. Then we, the tree and the world of which we form a part cannot be analyzed, according to

[1] Grote, EP, II, 153, 154.

Grote. In the indistinction resulting is the basis of the truth of the tree. Of course, if reflection is added then there is perception, and consequently the problem of the two points of view, namely, the 'philosophical' and the phenomenal, is evident. It seems that Grote follows the line of thought taken by Bergson much later as the latter distinguishes between intuition and intelligence, for example, in referring to time: "We do not *think* real time. But we *live* it, because life transcends intellect." [1]

Immediateness and intuition are not concerned with the problem, but reflection and perception are. No *distinct* object, or thing (whether of sense or reason), can *intuitively* be known, in the sense in which Grote speaks of intuition in its character as immediateness.

Intuition is true, or real knowledge, in its character of immediateness, so far as immediateness can give knowledge, but not necessarily true, or real knowledge, in its character of distinction. We have no proper right to say, we know this or that intuitively, because 'this,' and 'that,' imply a distinction of objects which does not belong to intuition as immediate. We have an intuitional knowledge of the external world: [2] but our distinction of objects from our selves and among ourselves, and our consequent view of their relations to us and among each other, which makes up our notion of the external world in its characters and variety – all this is not at all intuition, though it need not be inconsistent with it. Intuitive knowledge, as immediate, is a state of undistinguished and common being uniting us with what we know: [3] as soon as we separate it off from us, intuition passes into reflection. [4]

b. *Trueness of 'intuition'*

Concerning the trueness of intuition Grote has the following to say. Truth is a property of intuition in its character of immediateness (but not in its character of distinction). In its purest form truth is in intuition, not in reflection. This intuition *is* immediate 'knowledge,' except the extreme of immediateness seems to be, for Grote, a limit rather than an actuality. The closest that it is possible to get to truth is through intuition. When reflection enters so also does error, for when the inactive immediateness is put into activity by reflection nothing new in the way of truth can be added. Activity as mere activity is the fountain of error. Grote seems to take a position regarding intuition and reflection akin to that of Bergson regarding intuition and intelligence. [5]

---

[1] Bergson, CE, 53.

[2] Obviously Grote means intuition 'in its character of distinction' here.

[3] When we are united with what we know, there is then no 'subject' and 'object,' but only 'subject' (in the sense of the subject being characterized by immediateness), giving an idealistic metaphysics.

[4] Grote, EP, II, 154.

[5] Bergson, CE.

x. *Antithesis between immediateness and reflection*

Grote calls attention to the antithesis, indicated by 'immediateness' and 'reflection' or 'intuition' and 'reflection,' as asserted by different terms in English usage, such as 'intuition' and 'experience,' or 'ideas' and 'sense.' Intuition in its character of immediateness is truth. For when reflection enters no more of truth can be added, and there is the possibility of error. Now intuition in its character of immediateness, plus reflectional activity, gives intuition in its character of distinction. This plus portion is what Grote considers responsible for a great deal of confusion.

By reason of this meaning 'intuition' (in its character of distinction) as used by almost all English philosophers is practically equivalent to Grote's 'reflection.' Therefore the place which Grote reserved for 'intuition,' in its character of immediateness, is left vacant (though intuition does occupy a place within reflection). It is 'pre-distinctional' immediateness. Confusion becomes somewhat worse confounded when the term 'experience' is regarded sometimes as equivalent to 'intuition' when, according to Grote, it should be the antithesis of it. Hence, the term 'experience' may refer to any one, or all, of the following, experience of the physical, of the mental, or simply to consecutive states of mind.

The word 'intuition' . . . in its English form, is used more or less to express a combination of two things, which are looked upon as one, viz. what I have called the higher intuitions, and the reflectional activity of the mind. It appears to me that this analysis or antithesis of knowledge is virtually admitted by almost all English philosophers. That is to say, those who most strongly urge that the former element, the English 'intuition,' is not real or important, nevertheless make their supposition of the other element, 'experience' (from which they derive all knowledge) much as their opponents would, leaving in this way, if we may so speak, the place for the former element vacant, though they will not allow it to be occupied. Or, to put the thing in another way, they keep it (I do not mean with any intentional bad faith) as a convenient ground to which their term 'experience' retires now and then, and we never can precisely be sure whether 'experience' means mental experience, succession of states of mind, or physical experience.[1]

What Grote is saying here is that we must recognize two meanings of intuition, one of which is 'immediateness' or "immediate 'knowledge,'" and the other 'reflection.' English intuitionists use the word 'intuition' for 'reflection' and hence leave intuition as immediateness, vacant. And Grote is arguing that if you follow the method of these intuitionists you do not really have intuition at all but reflection, distinction, and experience.

[1] Grote, EP, II, 157.

xi. Criticism of Kant's 'experience'

In his criticism of the use of 'experience' Grote attacks a rock of Gibraltar in his condemnation of Kant's use of the word. Kant's meaning is different from the above yet there is a certain lack of clarity about it. Kant speaks of 'the manifold of experience and intuition.' [1] There is too much distinctness involved in the manifold to suit Grote who would rather speak of 'the undistinguished' or 'the confused' which, the thinks, would better indicate the 'immediateness' characteristic of 'the undistinguished' or 'the confused' before attention or notice (or, reflection, one might say) is applied to it. This criticism of Kant is in conformity with the antithesis, which Grote advocates, between intuition and reflection. It is the same error, Grote asserts, that underlies both Kant and the English philosophers, namely, the lack of observing the 'indistinction' characteristic of immediateness in the case of Kant's manifold, and by the English philosophers who make an antithesis between experience on the one hand, and reflectional activity and the (pure or higher) intuitions on the other. In such an antithesis the 'indistinction' which should be characteristic of all that lies in contrast to experience, namely, immediateness, is violated.

xii. English philosophy unjustified in making antithesis between 'ideas' and 'experience'

Grote claims that in English philosophy ideas modify experience and experience modifies the ideas and both are placed in an antithesis, as in Locke [2] and Hume.[3] He sees no reason why the antithesis should be made. For if ideas fit experience (or *vice versa*), both ideas and experience are characteristic of immediateness. Unless reflection or activity became involved in the ideas or experience both these latter may as well be regarded as 'immediateness' and hence the artificial antithesis set up falls apart. Again if reflectional activity takes place in order to make the 'ideas' or 'experience' mean something, what happens is that there is no 'immediateness' but all is 'reflection.'

Grote seems to think that English philosophy tries to support a virtual antithesis between 'ideas' and 'experience' in the following way: One may see [4] a tree as oneness or as greenness, the oneness is the idea and greenness the sensation. Grote believes this is erroneous.

[1] Kant, CPR.
[2] Locke, EHU.
[3] Hume, THU.
[4] 'See' with the meaning of 'sense' or 'perceive,' that is, as phenomenal and 'philosophical.'

For the explanation usually given is that there is a correspondence between the greenness and certain nerves of our body while there is no such correspondence in the case of oneness. What is of importance here in Grote's criticism is that the greenness no more than the oneness is distinguished *without attention*. Attention at once brings both sides of the antithesis out of the realm of 'immediateness.'

xiii. Immediateness, and 'subject' and 'object'

Grote's exposition of 'immediateness' in its pure or complete form is that it is as subjective as it is objective. 'Subject' and 'object' are merged into one. The individual has no self-consciousness for all is conscious, and intuitive; there is no reflection in immediateness. As reflection combines with intuition the result is that the relation between thought and things becomes more subjective because things are looked at from the side of thought. One is concerned more with thought than with that which is *thought about*, or the 'object.'

Grote believes that William Hamilton and George Berkeley fundamentally would be of one mind if they really had been aware and impressed by the distinction which he makes between intuition and reflection. Yet Grote claims that neither saw consciousness in the sense of immediateness as he himself saw it, namely, as subject and object merged into one. Hamilton's philosophy deals with consciousness at one time as consciousness, and at another as self-consciousness (as Grote distinguishes these two terms). Grote believes that Hamilton's interchange of meanings makes for a great deal of confusion in philosophy. That is, Grote believes that Hamilton never saw such a fundamental distinction as he himself makes between immediateness and reflection. Berkeley was more concerned with one side only of the antithesis, and, hence, Grote thinks he too is a victim of error. Thus, thinking and what is *thought about* should be kept strictly distinct. The distinction was not maintained in Hamilton nor recognition given to it by Berkeley, Grote holds. When Reid and Hamilton broke out into controversy as to whether or not consciousness is a faculty, they were each wrestling with the problem for which Grote claims that he has found the solution.

One may state that Grote's comments are rather evidently appropriate when applied to Hamilton but it does not seem that they suit too well in Berkeley's case. For Berkeley held that there are no objects 'without the mind.' It is clear, then, that Berkeley could not be in error since he did not refer to 'subject' and 'object' in the ordinary sense. However, there is objectivity evident throughout all Berkeley's writings. This would violate the truth found only in immediateness, Grote would hold. However, one must say here what one cannot help thinking throughout all Grote's writing on immediateness, namely that, it seems impossible to make immediateness intelligible without bringing in 'subject,' 'object,' 'things,' etc., such as 'reflection' makes possible.

What Grote is distinguishing here, is aptly shown in the distinction between "Situations Experienced and Situations Believed-in." [1] "The only Situation Experienced by anyone is his own consciousness."[2] Immediateness is similar to a 'Situation Experienced.' As soon as we bring in such terms as, 'subject,' 'things,' etc., we are no longer dealing with immediateness but with reflection. Or, in terms of 'Situations Experienced and Situations Believed-in,' as soon as we are involved with other than consciousness we are dealing with Situations Believed-in.

It is necessary to distinguish between Situations Experienced and Situations Believed-in. A 'situation' means any state of affairs. No situation is a Situation Experienced unless it is actually present in consciousness. Experience is given only as a conscious state of affairs. To experience is to be aware. A man cannot properly say that he is experiencing a fire in his house merely because the fire is going on; he experiences the fire only when it makes a perceptible difference to his conscious experience. More exactly, the man can never say that he is experiencing the fire, even when perceptions of its odor or heat occur; yes, even when the fire burns his body, the Situation Experienced is excruciating pain, not actual fire. The fire is always a Situation Believed-in, no matter how painfully well-grounded the belief may be.[3]

xiv. Self-consciousness not dependent upon the 'objective'

Grote criticizes those who would place self-consciousness within the universe or dependent upon the universe, and would advocate rather the importance of observing an initial self-consciousness to which external objects are *objects for me, the self-conscious subject*. He believes that no possible physical discovery can change the primary importance of self-consciousness, especially of the 'self-self' as distinguished from the 'thought-self.' It is for this reason that Grote does not agree with Mill's language concerning sensation or consciousness being a function of matter or that matter is only 'possibilities of sensation.'

The truth is to be found rather in immediateness. Grote regards

[1] Brightman, POR, 347.
[2] *Loc. cit.*
[3] *Loc. cit.*

truth as existing only in immediateness where 'things' and 'thought' are indistinguishable. As soon as reflection enters so that there is self-consciousness this immediateness vanishes and gives place to distinction where there is no longer reason and meaning to hold things together in combination.

I said that the thing was the combination of its looks, not the sum or aggregate, and in respect of this we have to notice that the looks of a thing are in degrees, and of very different values: and that the difference between a combination and an aggregate is that, as to the former, we understand there is *reason* for it, *meaning* in it, not as to the latter. The looks are of greater or less value according as they tell us more or less of this reason or meaning. In fact, this reason or meaning might be described, if we like to use the language, as the look of the thing itself – it is what I have formerly called its 'thinghood.' [1]

The 'impressions' and 'ideas' of Hume and the ideas of Berkeley are not open to criticism when they are regarded as a part of consciousness (where immediateness is involved) but only become so when they are related to self-consciousness where 'distinction' enters, or when they are regarded in their atomistic nature as discrete.

xv. Sensibility and activity

a. Want

Besides 'self-consciousness' and 'perception' dealt with in the above, as related to our *intellectual* nature, there is also sensibility and activity in connection with the *active* side of our nature. The parent of both sensibility and activity is 'want' or 'immediateness.' When the 'state of things' passes into reflection, 'want' is *felt* as want. Further qualification of the above two factors of sensibility and activity should be made. Let us look at some of the terms Grote uses. 'Sensibility' is regarded as the capacity which an animate object may have for pleasure or pain. The fact of the presence of pleasure or pain is called 'sentience.' 'Sensiveness' is the instrumental operation that conveys information from the outside world to our bodies. It is the corporeal or nervous portion of 'perceptiveness.' Grote uses the word 'perceptiveness' in a wider sense than 'sensiveness.'

By sensibility I mean capacity of pleasure and pain, and I carefully distinguish it throughout from *sensiveness*, by which latter I mean the general operation or instrumentality of the nerves of our body in giving us *information* of what we then call external things. Sensiveness, as I use the term, is a portion, the nervous or corporeal portion, of the more general operation or faculty 'perceptiveness.' We are perceptive as intelligences: we are sensive as corporealized or incorporated intelligences.[2]

[1] Grote, EP, II, 177, 178.
[2] Grote, *op. cit.*, 185.

b. 'Reflectiveness'

Grote refers to 'reflectiveness' as halfway between immediate thought on the one hand and immediate or 'reflex' action on the other.

Some time since I said, that what I called 'reflectiveness' was intermediate between immediate thought and what I called 'immediate' or 'reflex' action. Immediate or reflex action, speaking roughly, is where there is action of one thing upon another, and continuous or spontaneous *re*-action from this other.

I only allude to this for the purpose of pointing out the difference – a difference, however, entirely gradational – between this and an action from without upon what we call an intelligence, with will leading to an action on its or his part, no longer to be called a simply re-action, but a consequence through a complicated intermediation. What I am saying now is from the physical point of view.[1]

When 'distinctiveness' enters through reflection there is more of *thought* than *what is thought of* in evidence. This is because we are always on the side of thought. Just as there is self-consciousness and perceptiveness when reflection enters so there is sensibility and activity where action enters. The former two, namely, self-consciousness and perceptiveness, deal with 'intellectiveness'; the latter two, sensibility and activity, deal with action. One experience of sensibility and activity leads on to another just as in the case of 'intellectiveness' one experience of reflection leads on to another.

c. Reflection as action

It seems that Grote here is trying to separate thought and the 'object' of thought, and in doing so he appears to be true to his professed basis of attempting to see the epistemological problem involved at one time from the 'philosophical' approach and at another time from the phenomenal point of view. In speaking about action he appears to mean physical action of one thing upon another, and upon the mind. But true to his position that reflection can differentiate the 'self-self' from the 'thought-self' he should regard reflection as action just as surely as corporeal activity. It is not likely that Grote did not see this point, yet in what he writes he does not always make this issue clear.

Reflection cannot, in Grote's view, be immediate. Corporeal activity is involved in reflection, for reflection has to do with phenomena representing the physical (or 'object') side, and also with 'philosophy' (in corporeal activity) which gives meaning to what is experienced through reflection. Also, it was said that reflection is *action* ('just as surely as corporeal activity'). By this is meant that there is a reflecting

[1] Grote, EP, II, 188.

and that upon which the reflecting is carried out. There is, therefore, a differentiation here which produces mediation.

d. Semi-consciousness

Grote speaks of self-consciousness being extended to semi-consciousness of corporeal activity.

> We pass onward from one experience to another, in respect of our activity, just as we do in respect of our self-consciousness and perceptiveness. As our self-consciousness is extended to that semi-consciousness, as I called it, which we have of our corporeal organization, so the experience of our power in directing our attention is extended to the experience of our power in directing corporeal movement, or (what is the same thing) to the experience of our body not only as a sensive organization, but as an active organization or machine for producing mechanical effects. Our experience of it in this way is exactly analogous to our experience of it in the other: we can move it partly, but it can be moved without our moving it.[1]

> I am not here concerned to consider the nature of this 'will' or what is called the 'freedom' of it. It is certainly not arbitrary, and our attention to one part of what is before us rather than to another is suggested by something independent of us: the nature of the suggestion is not matter for discussion now.[2]

This 'semi-consciousness' of corporeal activity, that is, this sensibility (at least the *thought* side of it) has the characteristic of immediateness. It corresponds to intuition which also is immediate. The same may be said for activity, in the primary sense of activity as the result of 'want' as a fact. 'Want' as a fact, and not as a feeling, underlies this activity.

> The common parent both of sensibility and of activity may be said to be '*want*' – '*want*' as a fact, which we must carefully distinguish from want as a feeling, or the feeling of want. Want, in what I have called immediateness, exists as a fact, and when this immediateness passes into reflection, this *fact* of want passes into *felt* want or uneasiness, and *concurrently* with this (*not* as a result of it) the *fact* of want impels action.[3]

When reflection enters in, the fact of want passes over into a *feeling* of want, and generates action. Reflection is the waking to a state of things which before the waking were included in immediateness. Reflection is half-way between immediateness and activity, or immediate thought and immediate action. That is, it is a state of semi-consciousness (or semi-self-consciousness) where we are aware of our corporeality.

---

[1] Grote, EP, II, 189, 190.
[2] *Op. cit.*, 189.
[3] *Op. cit.*, 190

By saying, some time since, that reflection was intermediate between immediate thought and immediate action, what I meant was this: that reflection, as we have seen, brings us into a region of what I called 'semi-consciousness,' which is the state of feeling in which we stand in regard of our body. From the other side, if we follow immediate action upwards or inwards, we come to a region of more refined physics, of vital physics, where there are phenomena of a very peculiar nature. This region corresponds, from the other side, with the semi-consciousness. In this region of the study of life we have consciousness and physical fact in very close proximity and entanglement. But for all this, we never can get both into the same view, any more than the two sides of the carpet.[1]

xvi. *Immediateness and reflection illustrated by carpet*

The epistemological problem involved in a discussion of immedi-ateness and reflection is carefully presented in an illustration of a carpet:

If we now recall to mind . . . action viewed from the side of physics, and compare it with what I have now said about action viewed from the side of immediate thought, we seem to see two portions, which put together, make up intelligent or volitional action as a whole. But this is not exactly so, and the supposition that it is so seems to me one of the errors which, in the present state of philoso-phy, we are most in danger of. We have to remember that they are seen from different sides. Looking from the side of consciousness and from the side of physical fact is like looking at a carpet, hung up, from the one side and from the other. What we see is the same, and yet not the same: and those who add the facts of body and facts of mind together as *two* constituents of the universe seem to do very much as if it should be said there are two carpets, which make up all of what we see: the one carpet rough and unfinished, the other smooth and polished: the one with a man in the pattern of it who has got a sword in his left hand, the other with a man who has a sword in his right. In a way, it may be said that it is two carpets that we see: but though we may *combine* them together if we know how, we must not *add* them or put them side by side with each other, for they are viewed each in a different manner, and cannot in *this* way be brought into relation.[2]

Grote looks at reality (the carpet), from the point of view of physics, or phenomena. Here there is physical activity, as though we are on the phenomenal side of reality and, for example, directing the eyes (as physical) on the carpet, from the physical side. But the eyes, as physical, tell us *nothing* about the carpet. Yet the eyes, as physical are *absolutely necessary* if we are going to conatively 'see' the carpet (from the other side). That is, there is physical action upon the carpet and a corresponding reaction, as when we stretch out the hand to touch the carpet, and find that there is a reaction to our touch as the carpet may yield to it, seem rough. etc. But this action and re-action do not yield meaning though they are necessary to the deri-

[1] Grote, EP, II, 193.
[2] *Op. cit.*, 191, 192.

vation of meaning. Where meaning is derived is from an approach to the carpet from the opposite side. This is the 'philosophical' approach. Here there is volition or will, as conation.

xvii. A paradox

Let us return now to consider briefly again the initial starting-point of this chapter, namely, intuition and reflection. It is untrue to say, Grote holds, that of intuition and reflection, that intuition comes first in time. Total abstraction of either intuition or reflection from each other is not possible. For convenience in analysis it seems fair to Grote's position to say that intuition as immediateness could be abstracted from reflection (if abstraction were possible at all) more readily than reflection could be abstracted from intuition. What is meant by this is that, for all thinking at all the 'self-self' underlies everything else. The 'self-self' is itself an abstraction, but it must be present *before* any possible reflection can take place. Now since intuition (as immediateness) is an abstraction it can not be said that intuition generates reflection. For, strictly, intuition is never present without reflection. And it would be impossible to say just what intuition by itself could do since we never find it by itself but always along with *some* reflection.

Reflection (specifically implied in the 'thought-self') is possible only because there is thought. 'Before' is emphasized here in order to call attention to a rather paradoxical position in Grote. For if the 'self-self' is itself an abstraction it cannot very well 'precede' the 'thing-self' from which it is abstracted. Grote seems aware of this paradox though he never refers to it by this term. There is a sense in which Grote is incorrect, and a sense in which he is correct. The sense in which he is incorrect (and he doesn't seem unaware of this incorrectness) is that if immediateness or the 'self-self' is an abstraction from reflection or the 'thought-self' then it is incorrect to say that it *precedes* or comes *before* reflection or the 'thought-self.' The sense in which he is correct (and he seems very aware of this correctness) is that immediateness or the 'self-self' is basic to all reflection, whereas all reflection is not strictly basic to immediateness or the 'self-self.' That it is not basic to the *self-self* is evident in the fact that as soon as reflection is considered it is the 'thought-self' that is considered and not the 'self-self.'

xviii. *'Knowledge of acquaintance' and*
'knowledge of judgment'

a. Intuition as 'looking on'

'Intuition' is a very inadequate term for what it represents. What is meant by the word is that mind and its object are so closely connected that they are one. This is immediateness. There is so intimate a contact between the object and the subject that the one cannot be distinguished from the other. The German word 'anschauung' has been used for intuition and implies 'looking *on*' the object, but there is a separation implied in this term that should not be entertained in the case of Grote's use of the word 'immediateness.' If the separation is to be made, it will be of the nature of an abstraction with two kinds of knowledge, first, immediate or intuitive, and, second, mediate, conceptual, or reflectional. The former Grote refers to as 'knowledge of acquaintance' and the latter as 'knowledge of judgment.' Judgment strictly could never enter into the former, for if it did the former kind of knowledge would be no longer immediate. Immediate knowledge may be referred to as knowledge of acquaintance because the element of reflection which enters into this knowledge is not sufficient for judgment. Of course both kinds of knowledge are abstractions for they never really are other than in conjunction. Knowledge of acquaintance and knowledge of judgment shade off into each other so gradually that they cannot be found, in actuality, separate.

b. Basis for distinction arises in immediateness and reflection

The basis for this distinction between knowledge of acquaintance and knowledge of judgment in Grote's writing arises in connection with the distinction he draws in dealing with immediateness and reflection. In the popular references to 'knowledge of acquaintance' and 'knowledge about' indebtedness has been acknowledged to Grote as the originator of the distinction between these terms. This distinction will be discussed later in this dissertation.

c. Analogy in Ferrier

How closely both kinds of knowledge are combined may be noted in Ferrier where he says that what we know is not the object of knowledge but 'our knowledge of the object of knowledge.' That is, the person who knows gets in the way of what is known. To speak of 'knowledge of acquaintance' is correct if by this term immediateness is implied; but, strictly, to speak of intuitive 'knowledge' is not correct. For 'knowledge' implies reflection and hence knowledge as reflective knowledge is not intuitive.

4. SIGNIFICANCE OF IMMEDIATENESS AND REFLECTION IN GROTE'S PHILOSOPHY

One of the most evident and significant points in Grote's analysis of immediateness and reflection is this distinction just made between 'knowledge of acquaintance' and 'knowledge of judgment' (or 'knowledge about'). This distinction has now become familiar in philosophy.[1] This significant issue out of an analysis of immediateness and reflection is explicitly presented by Grote.

There are other significant points that are both implicit and explicit – mostly implicit. Throughout his discussion of these two terms Grote is concerned with showing just what happens when epistemology is approached wholly from the 'philosophical' aspect. The result is the 'self-self.' One could make an extravagent statement by saying that this is pure unadulterated immediateness, a total abstraction – yes, an abstraction so extreme that Grote will not strictly allow it. This extreme and impossible position of immediateness at least shows that the 'philosophical' approach in epistemology may be so far-reaching as to be absurd.

Now immediateness as a total abstraction would have no reflection in it. This would involve an abstraction from reflecting upon the past or a considering of anything regarding the future. In that case pure immediateness would be wholly devoid of relations, for relations in immediateness would have to allow for *thought* as well as *what is thought of*. Immediateness wholly abstracted from reflection would not have any relations with spatial objects, nor could it have any relations with thoughts (as 'objects') in a time sequence. Immediateness, then, would be a theoretical limit rather than an actual one. In fact, Grote would have to admit that pure immediateness devoid of all relations, and abstracted from all reflection does not *actually* exist.

Sensibility and activity are represented in a view of knowledge from the physical side. These terms are not too specifically defined but they are reasonably adequate for Grote's purpose in showing the phenomenal approach possible in epistemology. Strictly, Grote should not use the term 'sensibility' here, for the term has 'philosophical' impli-

[1] Cf. 'Conclusion' of this book.

cations. It carries *meaning*, implies consciousness, and is also otherwise a philosophical term. He seems to require just enough *meaning* to allow use of such a term as sensibility in the sense in which he is using it, namely, capacity which an animate object has for pleasure or pain. Now, an animate being cannot have any capacity for pleasure or pain unless there is at least *some* meaning present in the mind of that animate being, though not necessarily very much. This permits Grote to speak of sensibility and activity as representing the phenomenal approach to knowledge. Both sensibility and activity together are referred to as volition, as conation. For there to be any volition at all there must be *some* meaning present. This necessary meaning implicit in volition is an additional testimony to the impossibility of wholly abstracting phenomenal reality from 'thought.'

There are, then, two sides to the carpet, the immediateness and reflectional side, and, the sensibility and activity side. But there is also a sense in which both sides of the carpet are involved even in immediateness and reflection. For reflection has a sort of 'subject' and 'object' nature. This is evident in the *practical* impossibility of ever being without the 'thought-self' or of having *only* the 'self-self' in thinking.

It should be noted that even though we begin with our own personal experience, such as Grote refers to by the term 'self-self,' yet we are always going beyond ourselves. If the given is so 'innocent' as it has been declared to be [1] then it can reveal little if anything. If this 'innocence' were perfect we would never know it – not even as the given. The given must be richer than mere perfect innocence. It is this issue that causes Grote to assert that the 'self-self' is an abstraction from the 'thought-self.' The 'thought-self' reveals the fact that the given is not innocent. It is intimately bound up with the 'self-self' so that the 'self-self' (wholly by itself) must be regarded as fictional. That is, the given is a given *for us*. This givenness involves a reflection on the past, anticipation of the future, and a whole network of other relations also.[2] For Grote, the given is always a given for consciousness or 'philosophy.'

5. CRITICAL COMMENT

Grote's remarks on immediateness and reflection make difficult reading – a trait not uncommon in Grote's writings, especially in the *Exploratio Philosophica* – because of the introduction of new terms with specialized meanings. Only a few terms are so used but these are

---

[1] Williams, "The Innocence of the Given," *Jour. of Phil.*, XXX (1933), 617–620.
[2] Brightman, in *Jour. of Phil.*, XXXI (1934), 263–268.

sufficient in number to require considerable qualification throughout this chapter, or in the chapter where they appear in Grote's writings. Grote may have been dependent upon others in his use of these terms but the fact that he does not acknowledge any sources implies that he is not using these terms in any senses other than the ones that he specifies himself. This seems true in the case of such words as 'self-self' and 'thought-self.' This practice of dealing in terms with precise and familiar meanings, as well as with precise and unfamiliar meanings, has its advantages. It enables the user to present his meaning more directly and with a minimum of words. This is the method most attractive to Grote, and the one which he frequently makes manifest to the reader. There is a second advantage, namely, that the word so introduced may present an argument that could not otherwise be presented by Grote. This point seems to be frequently brought out. Grote appears to be strongly of the belief that he must couch his argument in terms some of which are of his own coinage.

There are several disadvantages in this use of new terms to bring out one's meaning. It is the difficulty which the reader finds in some of Whitehead's writings.[1] New terms are coined in order that the reader may not mistake the meaning which he would be almost certain to do if shop-worn terms were employed. This use of new terms makes the reading slow and difficult. And if one does not carefully note the context, as well as the words actually being read at the time, one does not get any sense out of the passage under consideration – at least not the full meaning that the author wishes to convey.

Another disadvantage in the use of new terms, or in the new meanings given to old ones, is that a work otherwise very meritorious may fall into oblivion in which case the characteristic terms along with their respective meanings are lost. Probably this oblivion is somewhat justified – certainly not on the grounds that would lead to the adoption of 'basic English' on the view that all other English is unnecessary – for the slow adoption of terms gives more opportunity to weigh and consider, in order to find out the ones that are most valuable and most essential.

A third disadvantage arises, especially in the case of words already used with other meanings, from weighing down our language with new interpretations that could be expressed in some other way. This seems true in the case of the terms, 'philosophy' and 'phenomenon' as used by Grote. To the reader who comes upon Grote's use of these terms

[1] For example, Whitehead, PR.

for the first time, the old meanings (sometimes referred to by Grote as the ordinary accepted meanings) will recur again and again, making it difficult to see that the author is accurate when he seems inaccurate.

These advantages and disadvantages are characteristic of Grote's use of 'immediateness' and 'reflection' as one can readily see both from what has been presented in this chapter on the terms 'immediateness' and 'reflection' (neither of which is ever wholly abstracted from the other), and to a lesser extent on such terms as 'sensibility,' 'intuition,' and 'want.'

Regarding the use of 'immediateness' and 'reflection' comments have already been made under 'Significance of immediateness and reflection in Grote's philosophy' [1] and passing mention may be made here to Grote's use of terms that do not mean what they seem to say. For example, he uses 'immediateness' which is strictly not immediate, 'reflection' which is strictly not reflection, and 'sensibility' which strictly does not pertain to the senses alone. For 'immediateness' is never wholly immediate but contains some reflection, 'reflection' always requires something immediate upon which it may reflect, and 'sensibility,' in the sense of possessing capacity for pleasure and pain, cannot terminate in pleasure and pain unless there is an animate object to which pleasure and pain *mean* something (namely, pleasure and pain). However, it should be said to Grote's credit that he is concerned with showing what some terms can imply, if taken in their extreme form. And he wants to point out that a taking of terms in their extreme form, or meaning, is frequently characteristic of much of our thinking. Hence, for example, he wishes to show that this is quite all right *provided that* we be prepared to recognize the extremity of our analysis and not affirm that such extreme meanings are the *sole* ones. For example, he would hold that to regard 'immediateness' as *wholly* immediate is to be guilty of what has frequently been mentioned in this book by the term (which he applies to this mistake, namely) 'mis-psychology,' or 'bad psychology.' The sound advice, frequently true in dealing with propositions in logic, to understand what is written in the way in which it is meant rather that in all the possible and remote meanings that can be drawn from it, is good advice to follow in dealing with Grote's somewhat unusual and partially hidden meanings throughout the various expositions of his views. Yet it must be said on the side of the reader of much of Grote's work, and, for example, in connection with his exposition of immedi-

[1] *Supra*, pp. 181–182.

ateness and reflection, that it is frequently difficult to understand 'in the way in which it is meant' much of what Grote writes. Whatever Grote has contributed that may be judged of considerable importance will be forever vitiated by this weakness. That his thought is not completely vitiated but rather is of very considerable importance is a view to the testimony of which this book is written – which project is itself an *explicit* recognition of Grote's contribution in philosophy. It is the aim of this work, also, to signify *implicitly* (that is, meaningfully) how much recognition and importance should accrue to Grote because of the heritage received by his written contributions.

6. RELATION TO THE FOLLOWING CHAPTER

The chief significance in giving as exposition of immediateness and reflection preceding a discussion of personalistic elements in Grote's philosophy, is to show once again the importance of distinguishing between two approaches that are taken in philosophy, the 'philosophical' and the phenomenal. A mixture of the two is frequently found in the use of the words, 'immediateness' and 'reflection.' The closer a philosophy can come to complete 'immediateness' the less likelihood there will be of error. Grote's emphasis on the 'self-self,' which he regards as basic for everything else in epistemology, is as personalistic an approach to reality as any.

This 'self-self' may be compared to what has been called the 'Pure Ego.' This 'self-self' may be "conceived as a non-empirical principle, ordinarily inaccessible to direct introspection, but inferred from introspective evidence." [1] The 'self-self' therefore, is a sort of soul substance, implied in "the soul theory which regards the pure ego as a permanent spiritual substance underlying the fleeting succession of conscious experience." [2] The 'self-self,' Grote states, is that which contains thought which is immediate and unreflective. It seems, then, that the 'self-self' could be regarded as a spiritual substance – 'spiritual' in the sense of animated, and God-given – which is basic for all reflection, or for "the fleeting succession of conscious experience," as described above.

Grote's position regarding the basic importance of this 'self-self' appears to designate him clearly as a theistic personalist, who regards

[1] Wood, "Pure Ego," in Runes, DOP, 88.
[2] *Loc. cit.*

the relation of thought and 'thing,' or 'philosophy' and phenomenon, as inseparable aspects of one fundamental reality.

He has been referring to the way in which all 'things' must conform to this idealism. He contends, on quite safe ground, that we are always present in any realism, whether professedly or not. This point, so simple that critics of Grote might regard it as naive, is of extreme importance. It is Grote's way of acknowledging what later was called 'the ego-centric predicament.' [1] So we cannot take the position that we must forsake the considering of things in relation to us, and look at them for what they are *in themselves*.

Grote would say, they are nothing in themselves; 'they' are always in relation to us. One might comment on Grote's argument by remarking that to regard them as *in themselves* is an unwarranted abstraction. It is an abstracting of what never is found alone, namely, phenomenal reality; 'phenomenal reality' is always 'found' in relation with consciousness. It is that which can affect us even though we may not be conscious of it. And yet when we are conscious of it there is a mixture of consciousness and phenomenal reality.

When Hamilton, for example, speaks of the 'consciousness of matter' he unwittingly assumes matter in relation to us, and then deals with it as though it were *not* in relation to us already, by referring to it in the phrase 'consciousness of matter.' In reflection, as Grote deals with it, in this chapter, there is the self reflecting and that upon which the self reflects. Now, this 'thing' upon which the self reflects is in the very same position as Hamilton's 'matter' which is already unwittingly assumed as in relation to consciousness before we are said to have consciousness of it. If we may comment on Hamilton's position here, as it provides a convenient illustration of what Grote is dealing with in this chapter on immediateness and reflection, there is implicit truth in the self doing the reflecting – in the self that is self-conscious – in Hamilton.

Hamilton is not fully aware of this and mixes up a correspondence theory of truth with a coherence theory. But if there is a coherence theory of truth, then a correspondence theory of truth is both unnecessary, and superfluous (in the additional sense of being not only unnecessary but also erroneous). Grote seems to be sticking with a theory

---

[1] Ralph Barton Perry, defending his view that we are involved in 'the ego-centric predicament,' attacks James Bissert Pratt who in criticism of Perry stated: Let us "forsake dialectics and observe what actually transpires," for "observations will do the realist very little good," etc. *Jour. of Phil.*, X (1913), 454.

of truth as coherent.[1] And the greatest coherence that he can imagine is to be found in the 'self-self.'

This seems to be an extreme personalism that is wholly impracticable for a 'self-self' that doesn't admit even of a 'thought-self' not to mention 'things' (both mental and physical) as we have them in reflection, is impracticable. But the impracticability is only apparent, for Grote affirms that the 'self-self' is a sort of imaginary extreme which does not exist by itself, but always has some reflection combined with it however small the reflective element may be.

Throughout all his writing on 'immediateness' and 'reflection,' Grote is especially concerned with analysis. He has been so interested in the analytic approach to his subject that he might give the impression that what he designates as the 'self-self,' 'thought-self,' 'reflection,' 'immediateness,' etc., are entities which are valid when considered separately. This is one of the possible impressions that, his writing generally, and his views on the 'self' particularly, gives.

However, regarding the 'self,' it should be noted that Grote has persons, or personality, in mind. The 'self-self' is personal, though Grote does not wish to make it an object, for then it would become the 'thought-self.' But the atomistic elements which Grote presents, are misconstrued if taken in abstraction. Probably Grote could have said that the 'self-self' alone exists and that the 'thought-self' exists in it. But he has already stated that the 'self-self' is not an object of thought, and has implied that it exists only as a sort of theoretic extreme from which, because of his analysis, all reflection is abstracted.

Actually, the 'self-self' does not exist *as such*. Reflection is always present in some degree. A consideration of this immediateness and reflection together makes Grote's personalistic philosophy a practicable one which recognizes the basic and extreme (epistemological) personalism from which it stems. We will now consider it.

---

[1] Grote's criterion of truth is coherence. The greatest coherence is found in immediateness. The more reflective, and 'objective,' the elements are that comprise 'knowledge' the more likelihood there is of error.

CHAPTER IX

PERSONALISM IN GROTE'S WRITINGS

1. INTRODUCTION

As indicated at the close of the last chapter, Grote may be classed as an epistemological personalist. It may be added that he is also a metaphysical personalist. Let us look at each of these terms, both to see what is meant by them and also how they apply to Grote's philosophy. First, as an epistemological personalist Grote reveals his position by pointing out that the common source of thought and 'thing' is to be found in deity mediated through human personality. Man is a partaker of a nature above phenomenal nature. This higher nature is of "a Planner or Maker with his ideas and his purposes." [1]

There is also involved in this view of the deity, Grote's metaphysical personalism. By metaphysical personalism is meant the personal nature of reality. Now Grote's view of reality as personal is revealed in his conception of a Planner or Maker who possesses *ideas* and *purposes*. Ideas and purposes, considered on a level at least as high as human beings, are properly regarded as belonging to persons and are therefore, on that level, personal. Ideas and purposes considered as belonging also to "a nature above all this" [2] are likewise personal. That is to say, the nature of reality is personal and can have *meaning* and can be *understood* only through personality. This is what Grote seems to say and is what he accepts as a basis for the metaphysical expression of his personalism.

Grote's interest is taken up, in his chief writings, with epistemology rather than with metaphysics. Yet, metaphysics, dealing with the nature of being or reality, is basic for epistemology. There is no reality, for Grote, that is not a sort of reality-for-us. This is not a reality that can *ever* be regarded as separated from us. There is always a personal

[1] Grote, EP, II, 293.
[2] *Loc. cit.*

nature to reality. Here is Grote's metaphysical personalism. The monistic nature of his epistemology is evident in his view of reality as essentially one, but a reality that can be viewed from two different aspects, namely, from the consciousness or philosophical side, and the phenomenal or 'reality' approach.

These two aspects are of the same reality, Grote seems to say in various ways. Now this reality cannot overlook epistemological personalism where there is a blending of "ourselves and our being with the known." The epistemological monism evident in Grote's thought may be illustrated by referring to his comment on 'intuition.'

The word 'intuition' is in many respects about as bad a word as could have been chosen to express immediate knowledge, and in fact, it is almost the most confusing word in all philosophy. The looking *into* a thing implies a very high degree of attention and distinguishing, and is thus the mental process almost at the furthest remove from what 'intuition' is intended to mean. No doubt 'intuition' means also 'looking *on*' a thing, the metaphor simply taken from sight, and hence the Germans use 'Anschauung' to correspond with it, but even this metaphor expresses very poorly that which we want to express, viz. that blending, so to speak, of ourselves and our being with the known, that intimate contact of it with us and of us with it, which is the groundwork of our confidence in 'intuition' as necessary trueness.[1]

The essential part of Grote's meaning is "That blending . . . of ourselves and our being with the known." It is this meaning given to intuition which enables him to speak of immediateness in distinction from reflection, and the 'self-self' from the 'thought-self.' Thus, also, he contrasts intuition with experience.[2]

Grote makes this contrast because it seems to him that experience is concerned too much with a correspondence theory of truth which he rejects. It is only in intuition that reality is wholly grasped and where there is no analysis possible between knowing and the known. Here his essentially epistemological monism presents itself. If one were to say that intuition as used by Grote should be the most characteristic experience, Grote would raise no objection. Yet his use of 'experience' implies analysis into 'subject' and 'object' – an analysis which he rejects as unsound because dualistic. If we maintain that intuition is the most characteristic experience, Grote would agree. He is simply very cautious about the use of the term 'experience,' being careful to imply that it is characterized by dualism and therefore unacceptable.

Intuition, as Grote defines it, may be put differently as, "that intimate contact of it (i.e. 'the known') with us and of us with it, which is

[1] Grote, EP, II, 203.
[2] Grote, *op. cit.*, 152–159.

the groundwork of our confidence." [1] All knowledge, then, is essentially personalistic in the sense that personality is central. We may consider personality central, epistemologically, as a blending "of ourselves and our being with the known" thus, metaphysically, mediating reality through personality – so that the result is the personal nature of reality.

Now complete truth is found only in intuition, or in the 'self-self.' For Grote considers "intuition *the ground* of all knowledge." [2] Grote uses the term 'self-self' as an abstraction. If the 'self-self' is an abstraction and truth lies essentially in the 'self-self,' it looks as though truth is an abstraction and hence not complete truth. What Grote is trying to say is that it is only essentially through the 'self-self' that truth can be recognized. For once we admit any semblance of duality into epistemology we get the unacceptable correspondence theory of truth. Grote much prefers a coherence theory of truth, and coherence rests ultimately upon the self. All reality other than the personal nature of reality is a reality borrowed from the self.

2. EPISTEMOLOGICAL MONISM

This epistemology is fundamentally monistic. Hence it is akin to that presented by Royce, Calkins, and Hocking rather than to personal dualists like Bowne. But the monism is of an unusual variety. If one is to distinguish between the terms 'idealism' and 'panobjectivism' in regard to this monism, the choice must certainly lie on the side of idealism. Being *epistemological* monism the idealism is 'idea-ism' rather than 'ideal-ism.' Yet the 'ideals' are *metaphysical* personal norms in the sense of standards by which to evaluate. Ideals used in this sense characterize Grote as a Platonist. For Plato, as Professor Demos is careful to point out,[3] these ideals are reached by 'a leap.' These ideals are intuitively 'seen.' The idea is essentially personalistic in the sense that the common source of thought and 'thing' is mediated through human personality.

Truth is found primarily in the person. This person, as a conscious self is the 'self-self' in distinction from the self thought of, that is, the 'thought-self.' Grote's Berkeleianism is humanistic as well as theistic. The theistic nature of his personalism appears in such passages as the following:

[1] Grote, EP, II, 203.
[2] Grote, *op. cit.*, 218.
[3] Demos, POP, Chapter III.

To me human consciousness and freedom – suggesting to us a personal existence more real than that even of the universe, suggesting moral responsibility, hope of future life, relation to God, or the mind which originated the universe – are things quite unaffectable, *a priori*, by anything which physio-psychology can discover, and which any consideration how the human race has come physically to be what it is, or how it is related to other organized races, has nothing to do with.[1]

Here Grote definitely affirms his belief in, and relation to, God. God is declared to be the originator of the universe and therefore of consciousness and phenomena. Grote conceives of God as a being possessed of mind and a personal existence more real than that of any human person. The greater reality which he attributes to God is that of one who made all other reality possible in the sense of originating (and sustaining) it.

The metaphysical personalism characteristic of Grote can be observed in his conception of deity. Grote accepts Ferrier's position that "in the judgment of reason there never can have been a time when the universe was without God." [2] The reality of the universe is, therefore, characterized by divine personality. Hence, metaphysics is not excluded by Grote even though he seems to be more interested in epistemology than in metaphysics. And his interest in epistemology is also, necessarily, an interest in metaphysics. He is both concerned, that is, with the nature of reality and the character of knowledge. All true knowledge pertains to the 'self-self.' Grote is thinking specifically of the human self, here. But there seems no reason to believe that true knowledge does not pertain also to divine Selfhood.

That true knowledge pertains to divine Selfhood appears in such a statement as "the mind which originated the universe" and "a personal existence more real than that even of the universe." It appears therefore that Grote resembles Berkeley, in view of the following remark regarding Berkeley:

Of all the British thinkers Berkeley was perhaps the greatest, the most misunderstood and neglected and with the strongest metaphysical interests. Too often he has been taken as a pure subjectivist whereas he founded his objectivity in true personalistic fashion in the act of the immanent Supreme Creative Person.[3]

---

[1] Grote, EP, II, 332.
[2] Grote, *op. cit.*, I, 79.
[3] Flewelling, "Personalism," in Runes, TCP, 333.

3. MONISTIC, PLURALISTIC, AND THEISTIC
PERSONALISM

i. Grote's unique personalism

The 'self-self' of Grote's epistemology has part of the characteristics of the self of personalism. "By self personalism means a unitary, self-identifying, conscious agent." [1] However, Grote's 'self-self' has the additional characteristic of being non-reflective. For as soon as the self becomes reflective it is no longer the unreflective 'self-self' but the 'thought-self.' This 'self-self' of Grote is a theoretical and impracticable abstraction, which as an abstraction is therefore virtually and admittedly incomplete. He emphasizes it as the extreme limit of the 'thought' or philosophizing side of reality in contrast with the 'thing' or phenomenal side. The 'thought-self' is an aspect of the self it is true, but it is that phenomenal aspect with which there is a corresponding 'philosophical' aspect, the 'self-self.' Grote refers to his epistemology as "the idealism, personalism, or whatever it may be called, which lies at the root of all that I have said." [2]

Personalism has been defined as "the theory that to be is to be a self or a member of a self. Personalism may be singularistic or pluralistic, theistic or non-theistic." [3] It has already been pointed out that Grote is a monistic, epistemological personalist. It may be stated also that he presents a theistic and pluralistic type of personalism. The theistic nature of personalism is not as frequently presented as metaphysical pluralism. It is, nevertheless, convincingly present as has been pointed out already in this chapter in referring to deity. Additional evidence in favor of the view that Grote is theistic is manifest, indirectly, in a later part of the present chapter in dealing with the topic of a 'Critique of Materialism.'

ii. Monism and pluralism

a. Introductory

Now, the first issue that must be dealt with at once is the senses in which Grote is an epistemological *monist* and a metaphysically *pluralistic* personalist. There appears to be two strains in his philosophy, namely, monism and pluralism. In what senses can these strains be

[1] Brightman, "Personalism and the Influence of Bowne," in PCP, 161.
[2] Grote, EP, I, 146.
[3] Brightman, *loc. cit.*

present in any one, generally coherent, philosophy? Let us look at monism first.

b. Monism

'Monism,' a term that Grote does not seem specifically to use anywhere, has been defined as "in general, the theory that one principle or being will explain the plurality in the world. In *epistemological* monism that principle is the identity of *idea* and *object*." [1] The sense in which Grote is an epistemological monist is due to his identifying idea and object. 'Both' are one; 'they' are idea. Grote refers to himself as an idealist. It is only through mind which *has* the ideas that 'things' have any meaning at all. There are no 'objects' *out there*, for Grote. The meaning of all reality is to be found in the self, the 'self-self,' intuition, 'philosophy,' mind, etc. *Meaning* is not found, essentially, in 'objects,' the 'thought-self,' experience, phenomenal reality, matter, etc. The essential nature of things is revealed through *idea*, the self, the person. Hence Grote may be called an idealist, or a personalist.

c. Pluralism

Though Grote does not expressedly use the term 'pluralism' in his view of reality as pluralistic, let us now briefly analyze to see in what sense Grote is a pluralist despite the fact that in a certain sense (described immediately above) he is a monist. It should always be remembered that Grote is concerned with looking at both sides of the one 'carpet.' [2] One side reveals the 'philosophical' approach to reality; this is the view of reality revealed in idea, mind, self – monism. This monism is an abstraction from phenomenal reality. The other side of the carpet reveals a plurality, a plurality that is never found wholly dissociated from mind, or the self. In the reality of phenomena there is plurality, variety, a manifoldness. In reality, also, Grote admits that there is a plurality of selves and that reality is essentially viewed individualistically. These phenomena (which are real) affect us and affect each other, even when no human consciousness is present which might assimilate all the phenomena into a monism. One cannot deny the existence of these phenomena though we may not be conscious of them. Yet they are *not* things-in-themselves when we are not aware of them. That there is *variety* amongst phenomena cannot be denied. 'They' are *phenomena* not *phenomenon*. 'They' are pluralistic, because

[1] Brightman, ITP, 388.
[2] Grote, EP, II, 192.

all reality is 'seen' in parts, and individualistically. Hence the *plural-ism* that we seek to draw out of the epistemology of Grote. This combination of monism and pluralism lies at the foundation of all Grote's writing on epistemology and metaphysics. Grote is an epistemological monist and a metaphysical pluralist. His epistemological monism has been pointed out frequently throughout the body of this present work, in referring to his view that reality is one though approached from two different directions. That reality is one is a view evident in the "fundamental principle of psychology, that there is no awareness apart from a subject and an object." [1] His metaphysical pluralism arises from his basic individualistic approach toward reality. There is no metaphysical pluralism independent of man. Pluralism has meaning only in relation to the knowing faculty. Nothing exists, to which meaning can be attached, that is independent of us. Reality is as pluralistic as the many selves that view it. It is also pluralistic for any particualr self that views it through analysis. Moreover, there is the reality of many selves or consciousness; the term 'selves' is plural, also implying metaphysical plurality.

iii. Theism

a. Grote, a Berkeleian?

Let us now look at the theistic nature of Grote's epistemology. In many ways Grote resembles Berkeley. Like Berkeley he is a

pluralistic idealist, reflecting upon the spatial attributes of distance, size, and situation, possessed, according to Locke, by external objects in themselves apart from our perception of them, concluded that the discrepancy between the visual and the tactual aspects of these attributes robbed them of all objective validity and reduced them to the status of secondary qualities existing only in and for consciousness . . . The physical aspects of the world are reducible to mental phenomena. Matter is non-existent.[2]

There is a mild intimation of Berkeley's theism in this passage. The physical aspects are reducible to mind. Berkeley is thinking of the mind of the deity that sustains all human minds. Grote at least may be regarded as resembling Berkeley in pluralistic idealism but for Grote's theism we cannot go for direct aid to the fact that both are metaphysical pluralists and idealists. For both could be pluralistic idealists and yet not be theistic. However, it is the case that Grote believes that God creates or makes possible human knowledge. And Berkeley maintains that all human knowing is dependent on divine knowledge.

[1] Bertocci, EAG, 198.
[2] Fuller, on George Berkeley, in Runes, DOP, 38.

b. Resemblances to Berkeley

Let us now examine this likeness. Both are subjectivistic, idealistic, personalistic. They emphasize the supreme importance that mind has in all knowledge. That is, except in relation to the self there is no knowledge at all. Berkeley admits, of course, God's knowledge (where no senses are necessary) which is not dependent upon finite selves. Grote holds that God as the Creator of human beings is the origin of all human knowledge. He admits the existence of phenomenal reality even when we are unaware of it. So also does Berkeley; the phenomenal reality is in the mind of God. For Grote there is no phenomenal reality *for us* ('us' implying the presence of mind) unless there is some consciousness present. Grote is thinking particularly of human consciousness. All reality of which we can speak, talk, or think, is in relation to the self.

Grote will admit the existence of 'objects' as always related to us. These 'objects' are phenomena and never appear without an admixture of consciousness. For Berkeley there are no objects without the presence of mind. Berkeley would not admit the existence of 'phenomenal reality' in Grote's sense. Grote seems to be attempting an explanation of a reality, by holding that such reality exists, in its inter-connections and inter-effects, and its influences upon us, even though we are *not always aware* of it. In Grote, deity is not emphasized so constantly as it is in Berkeley. Yet deity is necessary to Grote's epistemological scheme for he admits that there is "in the Universe a Planner or Maker," and that we are in "relation to God, or the mind which originated the universe." [1] For Berkeley,

finite spirits are created by God, and their several experiences represent his communication to them, so far as they are able to receive it, of his divine experience. [2]

Human experiences are the result of a communication of divine experience, for Berkeley.

There is not any one mark that denotes a man, or effect produced by him, which does not more strongly evince the being of that Spirit who is the Author of Nature. For it is evident that in affecting other persons the will of man hath no other object than barely the motion of the limbs of his body; but that such a motion should be attended by, or excite any idea in the mind of another, depends wholly on the will of the Creator. He alone it is who, "upholding all things by the word of His power," maintains that intercourse between spirits whereby they are able to perceive the existence of each other. [3]

[1] Grote, EP, II, 332.
[2] Fuller, on George Berkeley, in Runes, DOP, 38.
[3] Berkeley, TPH, in Burtt, EPB, 575.

c. Grote is essentially theistic

Grote's essentially theistic view is evident in the following:

There seems to me to be a nature *above* all this: a nature of which man, in virtue of his consciousness and knowledge, is partaker, just as, in virtue of his body and its sensation, he is a portion of the phenomenal nature. And it is this nature which the one part of his thought points to with as much legitimacy as the other to phenomenal nature.[1]

Though Grote does not urge the theistic nature of his metaphysics so constantly, he, nevertheless, supports both his metaphysics and epistemology by a fundamental awareness of the importance of belief in God. He seems to feel the necessity for a theistic hypothesis in stating that "man, in virtue of his consciousness and knowledge, is partaker" of "a nature *above*," that of "a Planner or Maker with his ideas and his purposes." [2]

Again, Grote's theism appears in his remark regarding "God, or the mind which originated the universe." [3] He refers to God as Creator:

What security have we that our humanly natural thought is not a sort of generically private or individual imagination (as in fact some relativists go far to think it), except our feeling that we with our thinking are a part of a constituted, harmonious, self-consistent, God-created universe? [4]

There seems to be the implicit view in this statement that the awareness of all human beings is somehow related. Grote could not possibly mean that any human mind is immediately aware of what takes place in another human mind. But he does seem to hold that we are at least partly aware of what takes place in the divine mind. In short, our minds are unified by and part of the self-consistent and harmonious nature of the mind of God. God through his nature as Creator has made this relationship possible.

4. CRITIQUE OF MATERIALISM

i. The natural sciences

a. Psychical anatomists

Let us turn now from an examination of Grote's personalism to consider his attitude toward the natural sciences, or materialism, made possible becausei of his personalistic approach. The following is, therefore, a partial critque of materialism based upon Grote's personalism.

[1] Grote, EP, II, 293.
[2] *Loc. cit.*
[3] *Op. cit.*, 332.
[4] *Op. cit.*, 36.

Grote criticizes the natural sciences in general and psychical anatomy in particular for their failure to find an adequate explanation of mental experience. After asserting his disagreement with such science, Grote supports his argument by citing certain moral and intellectual difficulties of materialism. Probably the reason why Grote chooses psychical anatomy rather than another science is because this particular science was, in his day, coming to a position which up to that time it never had attained. Certainly psychical anatomy (called by various terms, psycho-physiology, physiopsychology, or psychological anatomy) or anatomy applied to psychology reached a place of importance not true of it two millenniums before. There were two reasons why psychical anatomy claimed to supersede philosophy: (1) philosophy no longer seemed to advance, and (2) philosophy dealt with unrealities while psychical anatomy dealt with facts. Psychical anatomy virtually seemed to explain away the view that all true being is personal. Grote does not express himself in this way exactly, but this comment seems justified because of Grote's professed personalism. It is also interesting to note the approach of Fechner's psycho-physics to epistemological problems:

According to Fechner, the connection of inner and outer experience in our consciousness makes it possible to investigate the laws of this correspondence. The science of this is *psycho-physics*. It is the first problem of this science to find out *methods for measuring psychical quantities*, in order to obtain laws that may be formulated mathematically. Fechner brings forward principally the *method of just perceptible differences*, which defines as the unit of mass the smallest difference that is still perceptible between intensities of sensation, and assumes this to be equal everywhere and in all cases.[1]

To assert that psychical anatomy has not been superseded and to give no reason for this assertion, beyond aspirations which cannot be explained by psychical anatomy, is to present a fear of philosophy. For psychical anatomy to claim that it possesses the last word for any philosophy is merely idle pretension.

My aim in trying to clear the ground from the wrong noö-psychology or mis-psychology, is in order that we may have instead of it a good physio-psychology, such as now seems possible. To me however it does not seem that we ever shall have such a thing, unless we can clear our minds from the thought that it will do anything, one way or the other, towards settling the higher questions and difficulties of morality and religion . . . But all physio-psychology seems to me to be vitiated by the want of clearness of view as to its relation to the higher philosophy and to morals.[2]

Philosophy, according to Grote, in contrast to materialism, must show that psychical anatomy does not account for the factor which gives to

1 Windelband, HOP, 645.
2 Grote, EP, II, 331.

philosophy a right to predominance. If psychical anatomy claims to deal with *fact*, philosophy must deal with something *higher* than fact. It seems justifiable to regard this something that is higher than fact as personality. It is only through personality that any reality can exist for us. And in the controversy between psychical anatomy and philosophy, desire to follow either one of the contestants rather than the other must not be entertained without good reason. In other words, one does not acquiesce correctly unless adequate support can be given for one's position.

b. Professed materialists

Supposing the professed materialist explains everything even to what thought or action are, he will still be confronted with the problem as to what *we* are. "Formerly it was supposed that the facts might be reduced to matter and energy, and the categories consequently to one type. This was the method of the older materialism." [1] Hence Grote refers to 'professed materialists,' who deal with phenomena only and yet adhere to their materialism as an avowed philosophical doctrine. Viscount Haldane is typical of modern critics of materialism who note, as Grote did, great deficiencies in materialism: "Morality cannot be reduced to mathematics, and no more can life be resolved into mechanism, or reason into mere instinct." [2] Materialists, Grote continues, regard matter as a thing-in-itself and believe that this gives a complete philosophy.

I have used the expression 'professed materialists' here to signify those who, from the point of view of psychical anatomy, consider themselves able to make out that the notions which men have at various times maintained as to another world and a future life cannot possibly have any foundation.[3]

Further concerning 'professed materialism' Grote makes the following remark:

All the corporeal explanation is really only a discussion of a portion of the fact: what I have called above 'professed materialism' is a taking of this portion of the fact for the whole. And the notion of the professed materialists, that they are right in doing this, seems to me a good deal confirmed by the dealing of their adversaries towards them.[4]

c. New Realists

Nor do the recent New Realists, with their reduction of reality to 'neutral entities,' offer any more satisfactory explanation of know-

[1] Cunningham, IBA, 244.
[2] Haldane, ROR, 133.
[3] Grote, EP, II, 235.
[4] *Op. cit.*, 237.

ledge, than Grote noted about the 'professed materialists' of his day.
For, these materialists resemble those about whom it was said by a
present-day writer, that

they undertake to put the universals and relations of thought into the non-
mental world, which for them confronts the mind as something from which
the latter is receptive. But herewith the mind becomes like a substance on which
impressions are causally effected from without. Among the causes are the very
universals whose significance seems to be possible only as belonging to the nature
of mind itself. And there is no justification for this, certainly not in scientific
methods of treatment.[1]

d. Imagination and memory

It is true that Hobbes looked upon imagination as decaying sense.
"Imagination therefore is nothing but decaying sense." [2] And Hartley
believed that mind and matter could be explained by the vibration
of delicate nerve fibres over all parts of the body.

As a man of science, he sought a physiological basis for this mental transfor-
mation, and concluded that simple ideas are the result of vibrations in the
brain, and that complex ideas arise from the coalescence of such vibrations.[3]

However, imagination and memory are still left unexplained. For
example, it is not the physical eye merely that sees; the 'we' has an
important place in sight. Imagination and memory are but two of the
various attributes included within the 'we.' One may comment on
Grote's position here by saying that 'we' is that upon which imagination,
memory, etc. in personality, is founded.

Grote mentions a possible argument which antagonists of the
psychical anatomical explanation of mind could give. The argument is
to the effect that if the professed materialists explain everything as
done by body then the idea of soul is superfluous. Grote advocates the
soul as the director of bodily activity. It is that which comprehends
and without which there could be no reality. Grote sees no reason why
the soul should not be regarded as directing the activity of the body.
But he prefers not to use the term 'soul' here because of its historical
and substantialistic significance; he prefers to use the term 'mind.'

The contention of Grote is that consciousness and personality cannot
be explained away by any materialistic system. He would seem to hold
that the view of *thought* as sufficiently explained by stating that it is a
modification of the body is erroneous. For what is not known, he would

[1] Cunningham, IBA, 244.
[2] Hobbes, LEV, in Burtt, EPB, 133.
[3] Wright, HMP, 225.

seem to agree, is the very point in dispute, namely, where the body leaves off and consciousness enters. Psychical anatomy, he *could* continue to maintain, furnishes no adequate explanation for consciousness.

It might be contended further, beyond the point where Grote leaves the subject, that psychical anatomy empasizing materialism can *not* offer an *explanation* without violating the virtually exclusive materialistic basis it accepts. If psychical anatomy were to insist on a parallelism it would run into the difficulty which has been illustrated by "two railway trains running side by side on a double track." [1] The trains are operating on different tracks, are moving together but have no causal relationship with each other.

But the psychical anatomists with whom Grote deals are virtual epiphenomenalists who hold that consciousness or mind is simply a secondary phenomenon which accompanies bodily processes. For these materialists, matter is the primary or real substance. For the materialists the laws of the natural sciences are universal. Psychical anatomy, in short, furnishes no adequate explanation for consciousness or mind.

Again, there is a moral difficulty in the professed materialists' philosophy. Grote regards knowledge, as well as other facts of phenomena, as greatly dependent upon imagination. If the developed thought of a human being is not regarded as having something to do beyond the 'facts' and processes of life, then the position of the human being may be given the status of the brutes. The point is that Grote believes that there is something beyond the material world (as interpreted, for example, by the psychical anatomists) with which man is concerned, and imagination provides for this. If knowledge, which is not alone concerned with materialism, is to be regarded as a phenomenal fact it must be given a place by professed materialists. It has its foundation like other phenomenal facts on imagination. And imagination cannot be divorced from personality. It aids in giving *being* significance. Imagination can reside only in a *person*. It cannot be explained away by any materialism. Imagination is concerned with the realm of morals as well as with the universe of phenomenalism and therefore morality deserves consideration by materialists.

ii. 'Proverse' and 'retroverse'

a. Significance of these terms

There are two words widely used by Grote that help us to see the relation between mind and its 'objects.' These are 'proverse' and

[1] McDougall, BAM, i.

'retroverse.' 'Retroverse' has a close relationship with consciousness and personality. 'Proverse' is closely connected with phenomenal reality. Let us look at these two terms and see their significance since they are closely related to Grote's personal idealism.

By the use of the words 'proverse' and 'retroverse' Grote attempts to further elucidate the relationship (or lack of relationship) between mind and 'matter.' By 'proverse' he means the phenomenal fact as in the case of the eye having brain and nerves closely connected with and essential to its function. By 'retroverse' is meant the consciousness which accompanies the phenomenal fact mentioned. Both are, really, facts, yet very dissimilar ones.

These are two contemporaneous facts, entirely, as facts, dissimilar, or if we prefer so to speak, one fact composed of two entirely dissimilar portions. I shall call the one of them the *proverse*, the other the *retroverse*, of the fact: and the latter of these terms is that which will come into use the most frequently, because by the 'proverse' I shall mean in general the fact, whatever it is, which is being spoken about, and by the retroverse the corresponding fact on the side of mind, or feeling, or consciousness, or whatever we may call it.[1]

It was said in the preceding paragraph that Grote attempts to clarify the relationship between mind and matter. Now, one may reflect on just what affinity there is between Grote and Berkeley regarding matter. For Grote, we *never* see matter *qua* matter, for we can, at best, say only that we can look at matter from the material side. But there really is no 'matter' as such for Grote. Yet there is *reality*. We may deal with this reality through our consciousness or from the 'philosophical' approach, so long as we admit that there is a sort of phenomenal language in regard to it that may be used also. Hylas [2] is using what Grote could well refer to as phenomenal language. Hylas's difficulty was that in using this language he did not recognize it as phenomenal but thought he was describing *real* 'things.'

Grote would not accept Hylas's metaphysical view. For, Grote would maintain, such a view is an abstraction from reality and reveals reality from one side only – it does not reveal reality itself as Hylas professed it did. Grote, then, resembles Berkeley in this rejection of (Hylas's) matter. But whereas Berkeley affirms that there is only the 'philosophical' (to use Grote's term) way in which we view reality, Grote maintained that we, frequently, at least *tend* to and *do* speak of reality from the phenomenal point of view. Grote asserted that phenomena may affect us through interaction even when we are

[1] Grote, EP, II, 251.
[2] Cf. Berkeley, TDH.

unaware of them. Berkeley maintains that the *realness* of reality, despite the fact that we may not happen to be 'seeing' it, is supported by the deity and is real for divine consciousness.

Let us now return to a further consideration of the proverse and the retroverse, having dealt in the last two paragraphs with a necessary supporting comment on Berkeley's and Grote's views of matter with which the proverse especially (as well as the retroverse) is concerned. In 'sensation' the proverse means the communication between the nerves of the body and the phenomenal universe, the retroverse is the consciousness or feeling of this communication. The proverse is known only as communication as fact; it is distinguished from retroverse as consciousness (or imagination, or conception, or thought). Yet it is only by virtue of the retroverse that the proverse is understood. Further, as an epistemological monist the retroverse and the proverse are one.

The retroverse has an object which may be the universe or something within it. This universe contains fact and the proverse of sensation which forms an essential part of it. Grote here is attempting to show that the retroverse may include the proverse in the sense of giving meaning to it. But we cannot have this relationship *vice versa*. That is, the proverse is not as comprehensive as the retroverse, since it is only through the retroverse that there is *meaning*. Consciousness is more inclusive and fundamental than communication between, for example, the human body and material objects. Since this is so, consciousness itself, or the retroverse, must be admitted as closely related to the facts of phenomena. But consciousness, or the retroverse as a fact closely associated with phenomena, was completely overlooked by the materialists.

The proverse of sensation is the communication of the phenomenal universe with the brain and nerves, as physical organs; the retroverse has a sort of double aspect because it is at once both sentience (feeling of pleasure or pain, or body) and perception (or conception). Sometimes in the retroverse there is very little perception, for example, in a case of the body pricked by a pin; sometimes perception and sentience are mixed, for example, as in the smell of a rose; and sometimes sentience is almost absent, as in the motion of parts of the body. This is the case (namely when the retroverse is not prominent), when the proverse is the fact of communication between the phenomenal universe and our physical organs.

b. Bain's psychology

For the sake of further illustrating the proverse and the retroverse Grote turns attention to a glimpse into Bain's exploration of nervous organization. For Bain sensation and volition are two sets of brain nerves. The sensory nerves may be referred to as 'receptive' and the motor 'editive.'

It seems to me quite possible that physiological research might make out our nervous organization to be of the following nature; brain, with two sets of nerves, viz., of sensation and of voluntary motion starting from it: the brain a source of force, but of force communicable with, and therefore to a certain extent of the same nature as, the existing physical forces of the universe: this force supported by corporeal nutrition: and again a special adaptation of the nerves of sensation to particular physical agents. We should then have the brain with the two sets of nerves starting from it, both sets in a manner alive and in action: we might call for the moment the sensor nerves 'receptive,' the motor 'editive.' Both sets of nerves are then at work in their way: the *editive* transmitting the force from the brain, and with it contracting the muscles, which is our immediate or proper *motion:* The *receptive* seeking out, as it were, for something to receive.[1]

The receptive nerves may be regarded as seeking for something to receive while to the editive belongs motion. To both working in conjunction Grote gives the awkward name 'nervicity.'

All this may be conceived to be *one* force in the nerves analogous in some measure to electricity, galvanism, &c., but still peculiar: I will call it 'nervicity': it is generated by the brain, supported by corporeal nutrition, has the occasions of its energizing supplied to it by the receptive nerves, and passes out through the editive nerves into contraction of the muscles, where it becomes (or produces) mechanical movement.[2]

The whole physical process of the above is what Grote means by the proverse. To the proverse corresponds the retroverse. All the terms used in referring to 'mind' are covered by the term 'retroverse.' To mention an example of the complication involved in the retroverse the following will suffice. 'Perception' refers to the retroverse of the simple action of the receptive nerves; 'imagination' deals with the retroverse which lasts even after the communication between one's body and natural objects is finished; and 'conception' of the retroverse refers to the complicated internal action of the nerves when the communication takes place. The reason why Grote deals with the terms 'proverse' and 'retroverse' at all is to illustrate as well as possible what is meant by ambiguous language such as this: "Impression of light on the eye and optic nerve produces sight or perception." [3]

[1] Grote, EP, II, 254.
[2] *Loc. cit.*
[3] *Op. cit.*, 255.

5. CRITICAL COMMENT

i. *Intuition*

Intuition is true or real knowledge if it has the characteristic of immediateness, Grote states.

Intuition is true, or real knowledge, in its character of immediateness, so far as immediateness can give knowledge, but not necessarily true, or real knowledge, in its character of distinction.[1]

Just what kind of knowledge is this, one may ask, that has no 'character of distinction'? Grote seems to be narrowing the meaning of intuition to such a degree that it becomes the 'self-self' where there are no distinctions allowable, not even the distinctions involved in the 'thought-self,' or in reflection. It doesn't seem to make much sense to call this almost infinitesimally narrow meaning of intuition 'true, or real knowledge.' Or, to put it otherwise, this distinction between the 'self-self' and the 'thought-self' is unreal. Grote may be defended in presenting it, however, on the ground that he is trying to reveal in an extreme (though very exaggerated) form the two basic approaches in epistemology, sometimes referred to as idealism and realism.

ii. The 'self-self'

The 'self-self' also has a very narrow meaning. "I mean by it thought or feeling primary or by itself, as distinguished from *reflective* thought or feeling." [2] Grote has said that this 'self-self' is true knowledge, but that "as soon as we in any degree distinctly conceive of ourselves thinking, it is evident that thought is no longer simple or immediate." [3] He also acknowledges that the essential purity of the 'self-self' (where there is no admixture of the 'thought-self' in it) is non-existent. It always appears with some amount of reflection in it.

By speaking then, of 'intuition' and the 'self-self' Grote deals with what does not actually exist. He seems to wish to point out that if true or real knowledge were possible, then it would have to be wholly 'intuitive' or of the nature of the 'self-self.' Now, it seems important to point out the extreme to which we must necessarily *tend* if we are to have true knowledge. But true knowledge does not seem possible, in Grote's view. Moreover, when we ask what true knowledge is, then

---

[1] Grote, EP, II, 154.
[2] *Op. cit.*, 145.
[3] *Op. cit.*, 146.

we are left something wrapped up in an enigma, such as the 'self-self,' or 'intuition.'

Let us here consider a possible question that may come to the mind of the reader regarding the 'self-self' and the 'thought-self.' The problem could be presented as to why the 'self-self' and the 'thought-self' are not equally immediate as experience in the sense of experiencing. Now, if by the 'self-self' were meant what is frequently referred to as 'self' then it would seem that it could be regarded as that which experiences and therefore as possessing immediateness. And if by the 'thought-self' were meant the self *as* thinking then it would also be just as immediate as the self experiencing.

However, Grote means to set up a term that will be devoid of all reflection whatsoever – which is not the case with the 'self' – as a sort of extreme (and one must say, therefore fictional) limit from which all 'objective' elements are abstracted. The term he selects is the peculiar one, the 'self-self.' Now, the 'thought-self' as Grote uses this term, is *not* devoid of reflectional, and therefore of 'objective' elements because the 'thought-self' is the other extreme of the self where the self is not a sort of *self in itself* (as Grote seems to make out the 'self-self' to be) but a self *for thought*. It is for this reason that the 'self-self' and the 'thought-self' are not equally immediate as experience – in the sense of experiencing.

We have then noted why the 'self-self' and the 'thought-self' are not equally immediate as expereince. There is a kindred question, namely, why these terms are not also equally dualistic as *objective reference*. By the nature of the 'self-self,' possessing in its extremely abstracted form no 'objective' elements at all, dualism is necessarily ruled out simply on the grounds that Grote has accepted the 'self-self' as a term not possessing this character of dualism. Again, the 'thought-self' is objectivistic and – if we assume a necessary postulate of the *self* to which the 'thought-self' is an object – is also dualistic.

iii. Attitude toward materialism

In his comments upon the self-self, thought-self, intuition, immediateness, reflection, etc., Grote reveals quite pointedly that he is an epistemological personalist. His strong adherence to the view that only in relation to the self can any reality exist in the whole universe – however he may express himself regarding this view – furnishes convincing evidence that Grote is what he claims to be, namely, a personalist, or idealist. This personalism is essentially epistemological since practically all of his writings – and this is especially true of the whole of the *Exploratio Philosophica* – are epistemological. The essential purport of this work, though frequently embracing a cumbersome and unnecessarily involved style, is to reveal the relationship between the mind and objects, consciousness and matter, or 'philosophy' and phenomenal reality.

Materialism, Grote maintains, does not offer an adequate explanation of mental experience. This is a criticism characteristic of non-materialistic theories. It is, of course, supported by Bowne:

> Materialism, so far as it claims to be scientific, must build on the notion of fixed elements with fixed forces and fixed laws; and hence, if matter should attain to thought, the laws of thought must be viewed as a part of the nature of things, as much so as the laws of physics and chemistry. The mental manifestation, when it comes, is as much rooted in the nature of matter as any physical manifestation.[1]

Grote holds that the province of materialism is to deal with 'facts'; the field of 'philosophy' is to deal with something higher than facts which can be accounted for only through self, mind, consciousness, awareness, or personality. The fundamental error in materialism is the neglect of the personal factor.

The question may well arise in dealing with Grote's attitude toward materialism, namely, What is the metaphysical status of Grote's 'phenomena' in relation with 'matter'? The term 'matter' falls under the same criticism as does 'object.' Matter is regarded, either in ordinary speech, or in the materialistic approach, as something already *out there* independent of the mind that thinks about it. This *out-thereness* of matter is what Grote strongly objects to on the ground that matter can be intelligible only because of mind that views it.

In this intelligible or meaningful connection we have 'philosophy' as Grote uses the term in a specialized sense, where the approach to reality is that of consciousness. Grote criticizes the view of all those, including the materialists, who hold that there can be matter without 'philosophy.' What Grote does grant is that there can be phenomena as well as philosophy, but neither can be found at any time wholly abstracted from the other. What is maintained by some, *not* including Grote, is that matter can be regarded wholly abstracted from mind.

Grote would substitute, therefore, phenomenon for matter as always implying a necessary connection either with consciousness, or, if consciousness is not present, with our organism in some meaningful

[1] Bowne, TTK, 348.

connection where we are affected, or acted on, by phenomenon and in turn affect or react on it.

iv. Analysis of sensation into two elements

This neglect of personality in epistemology becomes evident in the use Grote makes of the terms 'proverse' and 'retroverse' of sensation, where he points out that the retroverse element, which essentially is mental, gives meaning to sensation. The proverse element provides communication between the 'thing,' or phenomenal reality and the organs of sense. This proverse role is, indeed, frequently called sensation, but sensation *means* nothing unless the retroverse of sensation is present. This is certainly a qualified explanation of sensation, but it seems a very intelligible and sound one, and one that allies Grote with epistemological monism. A less qualified explanation of sensation leaves the significance of the word vague, or restricts it to a *purely* physical plane characteristic of materialism.

It seems that Grote is wholly justified in relating sensation with mind so that sensation may have meaning. It is a sort of internal end of the sensation process, in contrast to the external end which is closely related to phenomenal reality. This internal, or retroverse, end of sensation is, of course, personalistic. Also, the external, or proverse end, having no meaning whatsoever aside from its relation to a human organism in some way, is also personalistic.

This reference to the proverse and retroverse factors of sensation simply provides another way for Grote to present his main thesis regarding 'philosophy' and phenomena. As there are no phenomena (that is, phenomenal reality) that haven't some element of awareness in them, so the proverse element of sensation is never found wholly separated from the retroverse.

6. SUMMARY AND TRANSITION TO NEXT CHAPTER

In short, Grote is pointing out by reason of his personalistic tendencies that all true being is personal, metaphysical as well as epistemological. The "theory that only *persons* are *real*," [1] holds true of Grote's idealism. Even phenomenal reality is real only because of persons. For Grote there is no reality that is reality altogether by itself. Strictly, reality is real, due to persons who perceive it. The 'retroverse' part of sensation is what gives any meaning to sensation. The 'proverse' portion communicates between our sense organs and 'objects.' For

[1] Brightman, ITP, 389.

Grote there is no matter as such at all. The whole of his analysis of
materialism is to show the necessarily restricted view in epistemology
that is common to all materialism. He could say the same about all
naturalistic or positivistic sciences that overlook the place that thinking has in all epistemology. If one follows Grote's argument it seems
impossible to regard anything as real that is not also personal. His
system is personal realism, or personalism. This system admits of
pluralism in the sense that there are many substances. But, as pointed
out earlier in this chapter, none of these substances are real except
when considered in relation to a personality. If, then, there is no
substance except that which is such for thinking, the conclusion is
that there is a sense in which substance is *one*, and "that the real object
and the idea of it (perception or conception) are one in the knowledge
relation." [1] This personalism of Grote's is, then, both metaphysically
pluralistic and epistemologically monistic. What these specific senses
are has been briefly stated immediately above, but the whole of the
Exploratio Philosophica forms the basis upon which Grote develops
this monistic (and pluralistic) personalism.

It was stated, in the paragraph immediately above, that Grote's
system is personal realism. The question may well be asked, How is
Grote both a personal realist and a Berkeleian idealist, for he has already been designated as both? His personal realism is metaphysical
realism which is *significant* because it would be utterly meaningless
except in relation to persons *to* whom it is reality. His Berkeleian
idealism also is evident when considering epistemology. It is Berkeleian
inasmuch as both agree that nothing can have any *meaning* apart from
consciousness. However, Grote's epistemology differs from Berkeley's
because Grote affirms that communication (and effects) can take place
without any consciousness being present at all. In that case there
would be effects made on us but they would carry no meaning for us.
Berkeley would say that there is meaning, if not for human beings then,
for God. Grote does not emphasize persistently that meaning could be
entertained by the deity and consequently inclines to say that phenomenal effects may be produced without the presence of a mind. But
they cannot be effects, for Grote, that are meaningful unless we are
aware of them.

The specific consideration of personalism in Grote's philosophy
seems appropriate. But Grote also presents an idealism that can be
classed as personal except that the emphasis appears to be on the

[1] Ferm, "Monism," in Runes, DOP, 201.

ideals of idealism. Persons are necessarily present, and ideals are also. This idealism, of course, cannot be decisively separated from personalism. But there are some factors in it that would seem to justify treatment under a separate chapter though the kinship between the present chapter and the following one is necessarily very close. Let us now consider "Grote's Idealism."

CHAPTER X

GROTE'S IDEALISM

1. INTRODUCTION

i. Ideal-ism

In dealing with Grote's personalism it was shown that his idealism as personalism was idea-ism rather than ideal-ism. Here we saw evidence of Grote's epistemological personalism in that thought and 'thing,' or idea and 'object' have a common source in deity mediated through human personality. Here we saw, also, that Grote presented a metaphysical personalism inasmuch as the personal nature of reality is revealed in conjunction with epistemological personalism where the common source of thought and 'thing' manifests itself through persons.

ii. Personal idealism evident in ethics and epistemology

We will consider in this chapter, his idealism as ideal-ism rather than as idea-ism; the latter involved a consideration of his epistemological personalism, whereas the former will deal with his Platonic idealistic tendencies in ethics. However, it is evident that Grote, especially in his treatment of happiness in the sense that Aristotle does (to be considered later in the present chapter), regards an aspiration toward happiness as (*personal*) activity in accordance with the highest virtue. Inasmuch as happiness involves personal striving toward an end, Grote manifests, in this ethics, personal idealism. Both in his epistemology and his ethics personal idealism is evident.

iii. Distinctions in idealisms

Some of what has already been stated, and what will be presented in this present chapter, regarding Grote's personalism and idealism, may be set forth in the following:

Personalism ⎱
Idealism ⎰ → personal idealism → ⎱ Idea-ism
                                    ⎰ Ideal-ism

Idea-ism ⎰ Epistemological monistic personalism
         ⎱ Metaphysical pluralistic personalism
         ⎱ Theistic personalism
         ⎰ (Platonic idealism)

Ideal-ism ⎱ Ethical personalism
          ⎰ (Platonic idealism)
          ⎱ (Aristotelian *idealism!*)

2. GROTE'S PLATONISM

i. Ideals

There is an important sense in which his idealism is Platonic, which will concern us now, where the ideals are forms, as in Plato's *Republic*, which never can be attained fully but nevertheless can be aimed at. The Platonic nature of Grote's thinking appears in connection with "A Discussion between Professor Henry Sidgwick and the Late Professor John Grote, on the Utilitarian Basis of Plato's Republic."

ii. Examination of a dialogue

Let us now examine this article and see what light it throws on the view that Grote is a Platonic idealist. In this discussion there is an imaginary conversation going on between George Grote and Socrates, with several others taking part also, in the discussion. John Grote is putting his own views in the mouth of Socrates. Let us look at various portions of the dialogue to see the particular portion that reveals his idealism. Thrasymachus speaks:

Justice is consulting the advantage of others to our own disadvantage and therefore there is *no* reason why we should practice it if we can avoid doing so. . .[1]

Then Adeimantus says to Socrates:

Without going so far as Thrasymachus, do you not think there is *some* truth in what he says?. . . and. . . that it is the resulting good reputation which, except when we act from fear of punishment, is the reason, and the only reason, why we should practice justice? [2]

[1] Grote, "A Discussion. . . Republic," in CR (Mar. 1889), 97.
[2] *Loc. cit.*

George Grote continues the dialogue:

I know our friend Socrates agrees with me. . . if you want your rights, you must
perform your duties. . . you will be done by as you do: and this is the reason
why you should practice justice. . .[1]

The answer which 'Socrates' (that is, John Grote, in the dialogue)
gives, favors a Platonic – in the sense of intuitive and idealistic – basis
for ethics, whereas George Grote's position is somewhat in agreement
with Thrasymachus'. George Grote believes to a large extent in
paying attention to the practical consequences of our actions. He
therefore partly favors Thrasymachus, in opposition to Socrates in his
(Socrates') view that justice has a regard for others and a disregard
of ourselves. Yet George Grote does not agree with the extreme position taken by Thrasymachus that "there is *no* reason why we should
practice it if we can avoid doing so."

John Grote, however, is strongly in opposition to Thrasymachus, on
the point that there is a reason why we should practice justice even
when we can avoid doing so. John Grote holds that there *is* a reason
for practicing justice in such a situation. This reason has the same
basis as it has in Plato, namely, intuition in the sense of being able to
see the good. For Plato, all things tend toward the *summum bonum*,
the ideal, *the Good*. John Grote, therefore, accepts an intuitive basis in
ethics.

But a consideration of intuition does not exhaust the bases on
which John Grote establishes his ethics. He implies in Adeimantus's
question to Socrates (above) that there is some small place for a consequential or experiential approach in ethics also, as Adeimantus
states: "Without going so far as Thrasymachus, do you not think
there is *some* truth in what he says?" John Grote, being very Platonic,
is not too willing to admit a consequential basis. And this is the very
point that John Grote seeks to establish, namely, that there is both a
Platonic basis and a consequential basis for ethics, but that the Platonic
basis is by far the more important. John Grote's ethical idealism,
therefore, is to a small extent tempered by an experiential (i.e. a consequential) approach in ethics; he is therefore a slightly mitigated
Platonic idealist.

Let us look further at the dialogue, and specially at Thrasymachus'
pointed question and Socrates' reply, in support of the above critical
reflections on John Grote's idealism in ethics. Thrasymachus asks:

---

[1] *Loc. cit.*

My question to Socrates was in effect: supposing a man has reason to know this trust will be abused, and that he will meet, for his justice, with treatment from men exactly opposite to what Mr. Grote calls the 'natural consequence' of justice, is there still reason why he should practice it?

There is, and the main reason of all. I do not say, and never said, but that a good reason for practising justice may be the reputation and praise that it brings – one kind of natural consequence: nor again but that another good reason may be that in practising it we are taking our part in the general commerce of mutual service among men, and may fairly expect to receive service from those whom we have served – another natural consequence: nor again but that another good reason may be that which Thrasymachus thinks a reason against it, that it *is* for the advantage of others.[1]

Socrates continues:

All education, as well as all moral philosophy, takes account of something more than fact, takes account, in some way, of an *ideal:* the father forms in his mind his ideal of the best life for his son, and tries to produce it: I form my ideal of the best life for man, and 'preach' that. Mr. Grote's use of the term 'preaching' seems to me to imply a notion on his part that all attempts to raise or improve human nature is [2] humbug, and with this notion I think he need not have troubled himself to criticize me: it is but going a step lower to think with Thrasymachus that all human society is a humbug, in which everybody is preaching to others and trying to shirk practising himself.[3]

If Mr. Grote says, We will have no ideals, we will keep to the practical: I think what he will come to is not *his* morality, but Thrasymachus'. It is Ideals and moral 'preaching' which have brought human society so far as it has been brought.[4]

iii. Grote's idealism evident

Now, the remarks of Thrasymachus and Adeimantus provoke replies from both George Grote and 'Socrates.' Socrates clearly reveals idealism when he asserts that all education as well as moral philosophy is concerned with *ideals* and not merely facts. The father has his ideal for his son; Socrates forms his ideal of the best life. Yet, Socrates continues, George Grote seems to mock ideals by using the term 'preaching,' implying that the ideals 'preached' are impracticable, and "that all attempts to raise or improve human nature are [5] humbug."

iv. Anti-relativistic, generally

Moreover, John Grote does not agree that "the reason why you should practice" justice is that you desire that "you will be done by

---

[1] Grote, "A Discussion. . . Republic," in CR (Mar. 1889), 98.
[2] Obviously an error; Grote meant 'are.'
[3] Grote, *op. cit.*, 99.
[4] *Loc. cit.*
[5] Correct verb form.

as you do" – as George Grote suggests. It is only one step further down to Thrasymachus' position where "all human society is a humbug, in which everybody is preaching to others and trying to shirk practising himself."

If anyone, John Grote is maintaining, insists on forsaking ideals, such as justice, while insisting on being practical, then ethics becomes very relative, individualistic, and selfish, according to the type displayed by Thrasymachus. And, as for the 'preaching' which George Grote is deprecating, the truth is, rather, it is by "ideals and moral 'preaching' " that human society has advanced.

In order further to clarify the wider view of 'Socrates' in distinction from George Grote's narrow conception that we have already presented [1] where ideals are not placed in the forefront, the dialogue continues: George Grote

charges me with making too little of the natural consequences of justice in the way of worldly success and men's approbation. I may have made too little of them; but still I think I was right in saying that the fathers of families should bring up their children rather to love justice for itself than to love it on account of these. I may be open to Mr. Grote's criticism as suggesting a wrong notion of human society by leading people to forget about these natural consequences of justice as if there were no such things, and to think only about their own state and feeling as their motive and reason for doing justly: the truth, putting all things, idea and fact, together, may lie rather between him and me; but I think it lies nearest to my side.

Glaucon: – Yes, and I think it does also in regard of the question of the improvement of society. Mr. Grote, in making credit and the approbation of men so important a natural consequence of justice as he does, is brought in face of the question that this consequence will not follow on doing justly except in a tolerably good state of society. Here appears a fundamental difference between his way of thinking and yours. You have given us what you conceive a perfect society, could we have it, but in the meantime you make a man's doing justly depend on himself, and not on the approbation of other men in our actual societies.[2]

v. Of utmost importance to teach ideals

John Grote reveals his attitude regarding a particular ideal, like justice, by maintaining that it is of utmost importance to teach ideals. His brother, George Grote, is maintaining that it is more important to consider practical consequences and moral approval than to be primarily concerned with ideals. Glaucon intercedes as a sort of mediator between the two extremes of the argument in which George and John Grote are involved. He maintains that George Grote's emphasis upon

---

[1] Under "iii. Grote's idealism evident" (above).
[2] Grote, "A Discussion. . . Republic," in CR (Mar. 1889), 102.

'natural consequences of justice' assumes a tolerably good society in which these consequences are brought about, whereas John Grote sets forth the perfect, or ideal society. Glaucon states that John Grote makes man's doing of justice depend upon himself and his ideals, while George Grote makes the doing of justice depend upon the approval of others in actual society.

vi. Ideal and approbative ethics

John Grote agrees that he himself may have overemphasized ideal ethics and feels sure that his brother has advocated approbative ethics too much at the expense of ideal ethics. He inclines to agree with Glaucon. But if it is a case of deciding whose extreme position should be accepted, John Grote feels that his own position is safer. Since John Grote is, of course, the author of the dialogue we know that his decision is in favor of idealistic normative ethics rather than consequential normative ethics, that is, if it were to be a case of bifurcation where one or the other was to be chosen. However, to affirm that the choice must be one or the other would be erroneous, Grote seems to imply. The error arises from what is popularly known today as the 'fallacy of bifurcation.'

So John Grote allows Glaucon to present his position more fully, in order that it will include regard for ideals but may also be concerned with the importance of consequences. Thus John Grote in a rather unique fashion reveals his Platonic idealism by introducing his views through the medium of an improvised Socratic dialogue. His position is revealed through the words of 'Socrates,' supplemented by Glaucon who also presents further details in John Grote's view.

3. CRITIQUE OF UTILITARIANISM

i. Relation of this critique to views on Plato

Another way in which John Grote reveals his concern for absolute standards is through his critique of utilitarianism. This he does through the posthumously published work *An Examination of the Utilitarian Philosophy*. Now, it is evident when one examines the preceding dialogue that there is a main tenet in it which also appears in Grote's examination of utilitarianism. Let us look at another of the statements made by 'Socrates' in that dialogue:

The reason why we should practice justice, right-doing, virtue, is because, in

so doing, we are acting with or from our better and higher selves. . . . What is
we? Not merely ourselves capable of happiness, but ourselves altogether.[1]

The whole foundation of Grote's criticism of utilitarianism rests
upon his conviction that it is "not merely ourselves capable of happiness, but ourselves altogether" that furnishes "the reason why we
should practice justice, right-doing, virtue." The *we* does not refer
simply to "ourselves capable of happiness" but to ourselves *altogether*.
Here Grote is thinking of each person individually in speaking of 'we.'

What Grote means is that each person should practice "justice,
rightdoing, virtue," *not* on the basis of having simply one capacity, a
capacity for happiness, but rather on the basis of what we, each one,
possess in our complete selves, namely, something that is much more
inclusive than one capacity. That is, we are possessed of many more
capacities than just simply one capacity – for happiness. These other
capacities – such as, he seems to hold, the capacity for recognizing
intuitively the nature of many goods such as justice, courage, etc. –
should *also* be taken account of, in moral action.

ii. Problems not settled in utilitarianism

All utilitarian doctrines fall victim to the same criticism by Grote,
namely, that they overlook our capacities for things besides happiness.
Though J. S. Mill was the first to use the term 'Utilitarianism,' there
were happiness theories previous to the time of Mill. What may be
described as the 'old utilitarianism' existed before Mill's time in
various forms. A view closely related to Mill's theory, is the hedonism
of Jeremy Bentham, with its basic tenet of, 'the greatest happiness
of the greatest number.' J. S. Mill defended the utilitarianism of
Bentham at the same time as he modified it by the introduction of
qualities amongst pleasures. The changes he instituted are an acknowledgment of the difficulties in the old utilitarianism. Mill, however,
did not surmount all the obstacles with which utilitarianism was
impeded. He made additions in clarity, and presented an introduction
of qualities among pleasures. But the main trouble with his utilitarianism, according to Grote, is that it is a *happiness* theory!

iii. Descriptive and normative ethics

Grote's idealism appears also, in his criticism of Mill for his (Mill's)
analysis of what *is* rather than what *should be*.

---

[1] Grote, "A Discussion. . . Republic," in CR (Mar. 1889), 98.

By the side of this discussion I have placed another, with the view of showing that though man, if we look at his past history, has proceeded along a course which has been one of real improvement, still it is not from the fact that such and no other has been his course, that we are able to judge that it is improvement, but we must further be able to give reasons why we call it improvement rather than the opposite. That is to say, we must have the *idea* of improvement: an idea of what *ought to be*, or what it is desirable *should be*, as well as a power of observing, recording, and analyzing what *is*.[1]

That men actually *do* desire happiness is descriptive rather than normative. And even if the objective is 'the greatest happiness of the greatest number' it is an objective that has to do with people in regard to their actual capacities *for happiness*. Grote wishes to have ideals that may be aimed at by *the whole of our being* rather than simply by our capacity for happiness.

Grote seems to think that 'our capacity for happiness' does not involve our whole being. Now, it is true that for Aristotle *eudaemonia* signified complete happiness. Grote would seem to leave himself open for some valid criticism here, especially *if* he meant that we have capacities for other than the *summum bonum* (such as *eudaemonia*) resulting from a fulfilment of function as in Aristotle. But, apparently, Grote did not mean that we have other capacities (than the capacity for happiness) for attaining the good, in the Aristotelian sense of *eudaemonia* (happiness). Grote seems to have been emphasizing happiness in utilitarianism which he tended to interpret in the sense of satisfactory or pleasant consequences. An emphasis on happiness of this sort where consequential ethics are involved is narrower, Grote would seem to hold, than happiness (in the sense of living in accordance with right reason, as) in Aristotle, which is dependent upon all the rational faculties, or in Plato where the internal *daemon* intuitively sees and knows the good.

iv. Why *adopt 'the greatest happiness', standard*

Moreover, Grote is more concerned with finding out the *reason* why Bentham and Mill accept 'the greatest happiness principle' rather than in knowing how this principle is elaborately worked out in all its details. Why 'the greatest happiness' standard rather than some other? To this question, Grote feels that neither Bentham nor Mill provides an answer.

---

[1] Grote, EUP, I, 2.

v. Activity and virtue

In *A Treatise on the Moral Ideals* Grote stresses the view that not
only *happiness* but also *activity* is necessary in order to have the
summum bonum. Moral philosophy dealing with the concept of 'ought'
must take account of activity as well as happiness. Grote is, therefore,
Aristotelian in his approach to the subject of happiness, The term
'eudaemonics' is derived from εὐδαιμονία, a word of prime importance
in the ethics of Aristotle.[1] The 'eudaemonism' of the ethics placed the
summum bonum in a life of activity in accordance with the highest
virtue or excellence. Into the Aristotelian or Peripatetic school there
crept the view that the chief element of this highest good was the feeling
of pleasure. Epicurus was an exponent of this view. Hence the word
'eudaemonism' in modern philosophy represents the theory of morals
which regards the chief end of life as happiness.

vi. Eudaemonia

a. *Relation to 'aretaics'*

The term εὐδαιμονία was used by the common people as well as
the learned for the highest good that it was possible for man to obtain,
and it is in this sense that Aristotle uses the word. Grote means by
happiness the same thing as Aristotle, and the deficiencies evident in
partial approaches to Aristotle's view, such as Mill's and Bentham's,
are subject to the criticisms which affect all theories that emphasize
only a part of Aristotle's meaning. Grote is idealistic in his view of
happiness. This idealism colors all his analysis of hedonism.

Though *pleasure* may accompany the realization of the highest good,
the term cannot be analyzed into the sum or succession of pleasures
but is an active condition. The virtue which accompanies such activity
is ἀρετή.[2] The highest conception that Aristotle held concerning this

---

[1] Εὐδαιμονία was used by Plato and Aristotle to signify *complete happiness*. Εὐδαίμων
pertained particularly to outward prosperity, as well off, wealthy. ὁ ἡμεῖς γελοίως
ἐπὶ μὲν τῶν δημιουργῶν αἰσθανόμεθα, ἐπὶ δὲ τῶν πλουσίων τε καὶ εὐδαιμόνων δοκο-
ύντων εἶναι οὐκ αἰσθανόμεθα. Plato, Rep., 206c. B. Jowett trans.: "This we remark in
the case of the artisan, but ludicrously enough, do not apply the same rule to people
of the richer sort." The notion of *happiness* is associated with good fortune (to which
well off, and *wealth* relate), as in ἀλλὰ μὴν ὅ γε εὖ ζῶν μακάριός τε καὶ εὐδαίμων, ὁ δὲ
μὴ τἀναντία. Plato, Rep., 354a. Jowett trans.: "And he who lives well is blessed
and happy, and he who lives ill the reverse of happy"? Also, Εὐδάδει δὲ τῷ λόγῳ καὶ
τὸ εὖ ζῆν καὶ τὸ εὖ ζῆν καὶ τὸ εὖ πράττειν τὸν εὐδαίμονα. Aristotle, Eth., I, 8. Edward
Moore trans.: "Others may say that happiness is living well and doing well."

[2] (1) Used in Homer for *goodness*, or *excellence*, especially of *manly* qualities: δὲ τότε
νηπιέῃσι ποδῶν ἀρετὴν ἀναφαίνων. Homer, Il., 20, 411. John Stuart Blackie trans.:
"He full of youthful light conceit his *limber* legs displayed."
(2) Used in Aristotle for *goodness* or *excellence:* ῥητέον οὖν ὅτι παρὰ ἀρετή Aristotle,

activity was a life of pure speculation even though, practically, such might never be reached. "What Aristotle ascribes to God is knowledge which has *only* itself for its object." [1] "The sole activity of God is self-knowledge." [2] The traditional renderings of the word, ἀρετή, are considerably different from the Aristotelian meaning.

b. Reason for including 'aretaics'

Grote's point in supplementing the word 'eudaemonics' by 'aretaics' is therefore much to the point in his arguments against the utilitarianism of Mill. If the theory of eudaemonism as it is generally known in modern thought had not acquired a special restriction to happiness but rather retained its meaning as a theory which fixed the chief good in an active life in accordance with virtue, as in Aristotle, it would not be necessary for Grote to introduce the word 'aretaics' into his work. In general, then, one may say that Grote takes the side of Aristotle as against Mill in *A Treatise on the Moral Ideals*. Moreover, there appears to be no conflict between Grote's treatment, here, of happiness and his presentation of the ideal in the dialogue considered at the beginning of this chapter. [3]

vii. Bentham's influence in popularizing hedonism

Jeremy Bentham usually writes as though he were the first propounder of 'the greatest happiness' principle. However, it would be difficult if not impossible to know how much Bentham is indebted to his predecessors in moral theory. Certainly Richard Cumberland, Shaftesbury, Francis Hutcheson, George Berkeley, John Gay, John Brown, David Hume, David Hartley, Abraham Tucker ('Edward Search'), and William Paley had dealt with pleasure or happiness in some manner. [4] These in their turn have been greatly indebted to

Eth., II, 6, 2, and Met., IV. Edward Moore trans.: "Now speaking generally excellence of whatever kind."

(3) The Attic sense remained, more with the meaning of *active excellence* than of the moral virtues, for example, in art of *skill*, in Plato. "Ὅταν μὲν περὶ ἀρετῆς τεκτονικῆς ἢ λόγος ἢ ἄλλης τινὸς δημιουργικῆς. Plato, Pro., 322d. Jowett trans.: "When the question related to carpentering or any other mechanical art." With this is closely combined the notion of *distinction*, hence ἀρετή seems to imply fame, *praise for excellence*, for example, noble deeds. Τοὺς δ'ἐπὶ γένεσιν καὶ προγόνων ἀρεταῖς. Plato, Rep., 618b. Jowett trans.: "For their birth and the *qualities* of their ancestors."

(4) Moreover, ἀρετή is the recognized word for 'virtue' in Plato and Aristotle. Plato, Rep., 500d; Aristotle, Eth., I, 13, and Pol., II, 3.

[1] Ross, *Aristotle*, 183.

[2] *Op. cit.*, 185.

[3] Grote, "A Discussion. . . Republic," in CR (Mar. 1889).

[4] Albee, HEV.

Plato, Aristotle, and Epicurus. To these Bentham may have turned before he read the words 'the greatest happiness of the greatest number' in Priestley's *Treatise on Government*. These famous words became the cornerstone of Bentham's ethics and the maxim which guided a life of study and reform.

Never does Bentham speak about non-hedonistic theories except in a tone of contempt. His contribution to ethics probably was not as great as to law, yet he likely did more than any other writer to bring the utilitarian theory into popular ethical controversy. He did this in spite of having stripped the happiness of Aristotle of much of its idealism.

John Stuart Mill was greatly influenced by Bentham as well as by his father, James Mill. More attracted by ethical questions than legal problems, Mill will remain outstanding in the realm of morals for his *Utilitarianism*. In one of his works,[1] Grote analyzes the basis upon which Mill establishes his argument. A brief exposition of the main points of this book at this point will be attempted, in addition to what already has been indicated in regard to Grote's compatibility with Plato and Aristotle.

viii. Difficulties which Mill's utilitarianism does not avoid

a. Whose *happiness, not answered*

Certain difficulties arise in Mill's treatment of Utilitarianism. One of the first of these concerns *whose happiness* is to be produced despite the fact that intelligent determination to do only what is most useful and productive of happiness may be exercised.

> The most important points of moral difficulty arise not in reference to the question about actions, whether they are useful or not, but in reference to the question, *who* it is, in the conflict of various interests in life, that they are useful to.[2]

The word 'happiness' is vague until the question, as to whose happiness is meant, is solved. Mill passes rather abruptly from the agent's happiness to the happiness of all people. There is nothing to authorize such a step for the charge of selfishness may still be made against utilitarianism. The problem of the amount of action necessary for the end of happiness is a constant obstacle to Mill. Mill's hedonism, as well as

---

[1] Grote, EUP.
[2] *Loc. cit.*, 4.

Bentham's, lacks the precision of the definition of individual activity in accordance with the highest virtue that we see in Aristotle's ethics and Grote's idealism. He appears unable to set a standard for judging how distribution of activity should be made. Apparently quite unconscious that he is referring to a standard apart from happiness, Mill appeals to sympathy. Human beings, he states,

only differ from other animals in two particulars. First, in being capable of sympathizing, not solely with their offspring, or, like some of the more noble animal who is kind to them, but with all human, and even with all sentient, beings. Secondly, in having a more developed intelligence, which gives a wider range to the whole of their sentiments, whether self-regarding or sympathetic.[1]

b. Mill's utilitarianism uses extraneous elements

Grote relates, concerning Mill,

Sympathy, he tells us. . . makes another the object with us of the same feelings which we have in regard of ourselves, desire, for instance, of happiness: and sympathy follows fact or, if we prefer expressing it so, answers to relation; that is, those we sympathize with are those who are brought into contact with us, or about whom we come to have knowledge, and whose circumstances or relation to us call for feeling on our part: and so the desire of happiness which begins of necessity with ourselves, (for all desire must in the first instance be individual,) is propagated, as to its object, around us, until it at last embraces the whole human race, or as I most heartily agree with Mr. Mill, the whole sentient creation. All this is almost moral common-place; but it is common-place most unworthily exchanged, in the utilitarian scheme, for the doctrine that the object of our desire and action for happiness, should be the whole creation divided into so many units, one of which is ourselves, and each of which is to be looked on by us as of equal importance.[2]

Better than happiness as a standard is 'duty,' Grote declares. Duty as intellectually perceived, and its accompanying feeling, refer first of all to the particular, and not to the general as Mill would have us believe.

The utilitarian maxim, that 'an action is right in proportion as it tends to promote happiness,' is incomplete without having apppended to it such an addition as this, 'and not merely happiness in general, but such happiness in particular as the agent is specially bound and called upon to promote,' the terms 'bound' and 'called upon' being explained by the ideas of duty and sympathy in the manner which I have just described. It is so that the question, '*Whose* happiness?' is to be answered.[3]

Duty is not sufficient to attain the *summum bonum*. There should be a natural moral overflow beyond what duty requires, and sympathy supplies this necessary part. The idea of duty as well as that of sympa-

---

[1] Mill, UTI, 47, 48.
[2] Grote, EUP, 90.
[3] *Op. cit.*, 97, 98.

thy is included within the required virtue. The weakness of utilitarianism at this point arises from its resolve to allow nothing to the *summum bonum* except happiness. Probably the only potent criticism here possible pertains to *action* which appears to be just as important as happiness. Action appears to have value as action apart from any pleasure.

Man is by nature *active,* as well as active to *an end*; his action has a character of its own, independent of its reference to an end; and therefore, though it must have an end in order to be reasonable, and our object must be to find the proper end for it, it is not necessary that it should have no value other than what is given it by this end.[1]

That is, there is a general tendency in feeling to elevate, intellectually. "Reason and moral imagination or sympathy supply to the feeling thus elevated an object and a purpose, and confirm its elevation." [1] The question is the one of *oughtness* rather than *existence*. Mill builds upon the foundation of what *is*.

The meaning that Grote gives to duty seems to have been strongly colored by Kant's maxim, of 'duty done for duty's sake.' It is very possible that 'the moral law' of Kantian ethics has been influential as the determining source of duty as the ideally right, for Grote.

Duty is the ideally right, or that which should be done, in so far as we consider it determined for us, and the principle which we suppose to determine it we call 'the moral law.' [2]

Yet Grote does not directly acknowledge that he was influenced by Kant, in his view of duty. Grote, rather, gives credit to others for his conception of the moral law as the determining source of duty.

If we suppose 'law' to mean a rule for individual action, of which rule we know nothing more than that, if we do not obey it, we shall be punished, then duty is bare, perhaps unwilling, obedience to something which we have no interest or pleasure in, but which we are afraid to resist. The moral law is then a yoke imposed upon us by the Deity (Paley), or by society and public opinion (some Socratic interlocutors and several philosophers in later times), or by arbitrary power in general (Hobbes).[3]

Just how much acknowledgement Grote gives to these others may be noted in the following:

I have thought it would conduce to clearness, . . . in accordance with the four views which I gave of law, and will now say about them, that in my view they all belong to the notion of duty.[4]

[1] Grote, EUP, 107, 108.
[2] Grote, TMI, 98.
[3] *Op. cit.,* 99.
[4] *Op. cit.,* 100.

c. *Mill's positivism helpless by itself*

In his remarks in connection with 'the old utilitarianism' [1] Grote states that he sees in Mill a somewhat diminishing attachment to the Benthamite school and yet a feeling of loyalty to it, a greater appreciation of a certain positivism the proof of which refuses anything of the ideal. Yet this positivism is helpless if unable to appeal to something beyond itself. Hence the references which Mill makes to what is beyond positivism in an attempt to show, paradoxically enough, that happiness is the *summum bonum*. That is, in Grote's estimation Mill imports into utilitarianism much that is foreign to it.

ix. *Non-idealist origin of Bentham's utilitarianism*

In the 18th century through the influence of Bentham and others, Utilitarianism was a revolt against jural ethics and gradually eventuated in legislative reform. Benthamite utilitarianism revolted against natural law as a basis for ethics. It gave emphasis to happiness as a standard rather than to duty, and through the former attempted a reconstruction of society without fear of consequences.

The utilitarianism of Bentham was one of reform. There was another utilitarianism of which Godwin may be regarded as a representative. This utilitarianism was revolutionary. The element of revolution smouldered in the utilitarianism of Bentham but the essential element in this latter was reform. The utilitarianism for which Paley advocated was somewhat akin to the Benthamite, more conservative, and based upon common sense. Paley, however, is less consistent than Bentham because the reform which he suggested was more on the side of 'utile' than 'dulce' the useful than the pleasant. Paley, says Grote,

describes happiness as *not* consisting in (1) self-indulgence, (2) idleness, (3) *greatness*; and *as* consisting in (1) sociality, (2) occupation, (3) what we may call moderation, (4) health. If his account had been given in perfect good faith, I do not see why he should not have added competent livelihood or fortune, for that is not more a matter out of our own power than health is and in the importance of it for happiness Aristotle and an English tradesman would alike agree.[2]

Bentham had the mind of a legislative reformer.

Bentham thought, and with reason, that if men could once be got distinctly to have the idea that happiness, well examined and systematized happiness, and that not the agent's own only, was the one thing worthy of being acted for, great results in the way of philantrophy would ensue.[3]

---

[1] Grote, EUP, 10.
[2] *Op. cit.*, 38n.
[3] *Op. cit.*, 103.

Generally, then, the element of suspicion was directed toward utilitarianism. It is significant to notice that Mill professed to recognize the authority of existing custom and hence becomes involved in inconsistency when happiness is taken as the standard.

x. Grote's idealism akin to idealism in Christianity

A word should be stated here regarding the relationship of Utilitarianism to Christianity. Mill relates that the ethics of utility are those of Christianity in its purest form. There are two main elements recognized by each, according to Grote, namely, importance of happiness and love of one's neighbor. Utilitarianism begins with the former; Christianity starts with the latter. It is Grote's belief that philanthropy is due to Christianity. Yet Christianity is as important for other ethical systems as it is for Utilitarianism. Grote's point here is that Utilitarianism cannot claim for itself, alone, practical moral philanthropy; Christianity can. This statement should be qualified. Grote apparently does not mean that practical philanthropy is not possible outside of Christianity but that Christianity *in its ideal form* provides for such philanthropy. Utilitarianism cannot do so because of its failure to give great importance to duty, and sympathy. To account for what Christianity has and Utilitarianism has not, Mill deals with worthiness which is inconsistent with his positive Utilitarianism. 'Worthiness' introduces a factor other than 'happiness.'

xi. Idealism haunts Mill's utilitarianism

Grote notes an important distinction here which, he claims, Mill fails to see very clearly.

We have then a philosophy of happiness as εὐδαιμονία, or a lofty ideal of what man may rise to, entirely different from a philosophy of happiness as ἡδονή, or the fact of enjoyment as unaffected by man's will and his moral nature.

Mr. Mill hovers between these two, between an aspiring and truly ideal utilitarianism or lofty eudaemonism, and a utilitarianism on the merely Epicurean basis of measurement of pleasures.[1]

This observation by Grote distinguishes him as characterized by a strong tendency to idealism.

xii. Quantity and quality amongst pleasures

Mill attempts to distinguish between 'quality' and 'quantity' in pleasures. "It is better to be a human being dissatisfied than a pig

[1] Grote, EUP, 46, 47.

satisfied; better to be Socrates dissatisfied than a fool satisfied." [1] But 'quality' here is merely a sort of 'quantity.' A standard that has to do with quantity and quality is an appeal to an element other than happiness, Grote states. Grote seems to be vulnerable in his criticism here, for surely Mill was justified in speaking about quality and quantity amongst pleasures. But if it is granted that qualities may be reduced to quantities where quantities fall short of an ideal amount, then Grote reveals Mill as a non-idealist, while advocating for happines (in Aristotle's sense) in its ideal form.

'Quality' of pleasures is unjustified unless the criterion of human experience is brought into consideration, Grote insists.

A consistent utilitarian can scarcely hold the difference of *quality* in pleasures in *any* sense: for if they differ otherwise than in what, speaking largely, may be called *quantity*, they are not mutually comparable, and in determining as to the preferability of one pleasure to another, we must then be guided by some considerations not contained in the idea or experience of the pleasure itself.[2]

xiii. Utilitarianism suffers from lack of sufficient and consistent idealism

Mill attempts to establish upon experience what cannot be proved from it, namely, that the sole standard of morality is happiness. He is constantly faced with the question of proving that happiness as the *summum bonum* is what *should* regulate moral life. Grote contends that Mill might have as validly taken 'duty' as the *summum bonum* (or the *summum bonum faciendum*) as happiness and defended *it*. In regarding 'happiness' as the criterion Mill has assumed more than what he ultimately proves.

If we have to recognize vast distinctions among the different sorts of utility, and to take into the consideration of utility other considerations of quite a different kind, as of different kinds of sentiment with which the utilities are accompanied; I do not see why the philosophy should be called utilitarianism more than anything else.[3]

4. A CRITIQUE OF MORAL IDEALS

i. Idealism basic in Grote's two works in the field of ethics

Turning now from a consideration of Grote's idealism revealed through his critique of utilitarianism we may look with considerable

---

[1] Mill, UTI, 9.
[2] Grote, EUP, 52.
[3] *Op. cit.*, 149.

satisfactory result at his treatment of moral ideals. There is a definite anticipation of much of *A Treatise on the Moral Ideals* in *An Examination of the Utilitarian Philosophy*. The *idea* of progress, elevation or improvement, as what *should* be, constitutes the greater part of the last four chapters of the latter work, and is the basis upon which moral ideals rest. Utilitarianism made an attack upon positivism in ethics for positivism attempted to construct a moral code upon the sole basis of experience and observation without assuming that there is any ideal at all. But utilitarianism insofar as it describes what *is* (even though it may go beyond this to what is not possible to obeservation, namely, ideas), is prone to error similar to that of positivism. Its failure and that of Comte is fairly explicitly presented in the following:

> The logic of the moral sciences, or what Mr. Mill considers such, will not at all in the same degree stand alone without Teleology, and the attempt to make it do so is almost certain to be an abuse of it as *logic* – that is, there will be a supposition more or less express and distinct, but always without reason given for it, that *it*, the logic, is to supply us with the *end* as well as the means. This is precisely what I understand as the proceeding of M. Comte, and it seems to me the proceeding, to some degree, of all those who, like Mr. Mill, put moral phenomena in the universe simply by the side of physical.[2]

Here Grote emphasizes teleology as necessary; it is not logic but rather ideals that furnish the end.

It may well be asked, What is meant by ethical idealism, and what is Grote's relation to it? Ethical idealism may be defined as a system of moral theory which is teleological in principle and accepts either one or both of the following: (a) a scale of rules of action, or a scale of values, and (b) moral freedom rather than natural or psychological necessity. Grote is an ethical idealist not only because (a) he adopts a Platonic scale of idealistic values, but also because (b) he believes in moral freedom rather than psychological necessity.

There is no necessity for personalism to be idealistic ethically. But Grote appears to present a personalism that is such. As already observed, the nature of metaphysics and epistemology is personal for Grote. Any metaphysic directs attention to four types of object, physical, conscious states, universals, and values.[2] Grote is attracted to Platonic ideas, or universals, as objects. These objects are metaphysical and idealistic. Some, at least, of the Platonic universals are ethical. And all objects for Grote have their distinctiveley conscious or personal side. The result leaves Grote with a personalistic meta-

---

[1] Grote, EP, I, 201.
[2] Brightman, ITP, 101.

physics that is idealistic ethically, for example, entertaining high regard for virtues *metaphysically* idealistic and by nature ethical. Here also, then, is shown the necessary relation between metaphysics and ethics for Grote. His position appears invulnerable.

ii. 'Aretaics' and 'eudaemonics' kept separate

Even though Grote's treatment of the moral ideals may appear inductive rather than deductive by reason of the separate treatment of happiness, virtue, duty, etc., yet there is an underlying consistency in his scheme for which this basic idea of progress is largely responsible. Grote keeps what he calls 'aretaics' and 'eudaemonics' as separate as possible in order to show that there are moral ideals which are not fully accounted for by Mill's utilitarianism. That is, besides happiness (eudaemonism) there is activity which is partly responsible for making moral ideals such as duty, virtue, etc., possible, and for which eudaemonics cannot fully account. Man is not only a sentient being (capable of feeling pleasure and pain) but is active as well, and this furnishes a basis for the distinction of the two sciences. "His activity and his sentience are two independent portions or features of his nature, each as early, as native, and as important, as the other." [1]

Man's nature, in fact the universe in general, has two portions or characters counter-fitting (if I may use the word) the one to the other, want and power in the universe, or, as I have called them in man, sentience and activity. I take as my principle, that man as early and as naturally asks for an employment of his activity as for a relief from his pain. [2]

iii. Criticism of Grote's sharp distinction between 'aretaics' and 'eudaemonics'

S'il en est ainsi, on n'aperçoit pas la nécessité d'établir, comme le fait M. Grote, une séparation profonde entre la science de la vertu et celle du bonheur, l'*eudémonique* et l'*arétique*. Cette distinction ne nous parait pas suffisamment justifiée; il n'y a, croyons-nous, qu'une science de la morale: celle qui détermine le principe fondamental et les règles secondaires qui doivent diriger l'activité, le but suprême auquel elle doit tendre. Ce but, c'est le bien, qui comprend, indissolublement unis, la perfection morale et le vrai bonheur. [3]

Probably the decisiveness with which Grote distinguishes between the two is due to the influence of Bain. Grote states:

[1] "Movement precedes sensation, and is at the outset independent of any stimulus from without: action is a more intimate and inseparable property of our constitution than any of our sensations, and in fact enters as a component into every one of the senses, giving them the character of compounds while itself is a simple and elementary property." Bain, SI, I, Chap. 1.

[2] Grote, TMI, 10, 11.

[3] Carrau, RP (1877), pt. 2, p. 537.

The fundamental fact of eudaemonics is, not that men do avoid pain, supposing this a matter of experience or observation, or in other words, supposing it conceivable that they might do otherwise, but that pain is something which has in it that which makes it avoided.[1]

The basal axiom of eudaemonics is that pain is undesirable and to be avoided, and the axiom of aretaics that pain is a thing not to be inflicted. The former, however, deals with man as an active being just as well as the latter. The distinction which Grote attempts to make between the two sciences is not quite so distinct as he claims that it is. If pain is undesirable as included within the axiom of eudaemonics, and to be avoided, it is undesirable and to be avoided for all people. However, this involves the fundamental axiom of aretaics. Yet Grote seems to separate aretaics and eudaemonics for the sake of convenience in analysis. It does not appear that he means to separate them because they have little or no relation to each other. They are fundamentally inseparable in the ecstatic character of happiness that Aristotle presents as the *summum bonum*, an ideal (happiness) accepted by Grote.

iv. Want or 'egence'

True to his idealism, Grote states that what *ought* to be sought after, cannot be determined by what *is*, or by the physical sciences alone. The starting-point of action is want or egence.[2]

What, in addition to intelligence and fact, has to be taken account of when we think of action, is *want*. And what in addition to this again, has to be taken account of when we think of *moral* action, is the existence of a plurality of *sentient*, some or all also *active*, beings.

Want or egence is the great fact conditioning, and stimulating real action (by which I mean action as different from conceivable chaotic movement). Satisfaction is the fact corresponding to it: good is the idea, i.e. this latter fact, extended, heightened and developed, by the intelligence.[3]

The feeling of want draws man out of himself. He wants the ideal. Man never goes beyond himself as *merely* acting and feeling. One might be quite satisfied with one's own feelings and one's own personal activity, but the experience and the idea of want demands action in accordance with higher ideals which pertain to the good. These are the moral ideals which Grote discusses. One may subscribe to 'egence' or 'want' which Grote describes as the starting-point of action without agreeing with his further treatment of it as in the following:

[1] Grote, TMI, 3.
[2] *Op. cit.*, 27.
[3] *Op. cit.*, 26, 27.

When we speak of moral attributes in God, we ascribe to Him an egence of the highest, but of the most imperious kind: for what are such attributes without other sentient and moral beings on which they may be exercised? Love with nothing to fix on – can we imagine a state of greater defect, imperfection, unhappiness? Suppose sentient beings created, there is a transfer of part of this original egence: they want *Him*, as He wants them.[1]

Against such words of Grote one might interject that the Absolute, considered as perfect, should not 'want' as He is presented here as doing. Such difficulty does not appear in the words: "Egence is the life of the universe: the highest forms of egence are variously called 'love': the lowest are simply appetance, perhaps merely physical." [2] This supplies the reason for Grote's use of the word 'aretaics.' And this 'egence' is a striving toward a goal. It seems to be an *Eros*, as recognized by Plato, toward the Good. "In the *Symposium* the *Eros* is described as the aspiration of the mortal for the immortal, of the actual for the ideal." [3] "*Eros* is the character whereby things are not, but are striving to be." [4] "*Eros* is the love of the good." [5]

5. CRITICAL REMARKS

i. Bases of Grote's idealims enumerated

The bases of Grote's idealism may be enumerated as follows:

(1) As shown in regard to the dialogue at the first of this chapter, he is a Platonic idealist in ethics, in the sense that, for example, 'the good' is intuitively conceived.

(2) Materialism, and kindred views, fail to account for thought, consciousness, awareness, ideas, etc.

(3) The whole of the self, personality, the '*we*' in the sense of the whole of us, possesses an *Eros*, 'egence.' or 'want,' toward the good.

(4) Realization that only activity in accordance with the highest virtue can give happiness, or 'eudaemonia.' This is a conviction inspired by Aristotle's *summum bonum*. Now both the Platonic and the Aristotelian views of the good are quite possible within a single theory inasmuch as Grote reveals a Platonic concern for absolute standards and also stresses the Aristotelian criterion of activity in accordance with the highest virtue.

[1] Grote, TMI, 31.
[2] *Loc. cit.*
[3] Demos, POP, 15.
[4] *Op. cit.*, 38.
[5] *Op. cit.*, 82.

(5) There is also a fundamental dissatisfaction with all non-idealistic theories because, as an epistemological personalist – believing that idea and object have a common source in human personality – none of these theories are satisfactory. They do not explain how we actually know, or what knowledge is.

ii. General criticism covering the foregoing bases

The dialogue dealt with in the first of this chapter presents Grote's tendency toward Platonic idealism in ethics. The dialogue is cleverly worked out in a way that presents Grote as not concerned too much with consequences, but primarily interested in ideals. Having regard for one's own interest chiefly, in a sort of free enterprise and competitive world, presupposes an orderly society to begin with, Grote points out. Now, the only safe basis on which an orderly society may be established is one in which ethical ideals exist.

The materialism which Grote opposes by his idealism appears so incapable of accounting for consciousness that one seems forced, as in the case of Grote, to find a solution for epistemology by dealing with 'objects' as meaningful only in relation to minds. Grote seems to be basically correct in his view that there is no phenomenal reality which has no connection in some way with the self as the possessor of ideas, if this reality is to be reality *for us*. Materialists would at least say that idealists, like Grote, have gone too far in approaching epistemological problems from the side of personality, but it may be said in Grote's favor that *wholly* from the side of matter epistemological problems cannot be 'seen' at all, and that knowledge of matter is as 'personal' as knowledge of ideals.

In contending for the 'we,' in the sense of the whole of us,[1] rather than simply for that portion of us possessed with the capacity for happiness, Grote reveals again a sort of Platonic idealism which holds that all things aspire toward *the good*. The emphasis here is not entirely on Platonic idealism. Grote seems to have an original contribution of his own to make, in emphasizing that it is not simply that portion of us possessed with the capacity for happiness but *our whole being* that must be considered. It is difficult to see how this position of Grote's can be readily disputed, for the whole of the self must be considered when dealing with the *summum bonum*. The *summum*

---

[1] Cf. '3. Critique of Utilitarianism' and 'iii. Descriptive and normative ethics' (above), pp. 318, 320, for an exposition of what is referred to here by the words: 'in the sense of the whole of us.'

bonum is not that which is concerned simply with our capacity for happiness but it is rather concerned with the whole of us, with our entire welfare.

This seems to be the case in Aristotle's view of the *summum bonum* where the complete welfare of the person is considered. The *summum bonum* is here, in Aristotle, concerned with personal activity in accord with the greatest virtue in such a way that ecstatic happiness will result.

Grote is strongly Hegelian, as well as Platonic and Aristotelian, in his emphasis upon the complete person being considered, in relation to the *summum bonum*. "The truth is the whole. The whole, however, is merely the essential nature reaching its completeness through the process of its own development." [1] There are two chief senses in which Grote placed emphasis upon 'the whole.' (1) In epistemology when expressing the *truth* as a sort of union of subject and object: Grote tries to show this essential unity by referring to the 'self-self,' 'intuition,' etc. Also, his basic position is that the 'philosophical' and the phe- nomenal approaches are different ways of looking at the *one reality*. (2) In ethics, by affirming that it is only as the entire person is con- sidered that we can have the truth regarding the *summum bonum:*

The reason why we should practice justice, right-doing, virtue, is because in so doing, we are acting with or from our better and higher selves . . . What is *we*? Not merely ourselves capable of happiness, but ourselves altogether.[2]

6. CONCLUDING NOTE TO THIS CHAPTER

Idealism is fundamental both to Grote's epistemology and his ethics. This book began with emphasizing what appeared at first to be considerably removed from idealism, with 'philosophy' and as, especially, apparently remote, phenomenalism. It seems appropriate now to recapitulate and survey the territory covered and to offer some general criticisms of the entire study. To this task we will now turn and complete the research undertaken by means of the conclusion and appendix on various miscellaneous writings.

---

[1] Hegel, POM, 16.
[2] Grote, "A Discussion . . . Republic," in CR (Mar. 1889), 98.

CONCLUSION

1. GROTE'S POSITION IN THE HISTORY OF PHILOSOPHY

i. Scanty position given to Grote in modern philosophy

First of all, let us look at the place given to Grote in contemporary philosophy. The position given is only scanty; there are various reasons for this meagre reference.[1] The following is an extract which indicates Grote's opinion regarding his own philosophy and his reason for criticism of various eminent contemporary philosophers. This statement is supported in the foregoing chapters by critical remarks on various writers such as Ferrier, Hamilton, Mill, and others:

> J. Grote, au lieu de ces doctrines qui se nuisent mutuellement, et dont les rivalités expliquent, dans une certaine measure, l'indifférence publique pour les spéculations sérieuses, voudrait voir se fonder, d'une part une philosophie *réele* [sic], qui ne se perdrait pas dans les abstractions et restituerait leur véritable valeur à l'intelligence et à la liberté humaines, si indépendantes, en elles-mêmes, des conditions de leur exercice; et, d'autre part, une science générale de la nature, qui comprendrait une physio-psychologie comparée, mais à laquelle ne seraient pas subordonnées les questions de philosophie proprement dite et de morale . . .
> Il étudie successivement les oeuvres maîtresses de Ferrier, de W. Hamilton, de Stuart Mill, de Whewell, et il projetait de continuer, s'il l'avait pu, avec celles de Spencer et de Bain; mais nous n'avons pas, dans le second volume, sur celles-ci les mêmes développements que sur les autres dans le premier. Ce sont autant de livres qui l'ont fait beaucoup penser, dont il a beaucoup appris, et dont il n'a pas été pleinement satisfait. En les critiquant, il nous découvre sa propre doctrine, plus éloignée de telle sutre, ou plus rapprochée, toujours originale, sincère et très digne d'être étudiée, même aujourd'hui.[2]

Criticism of well-known philosophers who appeared to be in the ascendancy at the time of Grote was not the type of work that would make one's scattered notes very popular. This is not alone what caused almost complete oversight of Grote's writings. There are several rather

---

[1] Whitmore, SJG, in PR, 36 (1927), 307–337.
[2] 'A.P.,' reviewing EP, I, II, in RP, 54 (1902), 435–436.

obvious reasons for neglect which were rather accidental. Henry Sidgwick succeeded Grote in the Knightbridge Chair of Moral Philosophy at Cambridge University. Sidgwick's philosophy was not especially epistemological and did not continue the discussion of any basic problems with which Grote dealt. A smaller reason for this neglect or oversight might be attributed to the prestige in which George Grote, the elder brother of John, was usually placed. Any reference to the name of 'Grote' recalled the name of the former whose work on Plato and Aristotle was much before the eyes of the public of his own time.

ii. John Grote overshadowed by his brother, George

At the age of fifty-three John Grote died, five years before his brother, and this may have accounted to a somewhat small extent for the lack of attention which John Grote received. Moreover, in the first part of the *Exploratio Philosophica*, John Grote criticized Mill, Whewell, Hamilton, Ferrier, Bain, and Spencer. During these various critical analyses Grote laid down his own position. Mill, Bain, and Spencer survived Grote and since they refer very little, or not at all, to Grote, this factor alone might be enough to stamp him into oblivion for a century.

iii. Bain's slight reference to Grote

Mill and Spencer do not refer to Grote. The references which Bain makes to Grote are only slight. However, he makes the following revealing statement:

John Grote was very hospitable and friendly, and was himself an interesting man to talk to. He had all the candour and metaphysical tastes of his brother, without the thorough-goingness in his conclusions. The two brothers rarely met, but held one another in the greatest brotherly esteem, while freely commenting upon each other's positions.[1]

Yet the reference to Grote's theory of knowledge alone, in the following remarks by various writers, indicates the very considerable regard in which his writing was held. But it is interesting to observe regarding Bain's view that Grote lacked "thorough-goingness in his conclusions," that Joseph B. Mayor in editing *A Treatise on the Moral Ideals* makes the following statement:

No doubt his mode of exposition is generally unsystematic. Writing, as he did, without any view of immediate publication, he thought more of putting his matter into the form which was most natural and expressive to himself than of

[1] Bain, AUT, 258.

putting it into the form which was most intelligible to his readers. Thus he suddenly diverges in the midst of an argument, returns again, repeats what has been said before, and not unfrequently passes over some point which had been previously left for further consideration.[1]

iv. Stephen's reference to Grote

Leslie Stephen writes favorably on Grote's epistemology. References to Grote have not been very numerous. Any estimate made concerning his work is to the effect that his writings are in a style difficult to read, though the thought is generally extolled. An example of such an estimate is made by Leslie Stephen, regarding the *Exploratio Philosophica*.[2]

This book is, I think, by far the most interesting contemporary discussion of Mill, Hamilton, and Whewell. It was, unfortunately, desultory and unfinished, but it is full of acute criticism, and charmingly candid and modest. Mill's *Logic* is especially discussed in Chapters VIII and IX. Grote holds, and I think truly, that Mill's attempt to divide metaphysics from logic leads to real confusion, and especially to an untenable mode of conceiving the relation between 'things' and thoughts. I cannot discuss Grote's views; but the book is full of interesting suggestions, though the results are rather vague.[3]

This note is appended after the remark is made to the effect that Mill handed over certain problems to metaphysicians, because, as metaphysicians, he considered they should be able to judge facts to be facts. Mill asserted that logicians need not enter into such judgment. Leslie Stephen questions Mill's distinction because "it is apparently relevant to inquire what are these 'ultimate facts.'" [4]

v. Remarks in an obituary notice

In an obituary notice of the death of Grote,[5] the writer of the article makes the following remark about Grote's first published volume:

His unfinished work called *Exploratio Philosophica*, hard to read, chiefly from the intense closeness of the reasoning, is a masterly review of modern theories of philosophy full of the soundest wisdom and opposed to the fallacies of popular metaphysicians . . . Professor Grote has left valuable papers, and it is hoped they are in a state for publication.[6]

These valuable papers proved to be more in the form of 'notes' than the first part of *Exploratio Philosophica*, and did not aid in advancing

---

[1] Grote, TMI, ix.
[2] Part I.
[3] Stephen, EU, III, 80n.
[4] *Op. cit.*, 80, 81.
[5] (No author nor title given) re Grote, in GM, 221 (o.s.) (1866), 550.
[6] *Loc. cit.*

Grote's reputation beyond what it was when he finished the second part. Moreover, the style of Grote's writings is not particularly attractive and gives the impression of hurried writing not intended for publication.

vi. 'Knowledge of acquaintance' and 'knowledge about'

a. James's debt to Grote

It is with Grote's epistemology that most people interested in philosophy have acquainted themselves. if they know anything of much account of his philosophy. At the foundation of Grote's theory of knowledge is the division of knowledge into two kinds. In the chapter entitled "Ferrier's Institutes of Metaphysic" Grote deals with how one "may speak in a double manner of the 'object' of knowledge." [1]

That is, we may either use language thus, we *know* a thing, a man, &c.: or we may use it thus: we know such and such things *about* the thing, the man &c. Language in general, following its true logical instinct, distinguishes between these two applications of the notion of knowledge, the one being εἰδέναι, noscere, kennen, connaître, the other being γνῶναι, scire, wissen, savoir. In the origin, the former may be considered more what I have called phenomenal – it is the notion of knowledge as acquaintance or familiarity with what is known: which notion is perhaps more akin to the phenomenal bodily communication, and is less purely intellectual than the other: It is the kind of knowledge which we have of a thing by the presentation of it to the senses or the representation of it in a picture or type, a 'vorstellung.' The other, which is what we express in judgments or propositions, what is embodied in 'begriffe' or concepts without any necessary imaginative representation, is in its origin the more *intellectual* notion of knowledge. [2]

This distinction of knowledge into two kinds is the basis of a whole chapter in one of Bertrand Russell's works.[3] William James states, also, that

there are two kinds of knowledge broadly and practically distinguishable: we may call them respectively *knowledge of acquaintance* and *knowledge-about*. Most languages express the distinction; thus, γνῶναι, εἰδέναι; noscere, scire; kennen, wissen; connaître, savoir.[4]

On the same page James adds the following note: "Cf. John Grote, Exploratio Philosophica, p. 60." The indebtedness of James to Grote is left unacknowledged in another of James's works.[5] Also, James has received credit for this distinction between two kinds of knowledge.[6]

[1] Grote, EP, I, 60.
[2] *Loc. cit.*
[3] Russell, POP, Chap. V.
[4] James, POP, I, 221.
[5] James, PBC, 14.
[6] Whitmore, SJG, in PR, 36 (1927), 310.

Grote in the first sixty pages of *Exploratio Philosophica*, Part I, prepared the way for his division of knowledge into two kinds:

A sizable, and solid body of doctrine precedes the 'page 60' by which Grote has thus far been chiefly known, and . . . his position is to be rightly judged only in the light of that doctrine.[1]

b. Eaton's debt to Grote

It is rather momentous to notice in a volume of a recent contemporary scholar[2] that the influence of Grote predominates certain pages. However, the author, Dr. Eaton, appears to have been unaware as to how much his chapter on "Meaning" (Chapter I) owes to Grote. To Bertrand Russell appears to go a great deal of credit for the distinction of knowledge into two kinds.[3] This is especially evident from Mr. Russell's article mentioned below,[4] the title of which indicates the division of knowledge made by Grote. W. R. Sorley makes the significant remark that

the distinction between acquaintance and knowing about was formulated by John Grote, 'Exploratio Philosophica,' Part I (1865), . . . More recently its importance has been emphasized by Mr. Russell, e.g., in 'Problems of Phil.,' pp. 71 ff, where universals as well as sense-data are regarded as objects of acquaintance.[5]

An elaboration of knowledge by acquaintance and knowledge by description has Dr. Eaton for its author in various places throughout *Symbolism and Truth*. The exposition itself is worthy but the source for the four chapters (to mention no more) on 'Meaning,' 'Universals and Individuals: Order,' 'Description and Analysis' and 'The Metaphysics of Knowledge' is very Grotian. The beginning of the trouble appears to have been in James's *Principles of Psychology* where Grote appears to have been overlooked though James possessed a copy of Grote's major work. Consequently, James has received recognition for what properly belonged to another. Dr. Eaton quotes the following from James:

Sensation, then, so long as we take the analytic point of view, differs from perception only in the extreme simplicity of its object or content . . . A pure sensation is an abstraction.[6]

---

[1] Whitmore, SJG, in PR, 36 (1927), 316.
[2] Eaton, ST.
[3] (1) Costello, in PR, 35 (1926), 574–580.
(2) Prall, in JP, 24 (1927), 71–80.
[4] Russell, in PAS, 11 (n.s.) (1910–11), 108–128. Cf. quotation (on this page) from Sorley, MVI, 193.
[5] Sorley, MVI, 193.
[6] Eaton, ST, 16.

Such a quotation breathes of Grotian language. Compare with the following words of Grote:

The description of knowledge as a course of experience and the description of it as a course of analytic and self-correcting judgments – as what many would call sensation, or as reflection in this view of reflection – are both what I call *abstractions*.[1]

Such similarities call for attention and especially so when "the scale of sensation or knowledge" is made the subject of at least one chapter in *Exploratio Philosophica* (Part I, Chap. VI) and is frequently referred to in some form in current philosophy.

c. Boswell's Life of Samuel Johnson

If James is indebted to Grote further than he indicates in *The Principles of Psychology* there is no reference to the fact, though it is clearly evident that James had the *Exploratio Philosophica* before him in writing his memorable work. However, it is quite possible that Grote himself may have been dependent upon *Boswell's Life of Samuel Johnson* where Johnson observes:

Knowledge is of two kinds. We know a subject ourselves, or we know where we can find information upon it. When we enquire into any subject, the first thing we have to do is to know what books have treated of it. This leads us to look at catalogues, and at the backs of books in libraries.[2]

Here, indeed, Johnson writes of 'two kinds' of knowledge. And he deals with *who knows* rather than with *what knowledge is*. It is possible, however, that the sentence, "we know a subject ourselves," might be regarded by Grote as having to do with 'knowledge of acquaintance,' and, "We know where we can find information upon it," would be regarded as only second-hand information and therefore to call it 'knowledge about' is a poor substitute of terms.

d. Robinson refers to 'William James's famous distinction'

Daniel Sommer Robinson refers to "the controversy initiated by William James's famous distinction between knowledge by acquaintance and knowledge by description," [3] to which he appends the note:

The history of these terms is obscure. James evidently did not coin them, because they are found in the form, "knowledge of acquaintance," and "knowledge about," in J. Grote's *Exploratio Philosophica*, Part I, p. 60, from which they were taken by Joseph.[4] Royce, in the article entitled "Mind," in Hastings' *Encyclopedia of Religion and Ethics*, attributes the terms to James. But the distinction itself is at least as old as Hobbes' *Leviathan*. He there said: "There

---

[1] Grote, EP, I, 30.
[2] Under the date, April 18, 1775.
[3] Robinson, POR, 109.
[4] Joseph, ITL, 68.

are of knowledge two kinds; whereof one is knowledge of fact, and the other knowledge of the consequence of one affirmation to another. The former is nothing else but sense and memory, and is absolute knowledge . . . The latter is called science and is conditional." [1]

It may be added that Professor Robinson's attributing of the distinction, made by Grote, to Hobbes is at least defensible in so far as he (Hobbes) refers to two kinds of knowledge, thus: "There are of knowledge two kinds." But that Professor Robinson is correct in labelling the latter kind as 'knowledge about,' is not clear. For the second type may be regarded as either causal or logical knowledge, and in either case it is not clear that such knowledge is 'knowledge *about.*'

Under the sub-title of "Perception and Conception as Fundamental Cognitive Processes" in the article 'Mind' [2] Josiah Royce gives credit to William James for a distinction which is at least as old as the time of John Grote. They are

two well-known types of cognitive process, perception and conception . . . These two have been recognized throughout the history of science and philosophy, and their familiar contrast has dominated epistemology . . . William James has use, for what is here called perception, the term 'knowledge of acquaintance.' He distinguishes 'knowledge of acquaintance' from 'knowledge about.' [3]

e. *Joseph acknowledges Grote's distinction*

H. W. B. Joseph remarks:

It has been frequently pointed out that the English language uses only one verb, 'know,' to represent two different acts, which in some languages are distinguished by different verbs: the knowledge of acquaintance with a thing, and the knowledge about it.

To this he appends the footnote: "Cf. e.g. J. Grote, 'Ex. Ph.,' Pt. I, P. 60 – a work and by an author less known than they deserve to be; the expressions 'knowledge of acquaintance' and 'knowledge about' are borrowed thence." [4]

f. *Whitehead's relation to Grote*

One might observe, again, in modern philosophy, an influence attributed to James which goes back to the time of Grote. Professor Whitehead in elucidating his meaning of 'the extensive continuum' [5] quotes William James in support of the essential relation among all actual entities in the continuum:

[1] Robinson, POR, 109n.
[2] Hastings, ERE.
[3] *Loc. cit.*
[4] Joseph, ITL, 55.
[5] Whitehead, PR, pt. II, Chap. 2.

Either your experience is of no content, of no change, or it is of a perceptible amount of content or change. Your acquaintance with reality grows literally by buds or drops of perception. Intellectually and on reflection you can divide these into components, but as immediately given, they come totally or not at all.[1]

The language 'acquaintance with reality,' and 'immediately given' suggests John Grote on "Immediateness and Reflection." [2] However, James supports his argument by reference to Zeno's 'Arrow in its Flight.'

g. Ward's adequate reference to Grote

The division of knowledge into knowledge as acquaintance and knowledge *about* is referred to by James Ward:

There is an ambiguity in the words 'know' and 'knowledge,' which Bain seems not to have considered: to know may mean to perceive or apprehend, it may also mean to understand or comprehend.

To this he appends the footnote,

Other languages give more prominence to this distinction; compare, γνῶναι and εἰδέναι, noscere and scire, kennen and wissen, connaître and savoir. On this subject there are some acute renarks in a little-known book, J. Grote, 'Exploratio Philosophica.' [3]

h. Sellars' reference to Grote

The distinction between the two kinds of knowledge is also recognized by Roy Wood Sellars:

For common-sense there are two kinds, or types, of knowledge: these are knowledge-of-acquaintance and knowledge-about . . . knowledge-of-acquaintance is, primarily, knowledge *due to* acquaintance, and knowledge-about is knowledge *due to* inference and communication. While the English language possesses only the word 'know' to designate these two kinds of knowledge, many other languages employ two words. Thus knowledge-of-acquaintance in Latin is 'cognoscere' and knowledge-about is 'scire.' In French, there are two corresponding words, 'connaître' and 'savoir'; in German, 'kennen' and 'wissen.' This distinction was emphasized by Grote, and, since his time, has become one of the recognized contrasts in knowledge . . . Mr. Russell regards the distinction of knowledge-by-acquaintance and knowledge-by-description as of fundamental importance for epistemology.[4]

i. Mackenzie gives proper credit to Grote

Professor John Stuart Mackenzie, of Glasgow and Cambridge, gave credit to Grote for the phrase "knowledge as acquaintance or familiar-

---

[1] Professor Whitehead states that his attention was drawn to this passage from reading *Religion in the Philosophy of William James*, where the extract appears. James's words, reproduced here, are from *Some Problems of Philosophy*, chapter X, p. 155.
[2] Grote, EP, II, bk. II, Chap's. I–VIII.
[3] Ward, PP, 86n.
[4] Sellars, CR, 257, 259.

ity with what is known" (along with a criticism of the phrase) in the
following:

A distinction is sometimes drawn between immediate and mediate knowledge,[1]
or, again, between what Mr. Russell calls knowledge by acquaintance and knowledge by description; but, if we are right in our general interpretation of the
meaning of knowledge, it would seem that all knowledge involves some mediation
and some element of description. We have, indeed, some immediate experiences
(e.g. of pain, colour, etc.), but these can hardly be called knowledge. They
become knowledge only when we reflect upon them and form beliefs about
them; and, in doing this, we are always going beyond what is immediately
before us.[2]

j. Brightman's informative reference to and acknowledgment of Grote

Professor Edgar S. Brightman acknowledges Grote's distinction
between 'knowledge of acquaintance' and 'knowledge about,' and
indicates indebtedness of James, Russell, Sorley, and others, to Grote:

The distinction between 'knowledge of acquaintance' and 'knowledge about'
was made by John Grote in the *Exploratio Philosophica*, Part I (1865), pp.
60ff., Part II (1900), pp. 201ff. It was taken up by James in his *Psychology*,
Vol. I, pp. 221f., by B. Russell, who introduced the term 'knowledge by description' for 'knowledge about' in *The Prroblems of Philosophy*, Chapter V;
by W. R. Sorley, *Moral Values and the Idea of God*, 2nd ed., pp. 194f., and by
others.[3]

vii. Two recent and peculiarly significant references
to Grote's philosophy

The foregoing references to John Grote are probably enough to
indicate the high regard in which his theory of knowledge is held. Two
recent philosophers, who have made use of some of Grote's thought,
are William James and Bertrand Russell. Both appear, inadequately,
to have given credit due to a predecessor whose thought perennially
had and has appeared in various forms. Outside the slight reference
to the *Exploratio Philosophica*,[4] no acknowledgment appears to have
been given to Grote either in the work of James or Russell.

It is probably unnecessary to carry on further investigation to indicate the debt of modern philosophy to one whose name is frequently

---

[1] (1) Grote, EP, II, bk. II.
    (2) Russell, KAK, in PAS, 11 (n.s.) (1910–11), 108–128.
    (3) Russell, POP, 88.
    (4) Russell, NSD, in MIN, 22 (n.s.) (1913), 76–81.
    (5) Russell, PM, I, 14.
[2] Mackenzie, ECP, 130n2.
[3] Brightman, ITP, 83n.
[4] Grote, EP, I, 60.

passed over but whose thought is quite alive in modern moral science and epistemology.

2. FURTHER CRITICAL COMMENT

To pass over Grote so almost completely as history has done, is scarcely fair to one whose thinking is characterized by frequent flashes of insight if not of genius. It was pointed out above (under "1. Grote's position in the history of philosophy") that Grote was largely responsible himself for this lack of recognition. He did not write with a view to publication but rather in order to clarify his own views. Much of what he wrote, therefore, is in the form of, what he himself called, 'rough notes.'

His posthumous publications were a complete and painstaking project, undertaken by the husband, Joseph Bickersteth Mayor, of his adopted niece. Had Grote himself been able to prepare these papers for publication he would have had the freedom, which his literary executor felt that he did not have, to make extensive alterations, in deleting some repetitions, clarifying the style of writing, and possibly putting his thoughts in considerably better order.

Much of Grote's criticism of Descartes, Berkeley, and, sometimes Hume and several others, does not seem appropriate. But there is some of it that is appropriate. And the appropriateness of it stems from his theory of reality as *one*, but reality as viewed from two possible approaches. Just which of these aspects is to be taken depends upon whether one wishes to speak in conceptual or phenomenal language.

The primary difficulty that one will most certainly encounter in becoming familiar with Grote's thought, especially as expressed in *Exploratio Philosophica*, is his meaning of 'philosophy' and especially of phenomena. What he means by these terms is of prime importance for the understanding of *Exploratio Philosophica*. It is by no means an exaggeration to say that this two-volume work can *not* be understood unless these meanings are grasped. This distinction is a basic requirement in the foundation of his epistemology.

For 'philosophy' Grote sometimes uses such terms as, 'consciousness,' 'logic,' 'thought,' 'reason,' 'knowing,' 'understanding,' 'mental,' and 'conceptual.' For 'phenomenon,' he substitutes 'object,' 'the known,' 'thing,' 'physical,' and 'phenomenal reality.' The one, 'philosophy' is never wholly separated from the other phenomenon. Phenomenon is always phenomenon for consciousness, or for us, in some way. It is a term that represents the 'thing' aspect of reality. The main trouble with referring to these phenomena for consciousness, as 'things,' is that in so doing we separate, or abstract, those 'things' from consciousness (or ourselves in some other way) as though they were such 'things' on their own merits. The fact is, as Grote is painstakingly careful to show, they are *never* 'things' in this way.

This seems like a very simple way of expressing what he means, but it is amazing how much writing in the field of epistemology seems to almost completely overlook this basic and essential distinction. Realistic philosophy, that attempts to analyze 'objects' as though they are 'things' *already* there for us to look at, runs against this impregnable rock which successfully defies all attempts to remove it. Behaviorism falls victim also to this particular and perennial psychological thrust. We simply can never deal with 'things as they are' since there are no such entities (altogether divorced from 'philosophy').

But one of the major types of 'offender' (who overlooks this fundamental distinction which Grote points out), is the one who will admit that we can not have 'objects' out of all connection with ourselves, and yet who will analyze those 'objects' as though they *were not* related to us primarily. This is a subtle danger lurking to catch the unsuspecting epistemologist unaware.

In some ways Grote's criticism of several outstanding contemporaries was judicious. At least, he attacked some important and well known philosophers whose strength was far more evident than their weakness. If he could successfully undermine the basis upon which they wrote, then this would be an accomplishment indeed. To the reader making a minute study of this approach to contemporaries, such criticisms of Grote are very convincing.

These critical remarks are frequently rather difficult to read. The reason for this is that the style is laborious and frequently interspersed with parenthetical clauses that prolong the sense and often require first a reading excluding the parentheses and then a reading including them. This is also a reason why a hasty perusal of Grote's writing on epistemology makes only a minimum amount of sense. One has to read on continuously in some sections, particularly in the *Exploratio Philosophica*, to get the meaning that otherwise one fancies one gets yet does not. This is surely an enigmatical way to write, and Grote could have improved on it greatly.

In his various writings certain main influences are noticeable. The modern philosopher who influenced him most was Kant. He was impressed, apparently, by Kant's thoughts on space and time, on the 'ground thought of Kant's Critique of Pure Reason' as the disengaging of 'the action of intelligence from all application and actual use of it' in order 'to see what it is in itself,'[1] and on the manifold and its relation to experience. He was also impressed by evidences of dualism in Kant.

Also, as pointed out in the last chapter of this book, Grote seems to have been much impressed by the idealism of Plato. What constitutes a 'thing' to be what it is, is "that in it which Plato conceived to correspond to the idea, that which I have variously called . . . the meaning, purpose, etc., the reason . . . of it."[2] His Platonic idealism becomes especially evident in his writings on ethics, where he insists that it is not simply our capacities for happiness that govern our conduct, but out total selves which seem to be motivated by something more than utilitarian pleasure. In short, Grote insists we are motivated by something that takes into account *the whole of us.*

I mean by 'ideal' anything which we mentally set before ourselves as the purpose or rule of our action, and (as will have been seen from all that I have said) I do not regard anything as a *proper* ideal for our conduct, a true ideal, except as being fact or part of fact, representing or expressing fact. But then it is not the fact of our ordinary understanding (which can only furnish us *means* for action, not purposes): it is the fact of our imagination, intuition, belief, inward vision, however we like to describe it.[3]

It should be noted also that Grote's idealism is personalistic. It is personalistic in two main senses. First, this personalistic idealism engages the whole person in aspiring after an objective or ideal, the *summum bonum,* which in Plato is *the Good* and in Aristotle *eudaemonia* or happiness akin to ecstasy. Second, this personalistic idealism is evident in the emphasis that Grote lays upon the 'philosophical' consciousness, or 'idea' side of his epistemology without which there is no *being* of any sort. All existence must be such for persons; there is no other existence.

Regarding Grote's belief in deity, it should be noted that he is professedly and actually a theist. He believes that the universe is God-created, and that human beings are a part of this harmonious and self-consistent creation.[4] Also, in addition to the natural world is "a nature *above* all this."

By reason of his knowledge and consciousness, man is a partaker of

[1] Grote, EP, I, 18.
[2] *Op. cit.,* 112.
[3] *Op. cit.,* II, 324.
[4] *Op. cit.,* 36.

this 'higher' nature. Man's thoughts point to this higher realm while his phenomenal being refers to phenomenal nature. In the universe there is "a Planner or Maker with his ideas and his purposes." In short, though Grote is neither frequent nor insistent in his references to the deity, yet there is sufficient evidence as noted above, that he is fundamentally theistic.

AN EXPOSITION OF THE MISCELLANEOUS WRITINGS OF JOHN GROTE

I. "ON A FUTURE STATE" [1]

1. Glorification of body and mind

In the first part of this article Grote speaks about the glorification of the body and of the mind. The glorification of the former as well as of the latter, must be through an *ideal*, in a manner compatible with its nature. Whatever form this glorification will take remains very indefinite and comparatively unimportant, in comparison with the glorification of mind. Grote does not explicitly state what he means by 'glorification.'

2. Simplicity of style and thought in this article

This article labors under the confusion necessitated by a Puritanical conception of a future life. It is somewhat different from what one might expect from the author of *Exploratio Philosophica*, where personalistic humanism is so prominent. One might readily conjecture that this fragment was written for people who had not adapted themselves to modern theological analyses. It is written from a popular standpoint and is exceedingly simple – much after the fashion of a Sunday School quarterly lesson. For example, Grote states that if we have lived an evil life up to the present we should make the best of what lies before us. The narrative takes the form of exhortation rather than of philosophical exploration which is so characteristic of the *Exploratio Philosophica*.

3. Effect of present life on the future

In the future state the body will have gone through a process of remodelling which will bear the traces of the present life. Just what

---

[1] These miscellaneous writings follow, generally, as close to a chronological order as it was possible to figure from some dates appended.

the remodelled body will be like Grote does not state. However, he attributes as much perfection as possible to it. The mind will be modified also but the nature of our present life will have an influence upon the future state of the mind.

4. *Manner of individual appearance in a future life is unimportant*

Grote does not consider the question important as to how each individual will appear before men and angels. This problem evidently was prepared for the unsophisticated theological mind somewhat incapable of independent speculation. "Minds," Grote states,

must there see into each other, far more than they do here; but they will have no desire and no care to do so in such a manner as to give plain; each will have his own burden to bear, and will only be considered with those of others in so far as there may be a possibility of lightening them.[1]

5. *Stress on the importance of* both *present and future life*

The future state implies another life as well as a continuance of the present one. If one were to consider future life as too important one would run into the danger of deprecating the value of present life, and if one were to consider future life as wholly unimportant one would give too much place to the present life. Grote does not wish to go deeply into any theological implications.

Grote remarks that injury done to one's fellow-man is injury done against God. Unwise conduct is the outcome of too little stress upon present life.

God showed how He took all sins upon Himself, made himself, so to call it, the great sufferer of all wrong that had been done, in order that he might have a right to forgive it *in that character*, as well as in His character . . . Christ in his death is at once the pledge of the completeness of God's pardon, and the universal Reconciler of all immortal men.[2]

We have no reason to think that our fellow-beings will be less interesting to us, or less cared for by us, there than here. It is the nearer presence and the clearer view of Him (God) which will be the source of the truer understanding of, and better sympathy with, them.[3]

6. *Comment*

In short, this article appears to have been prepared for a religious audience which for the most part were not expected to be interested in traditional arguments in favor of immortality, except Christ's view of

---

[1] Grote, CR, 18 (1871), 134.
[2] *Op. cit.*, 139.
[3] *Op. cit.*, 140.

the future life. Probably the article was prepared for such audience as *The Contemporary Review* reached, though Grote could have delivered the content as part of a sermon.

II. "ON GLOSSOLOGY"

1. Concerning terminology

i. Break in Grote's projected work on glossology – In 1872 two articles of Grote's appeared in *The Journal of Philology*, and in 1874 one article. The work was 'to be continued,' as pointed out at the end of the third article, in his periodical but was not, for some, apparently, unknown reason.

ii. 'Phone' and 'noem' – The key words for all Grote's work published in *The Journal of Philology* are 'phone' and 'noem.' The former of these is from φωνή, the latter from νόημα. 'Noem' refers to the 'thought-word.' "When I mean words as thought I shall use the term *noem*." [1] This is true not only for single words but even sentences (as well as nouns, verbs, particles, etc). 'Phone' refers to words as sounds. The adjectives 'phonal' and 'noematic' are employed in conjunction with the nouns. Modifications of the noems and phones have the term of 'phonal' or 'noematic' 'schematisms' applied to them. Languages differ from each other in two respects, (1) 'noematically,' in respect to what is expressed (i.e., what the sound expressess), and (2) 'phonally,' in respect to the sounds expressed. 'Noematism' refers to everything, generally, from the concrete to the abstract.

iii. 'Phonism' and 'noematism' – The whole 'noematism' of any language does not differ so greatly from the noematism of any other, though the syntactical difference may be considerable. The case is different with 'phonism.' Where radical 'phones' are used, the distribution of these among the noems are subject to various laws of schematism. What Grote means by 'schematism' is close to Kant's meaning, namely (and briefly) 'according to a rule.' All this is responsible for the various differences between one language and another.

iv. Ideas of physical 'things' – Phones are attempts to express the noems, and careful use must be made of these in order that the noems of one language may correspond with the respective noems of another language. What Grote wants to express by the term 'noem' is precisely what once must have been meant by the word 'thing.' The noem, however, has more general application than 'thing,' because

---

[1] Grote, JOP, 4 (1872), 55.

it has reference not only to what is supposed to be substantial existence, but to relations, actions, etc., of every kind. The noem has reference, then, to whatever is conceivable in the universe, on the one hand, and to whatever is expressible as a whole or in part, on the other. It would seem, then, that Grote holds that for every noem a 'phone' is possible however inadequate the phone may be in expressing the noem.

v. Stomatism – A synthetic approach may be taken toward the examination of the human vocal organism, exhibiting it with all of its phonic power, or the total of its vocal elements and the relation of these elements to each other. Conversely, an analytic approach may be taken where each actual existing utterance is examined and its physical constitution and conditions determined. For this latter process Grote uses the term 'stomatism.'

Stomatistic investigations, Grote maintains, are of importance chiefly in regard to writing, where there is a presentation of phones to the eye. But greatly independent of the phonism of a language, the noematism might deal with what is presented to the eye, or it could be written. Thus the noematism of a language could become far removed from the phonism. In the Chinese written language, for example, Grote points out, there is a close correlation between the noematism and the phonism of a language.

vi. 'Hypophonism' – A phone may be partly represented by phonograms. When these phonograms, considered individually, are put together, they cannot make up the complete phone needed. Much must remain to be understood which is unexpressed. Hypophonism is concerned with this great amount that is understood. Hypophonism must go along with phonogrammatism, and must be considered of great significance when we speak of a language being ambiguous.

This is probably what Reid had in mind when he stated that "when men attempt to define things which cannot be defined, their definitions will always be either obscure or false." [1] In order that a person may be able to master a language, not only the noematic elements must be understood but the phonal also. Moreover, the forming of a phonal sound and the forming of an idea are entirely different though they may readily accompany each other.

2. The philosophy of language

i. Four divisions – In the philosophy of language, according to Grote, there are certain main lines which should be noted; in regard to

[1] Hamilton, WTR, I, 220.

(1) 'noematism,' (2) 'noematoschematism,' (3) construction of a 'phonarium,' and (4) 'dianoematism.'

ii. 'Noematism' – In respect to the first of these, namely, noematism, the center of the noems are determined. What is meant by this is the maintenance of the relation of the primary meaning of the phone to the sub-meanings of it, or what Grote calls the 'protonoem' to the 'paranoem.'

A very good example of a book which illustrates the relation of the protonoems to the paranoems is Liddell and Scott, *Greek Lexicon*. Here the problem of subsuming paranoems systematically as species under the general noems as genus is very clearly presented. There are examples, Grote continues, of books that do not classify systematically paranoems under protonoems. One such example is Richardson, *Arabic and Persian Dictionary*, from which, Grote contends, one inclines to come to the conclusion that words have no definite meaning at all, since the catalogue of possible renderings is so arbitrary, unconnected, and multifarious. Lexicography has, generally, however, grouped lists of words in proper order and subordination, so the possibility of great variety of meaning in words can be understood. This is particularly evident in the case of the comparison of one language with another.

The noems not only must be defined in respect to their centers and boundaries but also must be classified or enumerated. Though this classification is somewhat the same as the determination of the centers of the noems yet it cannot be made the practical basis for language since the phones of language occupy such an important place.

iii. 'Noematoschematism' – 'Noematoschematism' is that which treats the noems through the arbitrary medium of phones. The phones exist merely for the matter of expression, but are very necessary as such in order that the noems may be expressed.

iv. 'Phonarium' – In an attempt to formulate a full 'phonarium,' which is the completion of the schematization of the phones, one must appreciate the arbitrary nature of the phones. It is this arbitrary nature which makes possible the communication by means of phones and forms a foundation for the elements of language. It is the purpose of etymology as commonly practiced to strip the phones of all the noematic quality with an attempt to find counterparts with words of other languages. This is done to the neglect of much of the essentially arbitrary characteristics of the phones.

v. 'Dianoematism' – 'Dianoematism' is that which is concerned with the expression of one noem or idea by means of another or others.

Thus by dwelling upon a word or its meaning, wide views as to the noems of the written words may be attained; this contemplation on the meaning of a word is 'dianoematism.' That is, to give a word a stereotyped meaning kills its dianoematism. For there is much more in a word than can be brought out by the word written, or by phones. There is really no such a process as 'transdianoematism' practicable. By transdianoematism is meant the process by which one language, wanting one word from another, would incorporate the actual phone, the idea or noem of which it does not possess. What, instead, is actually done is to translate the phones of which the other language is compounded. That is, it forms words with their own respective phones and with similar composition or dianoematism.

A word may be taken over by one language from another, to which a very different phone than that of the original may be attached, because the phone in the one language may possess a very different idea than the corresponding phone in the other.

vi. In extreme cases the modification in noematism is very great – The noematism of words undergoes a very great change in extreme cases which Grote indicates in his use of the word 'perinoematism.' [1] The feature of perinoematism which most readily presents itself is 'impejoration' or the change for the worse in the moral signification of words. This law (if one may call it such) is only part of a still wider one where a word becomes more and more impotent. This latter law is entitled 'trivialization' or 'evaporation.' These laws are the most important ones in perinoematism. The former is the outcome of 'euphemism' and the latter of 'grandiloquence.' Both euphemism and grandiloquence are the result of 'levity' of speech. When levity is employed so that exaggeration takes place, and a thing is given a name worse than it deserves, the result is what Grote entitles 'immelioration. Again there are the laws of 'generalization' and particularization' which correspond, respectively, to the earlier and the later growths of language. There is a sub-law called 'deflection' or 'side-change,' where the change of meaning takes place as in particularization or generalization. In particularization there is a tendency to extend the application of a word, while the opposite is the case in generalization.

3. *Criticism of Tooke*

All the words immediately above concern the dianoematism of words. Grote presents them in order to clarify glossology from his

---

[1] This word is explained above, in the paragraph immediately preceding this one.

point of view. In order to support his own arguments and manifest the futility of those of others Grote deals with Horne Tooke's treatment. Grote's general criticism of Tooke is that he mistakes the form of words for their dianoematism. Tooke's system of derivation of meaning from the form of words was admirable in consideration of the small amount of work that had been done previously on the subject. A single example of the general mistake that Tooke makes may be observed in the following:

His interlocutor is in doubt how the people of Melinda should be described, with whom it is the custom to use their left hand exactly as we use our right, and *vice versa*. Was Da Gama correct in describing them as all *left-handed*?

H. T.: "With reference to European custom the author describes them truly. But the people of Melinda are as right-handed as the Portuguese; for they use that hand in preference which is ordered by their custom, and leave out of employ the other which is therefore their left hand." [1]

What Tooke neglects is the dianoematism of the 'right' and 'left' hand. He derives the meaning of the words from what is decreed by custom; his mistake is the one of neglect to see that 'right' and 'left' are *facts of nature*. What Grote means by this is that the words 'right' and 'left' are called so *not* because of custom but by reason of something in thought which underlies the very words themselves. There is a meaning independent of and antecedent to the words, though to what extent different people mean the same thing must remain a problem of conjecture.

4. Criticism of Trench

After an examination of Tooke's etymological conclusion Grote next considers the glossology of Richard Chenevix Trench. Grote believes that Trench generally correctly examines words and their meanings. Yet he believes that he lays too much stress upon the dictionary meaning of words, for example, "plague means properly, and according to its derivation, blow or stroke." [2]

What Grote does not agree with is the etymology of the word taken as indicating the whole, and final, meaning. The dianoematism of words, Grote contends, is just as important. Due to changes in the meaning of words through generalization and particularization, the meaning of words constantly changes. This is true of words such as 'wretch,' which came eventually to involve wickedness when the original meaning would have reference to misfortune. Grote asserts

[1] Grote, JOP, 5 (1874), 161.
[2] *Op. cit.*, 169.

that the immoral bearing of the later word is due to the attempt to exaggerate what the original word 'wretch' signified. This exaggeration is the result of a certain levity of all speech. In contrast to Trench, Grote states that generalization and particularization caused by a certain levity of language is responsible for the differentiation of language, whereas if words continued in their etymological signification there would be a general tendency to less adaptation. In another manner of speaking, one might say in commenting on Grote's criticism of Trench, that this means that if Trench had things his own way at the beginning of language there would be no language at all.

5. Comment

At least Grote has shown in this article that it is possible to philosophize on the meaning and derivation of words. One basic note is sounded throughout this article by Grote, namely, that to regard dogmatically any estimate of the meaning, etc., of words as final, is an error.

Grote has used many terms in this article that are foreign to philosophy. Their nature is of little or no concern for philosophy generally. But he has shown to some small extent at least, what one may seem justified in calling a philosophy of etymology. This philosophy of etymology (if we may call it such) has a successor which is called by a somewhat different name, semantics, or "the study of the relation of sign to the objects to which the signs are applicable." [1] This later study is by no means remotely related to philosophy and a few present-day writers have very considerably enriched the field of semantics.

III. "THOUGHT VS. LEARNING"

1. A contrast

The sub-title of "Thought vs. Learning" is "An Address to Self-educated Men." The substance of the article may be conjectured to a certain extent. One might say that Grote here is attempting to indicate the clear distinction between 'intelligence' and 'education' even though he does not actually use these words in contrast to each other. Or the difference between the two may be further indicated by the method of Socrates and that of the Sophists as well as suggested by the words of the title, 'thought' and 'learning.'

---

[1] Morris, in Runes, DOP, 288.

2. Use of one's own mind is of chief importance

By 'thought' Grote means individual judgment or the using of one's own mind rather than plagiarizing from the minds or writings of others. By 'learning' he means, roughly speaking, the opposite, or, that is, virtual plagiarizing. To make the discussion of the contrast somewhat modernistic Grote attempts to show that it is true of his day as well as of centuries before to consider the importance of finding out what should be learned, rather than what may be learned. That is, it is of great importance to realize that those who have not had the advantages of education, may know the way in which education may be sought. Intelligence may remain unaffected whether books are read or not. It is more important to *think* than to *read*. An evident example is Descartes who felt that after all his reading he must yet find a method of his own whereby truth might be found. Hobbes said that if he had read as much as others he would have been equally uneducated as they, or have talked as much nonsense as they talked. The Socratic method was through *thought* rather than through learning. Socrates, Grote states, asserted that he had not been able to learn anything, at least after the manner of his own age.

3. Thought and learning stagnation

The worst form of mental disease is thought stagnation, not learning stagnation. Grote contends that the latter may even lead to the paralyzing of thought, unless it is wisely pursued. What is of very great importance is the use of one's own mind and lack of direct reliance upon the thought of others. There is much danger of relying too much upon the thought of others since man constantly recognizes himself as a social organism.

Of the two daughters of language, thought is far the more important, for this inward talk, where the sympathy is imaginative only, is very often the most real society.[1]

Books need not be relied upon too greatly for one's own thought may contain as much as they contain. This is not to discountenance the value of books but to recognize that it is of utmost importance to use the mind in thinking independently, concentrating, etc. To say that they possess what we cannot grasp without knowing something of history, for example, concerning the dialogues of Plato, is not the whole truth or even much more than a small part of it. The danger is that unless this fact is recognized one may come to the conclusion that

[1] Grote, TVL, in GW, 12 (1871), 820.

works, even like Plato's, cannot be understood except by the educated man. "What is wanted for. . . entering into much of the best thought. . . is not more knowledge, but that their minds should move better under the knowledge which they have already." [1] And again,

If we want something to think about, let us think about words. Our stock of language is a great book in our minds always ready for us to read, suggesting to us all kinds of images which as Milton could do not more than put together, and full of home-made philosophy of the kind which Socrates brought to bear against the book philosophy of the Sophists. We have all this in our mouths without giving it a thought, while we are murmuring that our minds are empty and stagnant, because what we want of other people's thought is perhaps denied us. [2]

4. Comment

The fact that this article was published in the journal, *Good Words*, is sufficient to indicate its simplicity. The sub-title is very descriptive, "An Address to Self-educated Men." The brief work is designed to be encouraging, adulatory and optimistic. It shows that it is of much greater importance to do one's own thinking than to be greatly dependent upon the opinions and views of others to the neglect of reliance upon one's own mental capacities.

IV. "PASCAL AND MONTAIGNE"

1. A brief comparison

Grote points out that Pascal was a great admirer of Montaigne and though he resembled him in certain respects he differed from him very greatly in others. He was alike Montaigne in his depreciation of human reason even to the extent of pessimism: "From the Port Royalists he may have learned to take a dark view of human nature, as he had learnt from Montaigne to take a depreciatory view of human intelligence." [3]

2. Pascal's devotion to religion

Pascal was not so wholly absorbed by the controversy of his time even though he entered into argumentation with the Jansenists and Jesuits. He was ardently devoted to any causes which opposed irreligion. Grote refers to "the old faith" before the rise of Protestantism. This faith embraced both outspoken opponents who were absorbed by Protestantism, and despisers who "were led to attach themselves

---

[1] Grote, TVL, in GW, 12 (1871), 819.
[2] *Op. cit.*, 823.
[3] Grote, PAM, in CR, 30 (1877), 288.

to the old faith, in the way of obedience and profession, more than otherwise would have been the case." Pascal was not so interested in this cleavage in the church as he was concerned with opposing irreligion.

3. Montaigne's neopaganism

Grote classified Montaigne (and also Erasmus to a somewhat lesser extent) as an adherent of neopaganism, a sort of 'mental Renaissance.' [1] This Renaissance was the outcome of a bizarre mixture of ancient philosophy used to the detriment of existing mediaeval religion and to the disrepute of the Ancients upon which it claimed to be based. This destructive criticism threatened to overwhelm mediaeval Christianity in the cause of which Pascal became an ardent exponent.

Montaigne probably was taken with levity by all of his readers with the exception of Pascal. Grote claims that Pascal was inclined to take Montaigne's utterances too literally and therefore missed much of the irresponsible inconclusiveness, which Montaigne intended. Not only was there a threatening influence hovering over philosophy and theology but over the conclusions of science also. Within science there were two elements one of which was hostile to religion, namely positivism, by reason of its refusal to accept anything as existing beyond physical fact. The other element was favorable to religion. This element was the scientific spirit which believed that there is truth and that it is obtainable, a fact which ultimately demolished a great deal of the indifferentism and inconclusiveness inherent within the work of Montaigne.

Pascal's *Pensées*, especially in the first chapter, is directly opposed to Montaigne's inconclusiveness. Pascal argues from the weakness and want of man and the reality of religion, and not from despairing scepticism. Though it was a last request of his father to translate Raymond Sebond's *Natural Theology*, Montaigne concluded in defense of the volume that since man was unable to judge properly of religion he must dogmatically accept it. To a certain extent, Pascal, too, depreciated human reason because of the weakness which he felt to be inherent in man. Pascal reasoned, therefore, to religion as supplying a great need for humanity, while Montaigne argued to irreligion with the assertion that it didn't make much difference whether the truth of anything might ever be found out. Grote believed that Pascal went

---

[1] Grote, PAM, in CR, 30 (1877), 286.

somewhat too far in starting with scepticism and ending with the importance of revealed religion:

> I have endeavored, in all that I have written about human nature, to avoid both the cynic indifference of Montaigne, and what we must call the complaint and repining of Pascal . . . We may have Pascal's earnestness without his bitterness or his determined looking at things on the worst side.[1]

> At one moment he writes as one who is himself painfully conscious of the weakness, the complications, and difficulties of human life; at another, as one who is simply satisfied to turn to account in proof of religion.[2]

4. Pascal on happiness

Grote quotes from Pascal's *Pensées* to support the importance of happiness: "L'homme est visiblement égaré, et sent en lui des restes d'un état heureux, dont il est déchu, et qu'il ne peut recouvrer." This is a much healthier attitude toward human life that Pascal takes here. Where he goes to an extreme incompatible with this statement may be observed in the following: "Why," says Grote,

> should it be necessary for Pascal to say that the desire for truth and happiness, impossible in our present state to be gratified, is left to us from our former one, not only to show to us that there has been such a former one, but *to punish us*? Would it not have been a greater punishment to us if it had not been left to us? This is what I have called his needless severity, and making the worst of everything.[3]

5. Comment

This article, written for a current journal with a wide circulation, was composed in a very simple style and presents rather obvious and contrasting traits in Pascal and Montaigne. It reveals Pascal's strong devotion to religion and Montaigne's professed irreligion. This brief work is chiefly descriptive of main traits in each man's thought.

V. "ON THE DATING OF ANCIENT HISTORY"

1. Dating of events by two methods – epochal and eponymous

In his article bearing the above title, published in the *Journal of Classical and Sacred Philology*, in 1854, Grote examines the various methods in use for the dating of events which took place before the Christian era. He makes the general statement that time is not only *measured* but also *marked*, and it is with the marking that Grote is

---

[1] Grote, PAM, in CR, 30 (1877), 288.
[2] *Op. cit.*, 289.
[3] *Op. cit.*, 291.

especially concerned here. If chronology is to be trustworthy it must be contemporary, or 'epochal,' so that comparisons may be made. The opposite of this is the manner of reckoning called 'eponymous,' or successional. Of course the epochal manner of marking may involve the eponymous but not vice versa. Grote's whole essay is based upon the manners of reckoning, epochal and eponymous.

2. Dynastical reckoning

Epochal reckoning was characteristic of the East rather than of the West. The first recorded epochal marking known in secular writing was the years of Nebonassar (called so, by the Greek astronomers of Egypt). The Nebonassar reckoning was a dynastical form which was contemporaneous with the reckoning of years of kings. This dynastical marking of time was modified later by the influence of Rome.

3. Olympiadic dating

In the West. in Greece, the reckoning of time was carried on variously by the many states. Probably the beginning of any other form of writing took place when the dynastical reckoning of the East first came to the attention of the Greeks. Timaeus, who was the first to give a complete history of the world, found it expedient to use a contemporary form of marking. He employed the Olympiadic dating which became recognized by all the states of Greece. Eratosthenes improved the method of Timaeus and chronologized records even before the first Olympiad, one of which was the Trojan War. This war became the starting-point of the traditional history of Rome, rather than of Greece. Timaeus may be regarded as the originator of epochal dating both in Greece and Rome.

4. Dating by lunar months

With the establishment of Roman dominion over the whole of the known world a more universal marking of time eventuated. The lunar months became fairly definitely established as the recognized form of dating. However, the neglected quarter of a day in three hundred and sixty-five was responsible for much error. Grote believes that the imperial dominion of Rome meritoriously supplemented the science of the East in the establishment of an accurate chronological dating.

5. Dating originating in Christendom

With the origin of Christianity, dating was improved. The Hebrew scriptures penetrated Greek thought and the establishing of events within these scriptures became the object of much attention chiefly because of the advantages afforded by contemporary dating. Moreover, the lunar reckoning of the Jews in establishing a proper date for Easter, gave a further impetus to accurate contemporary dating. Also, the Christian era began to occupy the minds of men so markedly that the beginning of it took on a particular significance even though due to various adjustments the birth of Christ is approximately fixed at 4 B.C. This was only one influence in the dating of historical events. The importance of Dionysius in fixing the date of the Incarnation as the beginning of an epoch should not be overlooked.

6. Other methods of dating

The dating of history before the birth of Christ occasioned much dispute. Because chronology was so uncertain no epoch could be agreed upon. Hence, the method of dating backward came into common use as early as the sixteenth century. The dating by epochs depending upon the particular country considered is the method favored by some, despite the backward dating.

7. Present and future methods of dating

Grote regards the present system of dating of events in ancient history as better than any other previous system. However, he believes that there is still a better method that might be used where time might be measured in 'chiliads,' each chiliad referring to 1000 years. The discussion of this system is the climax in all systems that have been used in dating of ancient history or of all possible ones, according to Grote. The system is rather elaborate and its study in detail appears unnecessary here.

VI. "ORIGIN AND MEANING OF ROMAN NAMES"

1. Significance of 'nomen,' 'praenomen,' and 'cognomen'

Grote states that a complete Roman name consisted of at least a 'nomen.' Frequently associated with this was a 'praenomen' which preceded the 'nomen' and a 'cognomen' which followed. 'Nomen' refers to what the person was called, originally. Generically, it was the name which referred to large numbers. 'Praenomen' particularized the reference since it applied to individual members. 'Cognomen,' when it appeared with 'nomen' standing as surname, signified a particular family. However, 'cognomen' did not usually appear since it was a sort of nickname applied to the person because of some peculiar characteristic. On the other hand, 'praenomen' was always a part of the name.

2. Criticism of Plutarch

According to Grote, Plutarch was a great offender in his attempt to trace the cognomen of names to some particular defect or peculiar trait in the character of the person to whom the name was originally attached. Although he is correct in so doing in some cases, yet in the later days of the Roman republic cognomination was rife and was an Oriental naming rather than Roman.

3. Change in a Roman name

Gradually the full Roman name underwent change so that the simplicity which once attached to the name by reason of the explicit 'nomen' changed to complexity and when the praenomen partially or wholly dropped away the cognomen or even a title might take its place. The general relation of the words of the complete name may be noted in the following:

> The relation of the cognomen to the nomen . . . is not difficult: that of the regular praenomen to the nomen is more difficult, and in some respects, so far as we can make it out, more interesting, as bringing us nearer the origin and principle of the whole system.[1]

What Grote means is that the original name consisted always of the praenomen and the nomen and this relation is more interesting than the relation of cognomen to nomen, even though the changes of praenomen may be more complicated. The cognomen was originally merely an appendage which variously took on considerable significance.

4. Criticism of Varro's view

The origin of Roman names appears to have been in binominalism, according to Grote, rather than in one name as Varro contends. Varro apparently would base his attestation upon the singleness of, for example, the name 'Romulus.' However, this particular name, like others, had a second name, namely, 'Quirinus.'

5. Present-day names based on Roman rather than on Greek

Grote makes the significant statement that the names of the present day owe more to Roman language than to Greek. That this is so may

[1] Grote, OMR, in JCP, II (1855), 268.

readily appear from the fact of the existence of the bivocabulary naming, which the praenomen and the nomen reveal. The Greek names may have been responsible for a certain portion of the 'cognomen' of the complete Roman name. That is, the cognomen when derived from the Greeks, as it often was, had no reference to a peculiar characteristic of the individual nor was it a nickname. From the Roman naming there has been a divergence because of the prevalence among European peoples of family naming. Hence what is now the Christian name is of least importance as compared with the surname, when in the Roman naming what stands for the Christian name today was then the most important name. Exactly how the change actually took place appears somewhat indefinite, Grote concludes. Use has established the present manner of naming. An example appears in the following:

> Once John or William was the proper or generic name, and Johnson, Williamson, or the name of the place of residence, additions for the purpose of differentiating or distinguishing one John or William from another: now use has altered this, and, if a man is asked his name, he mentions his surname, the Christian name serving simply as a specific differentiation, a distinction within the family.[1]

CONCLUSION TO MISCELLANEOUS WRITINGS

In the foregoing miscellaneous writings, Grote reveals his versatility of interests. The articles are summarized mainly in this work, with comments in various places throughout. Where the particular subject that Grote writes on seemed to call for it, a separate and brief comment was made at the close of the summary of the article.

The subjects on which Grote writes are somewhat generally technical and not designed to deal with what is ordinarily classified under philosophy. The audience that Grote reached was likely to appreciate the most of what he wrote in these miscellaneous articles. The type of journal publishing the writing is fairly indicative of the popular vein in which Grote expresses himself. Of course, a subject like "On Glossology" is specialized, not written from the popular viewpoint, and is of interest mainly in the field of philology. In his miscellaneous writings Grote reveals a considerable breadth of interest, though he can scarcely be classed as a prolific writer considering the importance of the Knightbridge Chair he held in Cambridge University.

---

[1] Grote, OMR, in JCP, II (1855), 257–258.

BIBLIOGRAPHY

CHRONOLOGICAL BIBLIOGRAPHY OF THE
WRITINGS OF JOHN GROTE

1849 "Commemoration Sermon." [1] Cambridge: Deighton, Bell, and Co., 1849.

1851 *Remarks on a Pamphlet by Mr. Shilleto entitled 'Thucydides or Grote.'* [2] Cambridge: Deighton, Bell, and Co., 1851.

1854 "On the Dating of Ancient History." *Journal of Classical and Sacred Philology*, 1 (1854), 52–82.

1855 "On the Origin and Meaning of Roman Names." *Journal of Classical and Sacred Philology*, 2 (1855), 257–270.

1856 "Old Studies and New." *Cambridge Essays,*[3] 2 (1856), 74–114. London: John W. Parker and Son, 1856.

1860 "Robert Leslie Ellis." *The Athenaeum,*[4] (1860), 205–206.

1861 *A Few Words on Criticism a propos of the Saturday Review.*[5] Cambridge: Deighton, Bell, and Co., 1861.

1862 Examination of Some Portions of Dr. Lushington's Judgment in the Cases of the Bishop of Salisbury v. Williams, and Fendall v. Wilson. *Essays and Reviews.*[6] Cambridge: Deighton, Bell, and Co., 1862.

1862 *A Few Words on the New Educational Code.*[7] Cambridge: Deighton, Bell, and Co., 1862.

1865 *Exploratio Philosophica.* Part I. Cambridge: The University Press, 1865.

1867 "What is Materialism." Macmillan's Magazine, 15 (1867), 370–381.

1870 *An Examination of the Utilitarian Philosophy* (ed. Joseph Bickersteth Mayor). Cambridge: Deighton, Bell, and Co., 1870.

1871 "On a Future State." *The Contemporary Review*, 18 (1871), 133–140.

1871 "Thought *versus* Learning." *Good Words*, 12 (1871), 818–823.

---

[1] A thorough search in reference books of Boston Public and Widener Librarie reveals no trace of this sermon. It was preached in Trinity College Chapel, Cambridge University, on December 15, 1849.

[2] No clue to this writing can be found in any library. The British Museum states that it contains ninety-one pages.

[3] This book cannot be found in the British Isles, Canada, or U.S.A.

[4] There are no volume numbers in *The Athenaeum*.

[5] A pamphlet of fifty-six pages, according to the librarian of the British Museum, but no copy available there.

[6] Cannot be found in any library. Contains 101 pages, according to the British Museum.

[7] A pamphlet that cannot be located after extensive search. Contains forty-eight pages. Information received from the British Museum.

1872 A small selection of sermons was published by Deighton, Bell, and Co., 1872.[1]

1872 "Memoir of (Robert) Leslie Ellis." *The Contemporary Review*, 20 (1872), 56–71.

1872 "Papers on Glossology." *Journal of Philology*, 4 (1872), 55–66, 157–181.

1874 "Papers on Glossology." *Journal of Philology*, 5 (1874), 153–182.

1876 *A Treatise on the Moral Ideals* (ed. Joseph Bickersteth Mayor). Cambridge: Deighton, Bell, and Co., 1876.

1877 "Pascal and Montaigne." *The Contemporary Review*, 30 (1877), 285–296.

1889 "A Discussion between Professor Henry Sidgwick and the Late Professor John Grote on the Utilitarian Basis of Plato's *Republic*." *The Classical Review*, 3 (1889), 97–102.

1900 *Exploratio Philosophica*. Part II (ed. Joseph Bickersteth Mayor). Cambridge: The University Press, 1900.

GENERAL BIBLIOGRAPHY

Abbott, Thomas Kingsmill. **SAT** *Sight and Touch*. London: Longman and Co., 1864.

Albee, Ernest. **HEU** *A History of English Utilitarianism*. New York: The Macmillan Co., 1902.

Alexander, Samuel. **STD** *Space, Time and Deity*. London: Macmillan and Co., 1920.

Aristotle. **BWA** *The Basic Works of Aristotle* (ed. Richard McKeon). New York: Random House, Inc., 1941.

Bain, Alexander. **AUT** *Autobiography* (ed. W. L. Davidson). New York: Longmans, Green, and Co., 1904.

——— **SI** *Senses and the Intellect*. 4th ed. London: Longmans, Green, and Co., 1894.

Baldwin, James Mark. **DPP** *Dictionary of Philosophy and Psychology* (ed. J. M. Baldwin). New York: The Macmillan Co., 1901–1905.

Bergson, Henri. **CE** *Creative Evolution*. New York: Henry Holt and Co., 1937.

Berkeley, George. **WOR** *The Works of George Berkeley* (ed. Alexander Campbell Fraser). Oxford: Clarendon Press, 1871.

Bertocci, Peter Anthony. **EAG** *The Empirical Argument for God in Late British Thought*. Cambridge, Mass.: Harvard University Press, 1938.

Bixler, J. S. **RPJ** *Religion in the Philosophy of William James*. Boston: Marshall Jones Co., 1926.

Boswell, James. **LSJ** *The Life of Samuel Johnson* (ed. Perry Fitzgerald). London: Bliss Sands & Co., 1897.

Bowen, Francis. **MWH** *The Metaphysics of Sir William Hamilton* (ed. Francis Bowen). Cambridge: Sever and Francis, 1865.

——— **TL** *A Treatise on Logic*. Cambridge: Sever and Francis, 1864.

Bowne, Borden Parker. **MET** *Metaphysics*. Boston: Boston University Press, (1882), 1943.

——— **TTK** *Theory of Thought and Knowledge*. New York: Harper and Brothers, 1897.

Brightman, Edgar Sheffield. **ITP** *An Introduction to Philosophy*. New York: Henry Holt and Co., 1925.

——— Art. (1934). "Immediacy?" *Idealismus*, 1 (1934), 87–101.

---

[1] A thorough search in reference books of Boston Public and Widener Libraries reveals no trace of these sermons.

Brightman, Edgar Shieffield. **MAN** *Manual for Students of Philosophy.* 3rd ed. Boston, 1940.
—— **POR** *A Philosophy of Religion.* New York: Prentice-Hall, 1946.
—— **PCP** *Proceedings of the Sixth International Congress of Philosophy* (ed. E. S. Brightman). New York: Longmans, Green, and Co., 1927.
Burtt, Edwin Arthur. **EPB** *English Philosophers from Bacon to Mill* (ed. w. intro. E. A. Burtt). New York: The Modern Library, 1939.
Carrau, Ludovic. Art. (1877). "J. Grote, *A Treatise on the Moral Ideals.*" (A book review.) *Revue Philosophique*, 4 (1877), 530–537.
Case, Thomas. **PR** *Physical Realism.* New York: Longmans, Green, and Co., 1888.
Clarke, Mary Evelyn. **SLV** *A Study in the Logic of Value.* London: University of London Press, 1929.
Contemporary Review, The. **CR** *The Contemporary Review.* London: The Contemporary Review Co., 1866 —.
Costello, Harry T. Art. (1926). "Symbolism and Truth." (Book review of R. M. Eaton, **ST**). *The Philosophical Review*, 35 (1926), 574–580.
Courtney, William Leonard. **LM** *Life of John Stuart Mill.* New York: Thomas Whittaker, 1889.
Cunningham, Gustavus Watts. **IAB** *The Idealistic Argument in Recent British and American Philosophy.* New York: The Century Co., 1933.
Davidson, William Leslie. **PTE** *Political Thought in England.* New York: Henry Holt and Co., 1916.
Demos, Raphael. **POP** *The Philosophy of Plato.* New York: Charles Scribner's Sons, 1939.
Descartes, René. **DOM** *Discours de la Méthode* (ed. T. V. Charpentier). London: Routledge, 1894.
—— **DOM** *Discourse on Method* (ed. Ernest Rhys). New York: E. P. Dutton and Co., 1912.
Dewey, John. **EAN** *Experience and Nature.* Chicago: Open Court Publishing Co., 1925.
Dictionary of National Biography. **DNB** *Dictionary of National Biography* (ed. Leslie Stephen). 63 vols. and Supplement. New York: Macmillan and Co., 1885.
Durant, Will. **SOP** *The Story of Philosophy.* New York: Garden City Publishing Co., 1930.
Eaton, Ralph Monroe. **ST** *Symbolism and Truth.* Cambridge, Mass.: Harvard University Press, 1925.
Encyclopaedia Britannica, The. **Enc. Brit.** *The Encyclopaedia Britannica* (ed. Walter Yust). 14th ed. 24 vols. New York: Encyclopaedia Britannica, 1929.
Erdmann, Johann Eduard. **HOP** *History of Philosophy* (tr. & ed. Williston S. Hough). 3 vols. London: Swan Sonnenshein & Co., 1890.
Ferrier, James Frederick. **IOM** *Institutes of Metaphysics.* 3rd ed. Edinburgh: William Blackwood and Sons, 1875.
Forsyth, Thomas Miller. **EP** *English Philosophy.* London: A. & C. Black, 1910.
Frost, S. E. **MOP** *Masterworks of Philosophy* (ed. S. E. Frost, Jr.). New York: Doubleday and Co., 1946.
Fuller, Benjamin Apthorp Gould. **HP** *A History of Philosophy.* 2 vols. New York: Henry Holt and Co., 1945.
Grote, John. Art. (1866). "The Rev. John Grote, B. D." (in sec. "Obituary Memoirs," 543–550, no authors given). *The Gentleman's Magazine*, 2 (n.s.) 221 (o.s.) (1866), 549–550.
Guthrie, Malcolm. **SUK** *On Mr. Spencer's Unification of Knowledge.* London: Trübner & Co., 1882.

Hamilton, William. **DPL** *Discussions on Philosophy and Literature*. New York: Harper & Bros., 1853.

—— **LOM** *Lectures on Metaphysics and Logic* (ed. Henry Longueville Mansel and John Veitch). Edinburgh: William Blackwood and Sons, 1859.

—— **PWH** *Philosophy of Sir William Hamilton* (ed. O. W. Wight). New York: D. Appleton & Co., 1855.

—— **WTR** *The Works of Thomas Reid*. Edinburgh: Maclachlan and Stewart, 1846–1863.

Hartmann, Nicolai. **ETH** *Ethics* (tr. Stanton Coit). 3 vols. New York: The Macmillan Co., 1932.

Hastings, James. **ERE** *Encyclopaedia of Religion and Ethics*. 12 vols. and Index vol. New York: Charles Scribner's Sons, 1908.

Hegel, Georg Wilhelm Friedrich. **HEG** *Hegel* (ed. Jakob Loewenberg). New York: Charles Scribner's Sons, 1929.

—— **PDR** *Philosophie der Religion* (ed. G. J. P. J. Bolland). Leiden: A. H. Adriani, 1901.

Hoffding, Harald. **HMP** *History of Modern Philosophy* (tr. B. E. Meyer). 2 vols. London: Macmillan and Co., 1924.

Hume, David. **THN** *A Treatise of Human Nature* (ed. Thomas J. McCormack and Mary Whiton Calkins). LaSalle, Ill.: The Open Court Publishing Co., 1946.

—— **EHU** *An Enquiry Concerning the Human Understanding* (ed. Thomas J. McCormack and Mary Whiton Calkins). LaSalle, Ill.: The Open Court Publishing Co., 1946.

James, William. **POP** *Principles of Psychology*. 2 vols. New York: Henry Holt and Co., 1927.

—— **PBC** *Psychology: Briefer Course*. New York: Henry Holt and Co., 1926.

—— **SPP** *Some Problems of Philosophy*. New York: Longmans, Green and Co., 1911.

Joseph, Horace William Brindley. **ITL** *An Introduction to Logic*. 2nd ed. (rev.). Oxford: Clarendon Press, 1916.

Kant, Immanuel. **CPR** *Critique of Pure Reason* (tr. Norman Kemp Smith). London: Macmillan and Co., 1934.

Lewis, Clarence Irving. **MWO** *Mind and the World-Order*. New York: Charles Scribner's Sons, 1929.

Locke, John. **EHU** *An Essay Concerning Human Understanding* (ed. Andrew Seth Pringle-Pattison). Oxford: Clarendon Press, 1924.

—— **EHU** *An Essay Concerning the Human Understanding . . . by John Locke* (ed. Benjamin Rand). Cambridge, Mass.: Harvard University Press, 1931.

—— **JL** *John Locke* (by James Gibson). London: H. Milford, 1933.

Lotze, Rudolf Hermann. **LSP** *Lotze's System of Philosophy* (tr. & ed. B. Bosanquet). Oxford: Clarendon Press, 1884.

—— **MIC** *Microcosmos* (tr. Elizabeth Hamilton and E. E. Constance Jones). New York: Scribner and Welford Co., 1886.

Mackenzie, John Stuart. **ECP** *Elements of Constructive Philosophy*. New York: The Macmillan Co., 1918.

—— Art. (1924). "Constructive Philosophy." *Contemporary British Philosophy* (ed. John Henry Muirhead). 2 vols. New York: The Macmillan Co., 1924.

Mansel, Henry Longueville. **LLR** *Letters, Lectures, and Reviews* (ed. Henry W. Chandler). London: J. Murray, 1873.

—— **POC** *The Philosophy of the Conditioned*. New York: A. Strahan, 1866.

Martineau, James. **EPT** *Essays, Philosophical and Theological*. 2 vols. New York: Henry Holt and Co., 1874.

Masson, David. **RBP** *Recent British Philosophy*. 3rd ed. London: Macmillan and Co., 1877.

McCosh, James. **SP** *The Scottish Philosophy*. New York: R. Carter and Brothers, 1875.

McCunn, John. **SRT** *Six Radical Thinkers*. London: Arnold, 1907.

McDougall, William. **BAM** *Body and Mind*. New York: The Macmillan Co., 1920.

Mill, John Stuart. **AUT** *Autobiography* (preface, John Jacob Coss). New York: Columbia University Press, 1924.

—— **DDP** *Dissertations and Discussions, Political, Philosophical and Historical*. Boston: W. V. Spencer, 1865.

—— **EHP** *An Examination of Sir William Hamilton's Philosophy*. London: Longmans, Green, and Co., 1865.

—— **SOL** *A System of Logic*. New York: Longmans, Green, and Co., 1941.

—— **UTI** *Utilitarianism*. New York: E. P. Dutton and Co., 1914.

Morell, John Daniel. **HCV** *Historical and Critical View of the Speculative Philosophy of Europe*. New York: R. Carter and Brothers, 1856.

—— **EOP** *The Elements of Psychology*. London: W. Pickering, 1853.

Murray, J. Clark. **OHP** *Outline of Sir William Hamilton's Philosophy* (intro. James McCosh). Boston: Gould and Lincoln, 1870.

'A. P.' Art. (1902). Book review of J. Grote, **EP**. *Revue Philosophique*, 54 (1902), 434–436.

Perry, Ralph Barton. Art. (1913). "Some Disputed Points in Neo-Realism." *The Journal of Philosophy*, 10 (1913), 449–463.

Plato. **DOP** *The Dialogues of Plato* (tr. Benjamin Jowett). 5 vols. London: Oxford University Press, 1931.

Pollock, Frederick. **SPI** *Spinoza: His Life and Philosophy*. 2nd ed. New York: The Macmillan Co., 1899.

Prall, D. W. Art. (1927). "Eaton's Symbolism and Truth." *The Journal of Philosophy*, 24 (1927), 71–80.

Pringle-Pattison, Andrew Seth. **PR** *The Philosophical Radicals*. Edinburgh: William Blackwood and Sons, 1907.

—— **SP** *Scottish Philosophy*. Edinburgh: William Blackwood and Sons, 1885.

Robertson, G. Croom. Art. (1890). Biographical Article. *The Dictionary of National Biography* (ed. Leslie Stephen and Sidney Lee), 23 (1890), 294–295.

Robin, Leon. **GT** *Greek Thought*. New York: Alfred A. Knopf, 1928.

Robinson, Daniel Sommer. **POR** *The Principles of Reasoning*. 2nd ed. New York: Appleton and Co., 1930.

Rogers, Arthur Kenyon. **EAP** *English and American Philosophy since 1800*. New York: The Macmillan Co., 1928.

—— **SHP** *Student's History of Philosophy*. New York: The Macmillan Co., 1938.

Runes, Dagobert David. **DOP** *Dictionary of Philosophy*. New York: Philosophical Library, 1942.

—— **TCP** *Twentieth Century Philosophy*. New York: Philosophical Library, 1947.

Russell, Bertrand. Art. (1910). "Knowledge by Acquaintance and Knowledge by Description." *Proceedings of the Aristotelian Society*, 11 (n.s.) (1910–11), 108–128.

—— Art. (1913). "The Nature of Sense-Data – A Reply to Dr. Dawes Hicks." *Mind*, 22 (n.s.) (1913), 76–81.

—— **POP** *The Problems of Philosophy*. New York: Henry Holt and Co., 1911.

Russell, Bertrand, and Alfred North Whitehead. **PM** *Principia Mathematica*. 2nd ed. 3 vols. Cambridge: The University Press, 1925.

Sabine, George Holland. **PE** *Philosophical Essays* (ed. G. H. Sabine). New York: The Macmillan Co., 1917.

Sellars, Roy Wood. **CR** *Critical Realism.* London: Macmillan and Co., 1920.

Seth, James. **EPS** *English Philosophers and Schools of Philosophy.* New York: E. P. Dutton and Co., 1912.

Sidgwick, Henry. Art. (1877). "John Grote's *Moral Ideals.*" *Mind*, 2 (o.s.) (1877), 239–244.

Sorley, William Ritchie. **HEP** *A History of English Philosophy.* New York: G. P. Putnam's Sons, 1921.

—— **MVI** *Moral Values and the Idea of God.* 2nd ed. Cambridge: The University Press, 1921.

Spencer, Herbert. **AUT** *An Autobiography.* 2 vols. New York: D. Appleton and Co., 1904.

—— **EMP** *Essays: Moral, Political and Aesthetic.* New York: Appleton and Co., 1865.

—— **POP** *Principles of Psychology.* 2 vols. New York: Appleton and Co., 1894.

Spinoza, Benedictus de. **ETH** *Ethics* (tr. A. Boyle). New York: E. P. Dutton and Co., 1934.

Stephen, Leslie. **EU** *The English Utilitarians.* 3 vols. New York: G. P. Putnam's Sons, 1900.

—— Art. (1894). "James Mill." *Dictionary of National Biography*, 37 (1894), 385.

Stewart, Dugald. **WOR** *The Collected Works of Dugald Stewart* (ed. William Hamilton). 7 vols. Cambridge: Hilliard and Co., 1829.

Tulloch, John. **MTP** *Modern Theories in Philosophy and Religion.* London: William Blackwood and Sons, 1884.

Veitch, John. **HAM** *Hamilton.* Edinburgh: William Blackwood and Sons, 1882.

Walker, James. **EIP** *Essays on the Intellectual Powers of Man* (ed. James Walker). Cambridge: Bartlett and Co., 1850.

Ward, James. **NA** *Naturalism and Agnosticism.* New York: The Macmillan Co., 1899.

—— **PP** *Psychological Principles.* Cambridge: The University Press, 1919.

Whewell, William. **PIS** *The Philosophy of the Inductive Sciences.* 2 vols. London: J. W. Parker, 1840.

Whitehead, Alfred North. **PR** *Process and Reality.* New York: The Macmillan Co., 1930.

Whitmore, Charles E. Art. (1927). "The Significance of John Grote." *The Philosophical Review*, 36 (1927), 307–337.

Williams, Donald Cary. Art. (1933). "The Innocence of the Given." *The Journal of Philosophy*, 31 (1934), 263–268.

Windelband, Wilhelm. **HOP** *A History of Philosophy* (tr. James H. Tufts). New York: The Macmillan Co., 1931.

INDEX

Extended things: 41, 43
Extension: 41, 42, 43, 131
Extensive continuum: 238
External: 142
External object: 88–89, 140, 147, 174, 194
External perception: 134
External test of truth: 146
External things: 131, 175
External to the mind: 143
External world: 40–44, 46, 69, 72, 75, 77-
79, 89, 94–96, 102, 109, 128–131, 133–
134, 140–141, 143, 170
Externality: 95
Extra-phenomenal: 25, 36, 38, 41–42
"Extra-phenomenal" *power*: 31, 32
Eye: 33, 37, 57, 140–141, 144, 199, 201,
203, 248

Fact(s): 52, 107, 109, 126–127, 130, 145,
168, 198, 200–202, 206, 213, 214, 221,
228, 234, 243
Fact *qua* fact: 127
Facts of body: 178
Facts of mind: 178
Facts of nature: 251
Faculties: 113
Faculties of comprehension: 113
Faculties of knowledge: 113
Faith: 115, 255
"Fallacy of bifurcation": 215
False: 248
Fame: 219
Familiarity: 235
Farber, Marvin: 117
Fear: 105, 211
Fechner, Gustav Theodor: 197
Feel(s): 72, 74, 139
Feeling: 14, 21, 23, 28–33, 37, 40–41, 46,
51, 68–74, 81, 87–89, 105–106, 119, 134,
156, 161, 162, 164, 177, 196, 201, 204,
221, 222, 228
Feeling of pleasure: 218
Feeling of want: 177
Fellow of Trinity College: 1
Fellow-beings: 246
Felt: 175
Felt want: 177
Ferm, Vergilius: 208
Ferrier, James Frederick: 7, 9, 47–52, 58,
60–64, 66, 180, 191, 232, 233
"Ferrier's Institutes of Metaphysic": 235
Fichte, Johann Gottlieb: 47, 53, 55, 64
Figure: 35, 130
Finite: 55, 56
Finite spirits: 195
Finiteness: 55
Flewelling, Ralph Tyler: 121, 191
Force: 28, 70
Foreward: 19
Form(s): 18, 51, 71, 77, 87, 90, 97, 251

"Form of the higher description": 71
Form of thought: 90
Form of words: 251
Formal Logic: 99–100, 102, 106
Forming concepts: 100
Forsyth, Thomas Miller: 82, 83, 132
Freedom: 177, 191
Frost, S. E.; Jr.: 123
Fulfilment of function: 217
Fuller, B. A. G.: 83, 194, 105
Function: 36
Future: 245
Future Life: 191, 245–247
Future state: 245, 246

Gama, Vasco da: 251
Gay, John: 219
Generalization: 250, 251
Genus: 249
Geometry: 108
Gibson, James: 132
Given: 111
Giveness: 182
Glasgow: 239
Glaucon: 214, 215
Glorification: 245
Glossology: 247, 250, 251
God: 16, 41, 43–45, 53–56, 64, 83, 140,
191, 195, 208, 219, 229, 246
God-created: 243
Good: 44, 212, 216, 217, 228, 229, 243
Good fortune: 218
Good Words: 4, 254
Goodness: 218
Gradations in consciousness: 153
Grammar: 102
Grandiloquence: 250
Gravitation: 37
Greatness: 223
Greece: 257
Greek names: 260
Greeks: 260
Grote, Arthur: 2
Grote, George: 2, 4, 211–215, 233
Growth of consciousness: 154
Growth of knowledge: 147, 149, 158
Guthrie, Malcolm: 147

Haileybury: 2
Haldane, Viscount Richard Burdon: 198
Hallucination: 45
Hamilton, Sir William: 5, 7, 9, 59, 60,
65–68, 71–73, 75–85, 87–89, 95, 96, 99,
100, 102–104, 106, 109–112, 132, 173,
186, 232–234, 248
Handling: 32, 34, 144
Happiness: 210, 217–225, 227–231, 243,
256
Happy: 218
Hartley, David: 199, 219